AMERICAN THEATRE

BAAS Paperbacks

American Theatre
History, Context, Form

THERESA SAXON

EDINBURGH UNIVERSITY PRESS

To John, Emma, Sarah, and Ma and Pa, with love

© Theresa Saxon, 2011

Edinburgh University Press Ltd
22 George Square, Edinburgh

Typeset in Fournier by
Koinonia, Manchester, and
printed and bound in Great Britain by
CPI Group (UK) Ltd, Croydon CR0 4YY

A CIP Record for this book is available from the British Library

ISBN 978 0 7486 4520 6 (hardback)
ISBN 978 0 7486 2592 5 (paperback)

Published with the support of the Edinburgh University
Scholarly Publishing Initiatives Fund.

Contents

Acknowledgements

I am grateful to Nicola Ramsey at Edinburgh University Press for her patience and care, and to Carol Smith, British Association for American Studies Paperbacks series editor, for her unstinting encouragement. Research for this book was funded, in part, by the Livesey Sabbatical Scheme at the University of Central Lancashire, the British Academy Overseas Conference fund, the US Embassy in London, and the School of Journalism, Media and Communication at the University of Central Lancashire, for which resources I am extremely grateful. I would like to thank my colleagues at UCLan for their material contributions in the way of research time, a commodity with value beyond measure. I am also particularly indebted to Heidi Macpherson and Will Kaufman, for duties above and beyond, and a constant supply of Prosecco; to Nancy West for her support and feedback; and to Lisa Merrill for her constructive advice and shared love of theatre in all its forms.

Introduction:
Critical Heritage

This book explores a long history of American theatre. The standard history of America's Puritan heritage, with its emphasis on theatre bans and rigorous policing of performance activities, has stood in the way of a fully developed understanding of theatre in America. Whilst critics have, in recent years, developed our knowledge of American theatre, the predominant focus has been the twentieth century, and this book sets out to redress that critical imbalance. Close examination of America's theatre history reveals a diverse, stimulating and relevant body of work, one that is crucial to understanding the range of cultural and social developments across the nation. Theatrical production not only responds to social issues, but actively participates in social debate, operating as a platform for examining construction of racial, ethnic, gendered, national and ultimately human identities. Accounts of American theatre tend to date themselves, chronologically, in accordance with records of theatre 'facts' that have been established alongside settled colonial communities. My exploration is also subject to those limitations. However, drawing on the cultural organisations of Native American and African non-print practice, I extend that concept of 'fact' to include performance histories in America that are not predicated on colonial record. In the production of an analysis that draws performance dramas into contact with theatre, I will demonstrate that the rich and compelling diversity of theatre in America is, and always was, more than a replication of imported European forms.

Until recently, what was considered to be a history of 'American theatre' worthy of critical discussion was carefully abridged, 'coming of age' with Eugene O'Neill in the early years of the twentieth century. Even then there was no sense of innovation or uniqueness about theatre within critical writing. More often parallels would be drawn between the European heavyweights and the 'good' American dramatists: to be 'good', therefore, was to match Ibsen or Strindberg. This dismissive attitude reflects opinions expressed by critics of the eighteenth and nineteenth centuries who were, albeit humorously, disdainful about what they witnessed in theatres. Writing his Jonathan Oldstyle letters for the *Morning Chronicle* (1 December 1802), Washington Irving appears bemused by the staging of *The Battle of Hexham; or Days of Old*. He observes a scene whose relation to the overall performance 'I could not comprehend. I suspect it was a part of some other play thrust in here *by accident*' (1983: 11). Dramatic content of the plays also found itself burning, unhappily, under the lens of the early critics. On 29 March 1845, Edgar Allan Poe reviewed Anna Cora Mowatt's popular and successful *Fashion* for the *Broadway Journal*. His review is damning: it 'is a good play – compared with most American dramas it is a very good one – estimated by the natural principles of dramatic art, it is altogether unworthy of notice' (1845–6: 204). To Poe and Irving plays are either derivate or poor, and altogether badly staged. Such were the voices of the inaugural critics of American theatre.

Under such influence, scholarly accounts of theatre have lagged behind other discursive bodies, notably that which has grown out of studies of poetics and the novel in America. The critical code that sagely sanctioned the emergence of 'good' theatre in America with Eugene O'Neill, albeit sparking some attention and controversy, has done little to propagate healthy or rich critical debate. Not until the latter decades of the twentieth century did American theatre begin to achieve anything like an equivalent level of academic attention.

Susan Harris Smith's statement 'think of American drama as America's unwanted bastard child' was seminal in articulating the dearth of critical material relating to America's dramatic output (1989: 112). What did exist, argues Smith, lacked the spirit of enquiry, of radical and rigorous study; criticism of the theatre had become 'unreflecting, unquestioning', inheriting 'a long-standing ingrained disposition to dismiss American drama' (ibid.). Smith suggests that this antipathy stems from a reluctance to recognise the viability of the dramatic text. Quite simply, a play looks 'inadequate', when compared with a novel, and, thus, hardly worth the probing of the cultural critic. Theatre has also, contrarily, been dismissed by such cultural materialists as elitist, a highbrow form of classicism that would not and indeed could not bend the way of the mass cultural output. Smith's essay was a landmark in theatre criticism, urging for and articulating a reconceptualisation of theatre and dramatic productions in America.

Smith's critical assessment focuses on 'drama' (the concept of the dramatic text, the play script – although this definition is subject to much slippage) but her argument can, even more forcibly, be applied to 'theatre' (all elements that go together to make the production of the dramatic piece, not necessarily requiring a written script).[1] If play texts have been marginalised, the art of the performance and the staging of drama have been extirpated even more rigorously from critical debate. Interestingly, though, literary criticism has, as Loren Kruger points out, repeatedly 'poached from theatre the notion of performance as a metaphor for strategies of reading and writing or, in the guise of the "performative," as a term of approbation' (1996: 699). Discussions of the 'theatricality' of the novel and the 'performativity' of language have proliferated, and in many ways this has been at the expense of serious and thoughtful interrogation of the function of theatre. Part of my purpose, in writing this book, is to reintegrate analysis of the dramatic with the theatrical and to reinvigorate critical approaches to theatre as a performative literary production and a relevant and viable area of academic study.

Since critics in recent years have been provoked to investigate American drama more thoroughly, a more expansive, albeit axiomatic, definition of American theatre has come into operation: the staging of plays and performances in the playhouses of the American nation. The preface to *The American Stage* (Engle and Miller), for example, explains its focus on the '250 year history' of American theatre, dating its research trajectory to the 1740s as a starting point of theatre (1993: xix). Such a definition, whilst infinitely preferable to the 'coming of age in the twentieth century' school of thought, pretty much disavows theatrical activity in America prior to the declaration of nationhood in 1776. Even more worryingly, this definition would exclude all staging effects that take place outside officially designated playhouses. Recent work in theatre criticism, drawing on the writings of anthropologists such as Victor Turner, Mary Douglas and Clifford Geertz, as well as Richard Schechner's influential *Between Theatre and Anthropology* (1985), has opened the door to other ways of thinking about what constitutes theatrical performativity.

Victor Turner argues that there is a distinction to be made between ritual and theatre:

Ritual, unlike theatre, does not distinguish between audience and performers. Instead there is a congregation whose leaders may be priests, party officials, or other religious or secular ritual specialists, but all share substantially the same set of beliefs and accept the same system of practices, the same set of rituals or liturgical actions. A congregation is there to affirm the theological or cosmological order [...] that all hold in common, to actualize it periodically for themselves. (1982: 112)

In ritual, there is an assumed accord between congregation and spiritual 'actor'. In theatre, there is a specific negotiation between performer and audience, where the audience are to be invited to observe, to 'see' or 'watch' in accordance with the Greek *theasthai*, from which the term theatre is derived. But, argues Turner, theatre relates *itself* to ritual: 'theatre is [...] a hypertrophy, an exaggeration, of jural and ritual processes [...] there is, therefore, in theatre something of [...] the sacred, mythic, numinous, even "supernatural" character of religious action' (1982: 12). Thus Turner argues that theatricality operates consciously (or even unconsciously) in response to ritualised performance.

Richard Schechner's detailed studies in theatre theory have stipulated several key points about the concept of performance and the role of the audience. In the first instance, when we speak of theatre we tend to be informed by Schechner's delineation of a spectrum of ritual and theatre that is framed by the concept of performance. Ritual is efficacious – 'performing' a job, delivering and processing a symbolic or mnemonic chain; theatre, in its fullest sense, is entertainment. In Schechner's analysis we see the liturgical control of political structures, during the era of the Holy Roman Empire, as dramatising experience based in efficacy and therefore a part of the ritualistic dimension of the performance spectrum. Where bourgeois forms are in the ascendancy, such as in the mid-nineteenth century, entertainment, therefore 'theatre', holds sway. But, we should note, the spectrum is not chronological; there is no sense that ritual 'becomes' theatre as a motif or emblem of a more sophisticated set of cultural operations.

Eli Rozik, however, argues that there is very little evidence to support such claims:

Theatre is a medium that can serve different intentions and purposes: and ritual is a particular mode of action, with definite intentions and purposes, which can be used in any medium. Ritual and theatre do not constitute a binary opposition: they operate on two different ontological levels. (2002: 337)

In response to the twentieth-century fascination with ritual in theatre, Rozik argues: 'directors invented artificial ritual elements, based on superficial knowledge of real rituals' (2003: 15). And indeed we should maintain caution: the work of theatre theorists can be aligned with an imperialist purview. For example, Antonin Artaud's admiration for the Balinese dancing that influenced his mandate for theatre states:

> One does not feel the presence of a certain number of themes introduced by what in modern Western theatre generally corresponds to the author. Instead we feel this organizer, or if you like producer, his or his own author, his own creator, working with exclusively objective stage means. (1968: 23)

In his assertion that the Balinese theatre is 'free' from the restrictions of 'Western theatre', in praising that form for achieving an objectivity unavailable to pan-European productions, Artaud conceptualises an orientalising narrative, an occidental account of Balinese theatre as something other than western dramaturgy. And something against which western theatre can be measured – if found wanting. Artaud's 'understanding' of the concepts of this 'other' theatre, therefore, articulates the skewed logic and liberalism of the paternal colonial benefactor. Artaud has imagined a form of theatre for the performers of the Balinese group and inscribed this imagery on the body of the performers. It is perhaps no coincidence to note that his attendance of the Balinese theatre took place at the Paris Colonial Exposition in 1931 – a celebration of the coloniser's control and beneficence (Savarese 2001).

Nevertheless, we can argue that whilst ritual and theatre are separate planes, ritual has become the subject matter of theatre. This is not to suggest that ritual enactments are merely progenitors of later theatrical forms, but to recognise that ritual and theatre entwine inextricably, developing through intercultural contacts, accretions and historical transitions. The opening chapter of *Theatre Histories: An Introduction* (Williams et al.), a significant work in the field of theatrical studies, states: 'theatre is not one "thing," but rather a complex set of human communicative activities involving, as does the practice of ritual, fundamental human desires to imitate, play, imagine, and structure our experience' (2006: 34). I am yet to find a finer definition of the flexible yet seemingly inextricable relationship between theatre and ritual, or of the function of theatre within human cultures and societies. I would only add that, to me, there is no evolution of theatrical modes: there is, rather, a productive and stimulating conscious or unconscious series of inter-referentiality.

Thus this book would like to de-emphasise any concept of a continuum in theatre. I have no desire to suggest that ritual or spiritual performance practices sit in any sense at the base of a 'better' and more substantial, European-inspired theatre. No theatrical family tree has sprouted in America, for example, with any 'primitive' system at its root. No chronology dates 'back' to a type of performance strategy that initiated theatre in America and I will not assert that there is a 'dawn' or a point of origin from which we can say American theatre 'began'.

But we should note that the concept of a point of origin, a 'dawn', has been the subject of critical wrangling with regards to American theatre. For example, William Dunlap's 1832 *History of American Theatre* argues that the Hallam Company, notable performers on London stages, 'introduced the drama to our country' (2005: 8). Dunlap's thesis sets the date 5 September 1752, and the place, Williamsburg, Virginia, for the 'first play performed in America by a regular company of comedians' (ibid.: 12). Later critics challenge Dunlap's 'dawn'. Indeed, George O. Seilhamer claims that 'the dawn of the drama in America is unfortunately without a historian. This is less to be regretted, however, because it was a dawn that emitted only a feeble light' (2005a: 1). Seilhamer continues, albeit paradoxically, to pinpoint his own version of the dawn: 'the performance at which that history [of American drama] may be said to begin was the performance of Addison's "Cato" in Philadelphia, in August, 1749' (ibid.: 2). Arthur Hornblow, like Seilhamer, declares that 'it would be an impossible task to attempt to ascertain when or where the first theatrical performance took place on the North American continent', but also states that 'the history of the theatre in America begins early in the Eighteenth Century, about the time the first rumblings were heard of the storm which was to break the ties still holding the Colonies to the mother country' (1919: 21). Odai Johnson and William J. Burling's meticulous study of theatre, *The Colonial Stage, 1665–1774: A Documentary Calendar*, argues that, amongst theatre historians who have tripped along the path of Dunlap, there has been a tradition of privileging professional troupes, which 'has led to the exclusion of many companies from the histories of the period' (2003: 21). Professional companies that travelled across the American colonies in the eighteenth century came almost exclusively from London. Thus the 'history' of American theatre, as a narrative constructed by Dunlap and co., is a colonial history specifically, one which retains close contact to the 'mother' country.

One of the key problems with such accounts of American theatre is their monolithic focus on American theatre as a product, untouched, unchanged, imported to America from Europe. This tradition of Eurocentrism continues even in recent criticism. Bigsby and Wilmeth's introductory essay to Volume I of *The Cambridge History of American Theatre*, for example, tells us that the 'tradition' of theatre in America 'was external to its country', the earliest playwrights being 'European, as were the popular actors. Theatre buildings followed European models, as did styles of production' (1998: 3). In short, argue the editors, the 'tradition' of theatre in America was European. Locating 'theatre' as 'external' to the 'country' is perturbing: critical accounts, therefore public consumption, of the history and substance of American theatre are circumscribed by a Eurocentrism which comprehends little in terms of theatrical forms and practices beyond a 'white' history of traditions and attitudes.

Such Euro-specific attitudes also assume a particularly vexed history of theatre in Europe – one in which pan-European theatre is sufficiently developed and sophisticated to be a 'tradition' that could be transplanted homogeneously to the New World. This is a specious 'tradition' of performance that rummages the history of Greek theatre, jumbling Shakespeare with Sophocles. James Hatch points out that 'Greek theatre stands at the door of Western Theatre History' (1989: 150) – a tricky door, fitted with hegemonic handles that opens one way. Reductive versions of theatre's history, that have written for us a specific narrative of 'western theatre history', formed within elitist criticism and, to borrow Hatch's term, 'colonial politics' (ibid.) have underpinned the concept of critical 'value', and effectively blocked the pathways to and from America's diverse theatrical landscape.

That monolithic pan-European version of America's theatre history has, in recent years, come under challenge. Felicia Londré and Daniel J. Watermeier, in their introduction to *The History of North American Theatre, The United States, Canada, and Mexico: From Pre-Columbian Times to the Present*, summarise critical conjecturing of theatre: 'dance, shamanism, and ritual enactments to propitiate the forces of nature' (2000: 15). Although Londré and Watermeier claim, problematically, that theatre is considered to 'originate' from these three performance structures, their axiom stands as a useful reference for what we should consider to be theatrical material. Evidence exists to demonstrate that, in America, 'all three kinds of performance activities were practised before the arrival of the first Europeans' (ibid.). Further, that there was 'a pre-Columbian equivalent to "theatre" as westerners traditionally conceive it', with 'performance events at which there is a clear distinction between the roles of the performer and spectator, and which are clearly intended more for entertainment than for ritual purposes' has also been verified substantially (ibid.). Londré and Watermeier's claims fall into the trap of suggesting that only European forms constitute theatre, and that there is some sort of unbroken, chronological 'western' tradition of theatre, but nevertheless, they make a crucial point: theatre, staged performances aimed at entertaining an audience as well as exercising ritual needs, existed in pre-Columbian, non-European American civilisations.

Susan Castillo's *Performing America: Colonial Encounters in New World Writing* explores the emergence of a range of performative, polyphonic texts which includes a study of plays alongside travel narratives and lexicography. Castillo's book is not, intrinsically, a study of theatre; but she makes an important argument: theatricality in America cannot be regarded as governed exclusively by European mores and codes. Colonisation was not a complete and total eradication of all aspects of cultural life in America by European colonisers. Encounter worked in a variety of ways to produce 'a cacophony of European and native voices attempting to make sense of each other' (2006: 2). *Performing America*, with its deliberation on performances as cultural and ideological exchanges between colonials and incumbent populations, whether aimed at dominance or resistance, offers another way of thinking about American theatre. When we speak of 'American theatre', we should be aware that we are speaking of a performance history prior to the introduction of that forced narrative of Renaissance-forged, pan-European conventions and we can confound, critically, that narrative of unity and continuity allocated to those European theatrical conventions.

The American scene, within European cognition, has been located as relatively 'new', born out of 'discovery' narratives from the late fifteenth century onwards. The burgeoning of the arts which was the cultural enactment of the Renaissance included an invigoration of the stage, enabling performances across Europe that were not circumscribed by the dominance of the Church. Pre-Renaissance performance structures had been controlled and managed by the Roman Catholic hierarchy, emphasising liturgical drama and performed within sanctioned church spaces. Between fifty and one hundred years would pass, from the 'discovery' of America in 1492, to the construction of specific theatre buildings for the staging of non-liturgical drama across Europe. The Hôtel de Bourgogne was constructed in Paris by the Confrérie de la Passion in 1548 but it was not until 1576 that the first theatre in England was approved in Shoreditch under a twenty-one-year lease granted to James Burbage. The Globe itself was not built until 1599. Indeed, the first play printed in England appeared post-Columbus; produced around 1516, *Fulgens and Lucres* appeared through the auspices of publisher Rastell.

The settling of America happens to be concomitant with the emergence of secular theatre across Renaissance Europe, and we can trace a 'polyphonic exchange' between the narratives of travel and exploration, and the narrative of European and American theatre history. In short, the flow of information about 'faraway places and distant horizons' fed into the theatrical imagination of Europe a good while before we can even begin to claim that a non-secular European theatre fed into the Americas (Edel 1989: xiv).

In the Americas, European explorers found, as Castillo contends, 'a dazzling array of performative practices' where 'there existed an extraordinarily sophisticated and vibrant tradition of performance' (2006: 8). Historians generally, however, struggle to piece together such pre-encounter performance traditions – the lack of scripted records of such activities leads us to rely heavily on imperial accounts that are inevitably flavoured by both ignorance and racialised ideologies. John Smith's *The Generall Historie of Virginia, New England & the Summer Isles* (1624), for example, gives an example of the performance practices encountered by the Captain. Whilst a prisoner of the Opechankenough, Smith records an account of a tribal performance that was conducted by a shaman, 'with a hellish voice and a rattle in his hand' (2006: 398). The ritual, which incorporated repeated performances of dancing and oratory, according to Smith, was explained to him by his captors as being a representation of Indian ways of life – the performative setting of a meal indicated Indian lands, whilst corn mapped the sea. We recognise the ideology of the western traveller – the Christian, Smith, hears 'hellish' voices – but we are also made aware of the performativity of the event. Smith's account, whilst drawing on the populist image of 'savage' behaviours, also reveals that he had been audience to a practised and polished, staged drama.

So merchants and court-sponsored adventurers wrote back to home shores with wonderful accounts of the strangeness they encountered. Although translating and in the process misdirecting understandings of traditional performance practices and productions within the Americas, such travellers, nevertheless, were clearly witnessing and accounting for performed events. That we cannot entirely reintegrate a history, or a textual record, of such performances should not prevent us from locating and researching carefully the material that offers us a range of explanations of theatre, one of the most important and telling cultural enterprises within any social order.

As theatre across Europe developed throughout the Renaissance period, therefore, it was also absorbing material fresh from this 'new world' space of the Americas. The emergence of print culture, also concomitant with the settling of the Americas, ensured that Greek scripts on theatre, Aristotle's *Poetics* as much as works by Terence and Sophocles, were very much alive and in circulation at the time that Renaissance writers were musing on the New World. We understand that the rediscovery of Greek theatricals – which were themselves an enshrinement of ritual dedicated to the worship of non-Christian Gods – informed Renaissance theatre. I would also suggest that the dominant modes of European theatricality that were allegedly transplanted unadulterated to America had been already fed by the narrative of the 'discovery' of that America.

And, as I have already pointed out, we should resist claims that there was such a thing as a monolithic European theatre. European theatre 'tradition' was hardly a tradition at all. Disparate histories and cultures, the diversification of religious ideologies including the break with Roman Catholicism in many nations, violence, plague and civil contestation, had divided the princedoms that formed the Holy Roman Empire. Throughout the medieval period, the concept of theatre in Europe was dominated by Catholic liturgical dramas, or mystery plays. Other forms of playing were suppressed assiduously by the religious authorities, who recognised the potential for transgression that resided in performance. The church recognised the power of playing and harnessed those energies to great effect. The Franciscan monks who set out to convert the Mayans did so armed with several versions of such dramas. But by the end of the fifteenth century, the Catholic Church was damaged by Lutheran and Calvinist theologies as well as by internal corruption and strife. Secular theatres emerged more and more into open view (although less so in

Spain and therefore Spanish colonies). Indeed, mystery and morality plays had been banned in England during the reign of Elizabeth I as they were inculcated with Roman Catholicism. The French parliament's ban on the overtly religious mystery pageants coincided with France's first purpose-built theatre in 1548 – although the Catholic Confrérie de la Passion did maintain a monopoly over what could and could not be performed in Paris. Across Europe, theatres themselves may have shared certain common features: the stage (albeit in differing shapes, styles and sizes), the auditorium, props and certain staging motifs; but the perfor-mances and performance styles were very different. Italian Renaissance theatre, drawing on the *commedia dell'arte*, bore little resemblance to the *commedias* or *capa y espada* of the Spanish Golden Age. In England, the mystery play, banned by Court, fed into the cycle and the interlude into farce. Reformation and Renaissance theatre in England also drew on a reclaimed humanist reading of the structures and strategies of Greek tragedy, though mainly through the auspices of Oxford and Cambridge Universities and performances at the Inns of Court. Claims, then, that American theatre is a product of European theatre are confounded by our recognition that those European forms were themselves diverse and discontinuous.

We should also challenge the concept that the importation of European forms was historically specific to the colonial period; immigration into American from the sixteenth century through to the present day has seen a plethora of ethnic forms of drama developing in the United States. Non-English-language performances were and continue to be a feature of the theatrical landscape, as do English-language theatricals that fuse forms of performance from a range of perspectives.

Critical mass has also tended to suggest that the 'European' impact on American theatre was specifically English. Certainly the impact of England in the New World, albeit slow to combat Spanish resistance, became more invidious in the seventeenth century. But the Spanish and Portuguese presence had been significant and not only in the regions of South America. Although France is credited with the establishment of the first colony in the North – at the coast where the St John's River flows into the ocean, this only survived briefly, finally succumbing to the Spanish conquistadors. It was, then, Spain that planted the first perma-nent European colonial town on the soil of the North – St Augustine in Florida, in 1565. Further permanent settlements sprang up across the lands now known as New Mexico, Texas and California. Over a period spanning three centuries, squabbling forces, in constant conflict with each other and with local populations, eventually divided into European colonies, and then formulated an independent North American nation. But England's permanent presence in the Northern regions was somewhat behind the times. Spain and Portugal had made their mark on peoples as well as places before the setting up of the Virginia Company and the founding of Jamestown early in the 1600s. Interestingly, one of the earliest attempts to entice new settlers to join the Jamestown settlement, produced by the Virginia Company in 1609, is in the form of a handbill, very like the playbill used to entice audiences into theatres.[2]

Garff Wilson declares emphatically:

> When European men first reached the New World they observed beautiful Indian ceremonies containing many of the elements of drama. The various Indian tribes had dance rituals that gave thanks to the gods, to animals, and to plants [...] they used imitation and mimicry and sometimes included the enactment of legends and stories associated with the tribe. Such rich material – the material of which drama is made – could be found everywhere in America when European settlers first arrived. But the settlers watched the dance rituals and turned aside. The theatre in America did not grow from such indigenous material. (1973: 4)

Wilson here provides a summary of that monolithically 'European' assessment of American theatre: no role was played by native performance practices. But it is an argument that is clearly suspect. European settlers did not 'turn aside' from the scenes of performative strategies before them.

Likewise African cultural operations are elided from the processing of American performance history. Africa was regarded in the imperial imaginary as an 'empty' continent, located as devoid of cultural life; yet one of the earliest moments of America's theatrical history recorded in *The Cambridge History, Vol. 1*, is 'captive African slaves forced to sing and dance' for the crew of the *Hannibal* in 1664 (Wilmeth and Bigsby 1998: 28). Edward G. Smith recognises the implications of this brief entry:

> The deck of the English slaveship Hannibal served as a stage for the imprisoned slaves, whose 'daily exercise' was to be forced to sing and dance for the crew. The crew found them highly entertaining, as did the slave masters who later purchased them. But the habits, customs,

and emotions that the slaves expressed in this entertainment showed that they were a people with a rich heritage; the demands of survival would have a significant impact on their contribution to American culture. (1983: 37)

Thus the first chapter of this book forms a specific consideration of the performance history of the northern American subcontinent, examining markers of Native American cultural dramas and the adaptation of African forms to the racialised environment of the 'new' world. In the first section of this chapter, I trace a performance history in the American continent that pre-existed colonial contact. I then move on to examine the cultural practices of Native Americans and African Americans that look to process and challenge ideological racialisation produced by the unique experiences of colonial settlement and slavery, and articulate concepts of agency through a range of autonomous and hybrid performance strategies.

The land that European colonisers travelled to was one that had already been explored. In spite of the ideologies that emptied the land of cultural operations, the practices of tribespeople made significant inroads into European performance history. My second chapter will assess the theatrical 'behaviours' of European colonisers in the sixteenth and seventeenth centuries, assessing the disparate theatrical landscape that emerged from Spanish, French and English colonial forces, and the role played by theatricality in negotiating the process of colonisation, conversion and conquest. Anxiously, with consciously acknowledged intent, a dominant majority of colonisers specifically set out to eradicate all native dramatic practices, obliquely and deliberately reading such performances as signs of deviltry and heathenism. In the southern regions of the continent, for example, in the name of Christianity – and gold – native theatrical rituals and behaviours were attacked through war, enslavement and the virulence of infectious diseases. There was not total success and although swathes of incumbent societies were indeed decimated, and conventional life was entirely disturbed, performance practices were maintained, if circumscribed by Catholic liturgical dramas, to resurface in differing formats. Other groups, influenced by the humanist thinkers of the Renaissance, such as Michel de Montaigne, sought to revel in the 'discovery' of 'other' modes of existence, which could, as enactments of the value of 'primitive' human interaction, teach Renaissance Europeans life lessons. We would be naïve if we claimed that the works about 'native' life produced by the latter group offer accurate accounts of cultural events and theatrical passages. My second chapter argues, though, that we can certainly claim that such accounts fed European culture and cultural documents with a concept of the dramatic that was new and fresh.

The third chapter will consider the development and significance of theatre and dramatic writing in the exploration of the colonial space and the political antagonisms of colonial existence. This chapter focuses on the consolidation of colonial power within the thirteen colonies that fell within England's governance, and the diverse forms of performance practices that came into being in these regions. The antipathy to theatre that was a feature of English law in the seventeenth and eighteenth centuries found its way to America. This chapter will assess the emergence of theatrical endeavours and the function of theatrical audience, in the context of disparate social structures, including the various attitudes towards racial identities that were under scrutiny at this time. The distinct approach to theatre that operated in the colonies are discussed in this chapter, and the preferences for certain types of drama distinct from the popular plays on English stages that were beginning to be imported at this time. Whilst there were some similarities between English and colonial American performances, there were also significant differences, and the touring companies developed a portfolio of plays for the consumption of colonial audiences, as a reflection of general as well as specific and local concerns and tastes. This chapter then engages with the revolutionary nation and its inherent drama of subterfuge, where theatre and theatricality, both on stage and in the street, provided a stage for acting out political tension. The plays performed were still, almost entirely, imports from Europe; but the distribution across the main centres offers an insight into the developing attitudes of local populations to current debates about the political and economic climates, and also about the shape of theatre itself on the diverse stages of this New World. Despite the repeated attempts to enforce anti-theatre legislation, over the decades leading up to the era of the revolution, theatre expanded and even proliferated across the colonies, and certainly, as the Douglass Company became established as a major touring company, we see an enlarged theatrical landscape. At the same time, though, we see that attempt to produce theatre repeatedly challenged, delayed and, occasionally, successfully thwarted.

The fourth chapter will consider the institutionalisation of theatrical endeavours in the nineteenth century, as a 'mainstream' theatre emerges, and the division between legitimate and non-legitimate stages comes into sharp relief through 'lines' drawn between race, gender and class. This chapter draws attention to attempts by the African Company, in the 1820s, to establish a theatre in New York. This enterprise was opposed by both white theatre managers and authorities of the time and, under increasingly violent pressure, folded in 1824. This chapter will also examine the relationship between the wider political landscape of territorial expansion and the structure of theatrical endeavours. I consider the proliferation of Native American and African Americans' characterisations in plays written and performed during this time. The distinction between mainstream legitimate and non-legitimate theatres informed the conceptualisation of gender within theatrical performances and structures. The prevalence of prostitution in and indeed around theatres meant that women in the audience could find themselves involved in complex discourses of social propriety. In the *New York Morning Herald* of 19 September 1838, an article titled 'Ladies of New York, Look Well to this Thing', stated that:

> On Friday night the Park Theatre contained 83 of the most profligate and abandoned women that ever disgraced humanity; they entered in the same door and for a time mixed indiscriminately with 64 virtuous and respectable ladies [...] Men of New York, take not your wives and daughters to the Park Theatre, until Mr Simpson pay some respect to them by constructing a separate entrance for the abandoned of the sex. (Cited in Bank 1997: 134)

The burgeoning role played by women on stage and off, therefore, will form part of my analysis in this chapter.

The nineteenth century theatre in American has become synonymous with a particular type of sensationalist melodrama, whereas the twentieth century sees the emergence of Eugene O'Neill and 'serious' drama. In my final chapter, though, I look to unravel that narrative. Drawing on work undertaken by Thomas Postlewait, who has argued for recognition of the 'suspect' history of progression and improvement in American theatre, I suggest that what happens in American drama in the twentieth century cannot be confined to a shift between forms of melodrama and realism that are inherently linked. At the same time, though, there was a marked change in focus within theatre, from the actor as 'star' of the show to the role of the playwright, as critics began to take American theatre more seriously. This chapter will therefore investigate the increased critical acclaim associated with theatrical endeavours of the twentieth century, which both supports the concept of staged drama as a body of work worthy of study and at the same time sets boundaries on what can be included as 'good' theatre for that study. This final chapter will conclude with an assessment of North American theatre for the twenty-first century.

CHAPTER I

Defining American 'Drama'

In my introduction I argued that definitions of American drama have been subjugated by a Euro-American, or even more reductively, an Anglo-American critical monolith. Yet evidence of performance practices indicates that America's dramatic heritage is far more encompassing. This first section of chapter, therefore, explores cultural exchanges that fed the settlers' theatrical imaginary, through an examination of a series of tribal stagings, some of which persist in mediated formats. The inter-racial dialogue of Africans, black Americans and Native Americans is also assessed as a series of intercultural communications that inspired and informed the dramatic shape of the nation. I will shape my discussions through regions based on the geography of tribal groups. I recognise, however, that communities were often mobile, in response to living conditions, tribal conflict, colonisation, trade and colonial wars.

The latter sections of the chapter explore Native American performance practices and African cultural dramas in the context of colonial encounter, but also in the context of extra-colonial development. The myth of America as a stockpot, or melting bowl of assimilation, has long since been debunked and this section looks to explore the reclamation of performance strategies within distinct groups. Native communities, through contact with colonising forces on the American continent, became caught up in the dramatic decline of populations, the exploitation of communities' land rights and the degradation of cultural practices. African communities that came to America, though, were already informed by contact; diaspora was a condition of life as it came to be played out in the Americas. These latter sections, therefore, discuss performance practices that were, or came to be embedded, as a product of encountering America for non-European cultures.

'Native America'

Prior to European settlement in the regions now known at the United States, over 500 indigenous nations populated the subcontinent and, according to the official online catalogue at the Smithsonian, over 1,700 languages were spok en (1987: 1). To discuss the varieties of performance strategies associated with the distinct nations would be a monumental task and falls outside the remit of this volume. Research findings are scant and written accounts of witnessed performances frequently flavoured by colonial ideologies. Styles of dramatic ritual within Native American communities, like the political shape of the nations, are dynamic. This consistently shifting structure also defers the possibility of a defined and final performance report.

Whilst, therefore, we cannot access any 'inaugural' performance of ritual drama, we can construct a narrative, albeit tangled and patchy, from historical records of those performances, not only via reports written by colonial settlers, whose stance tended to be governed by particular racial and theological perspectives and anthropological studies, which can appear as 'objective' accounts of scientific value; subject to the 'logic' of scientific discursiveness, such accounts lose vitality for assessments of flexible performance traditions. We should therefore recognise the intrinsic historicising value of contemporary stagings of traditional dramas, and accounts of performance practices and their function as assessed by contemporary Native American dramaturgs. This study cannot and has no intention of pretending to represent what 'all' Native American groups incorporate, but to demonstrate the diversity of theatrical styles and stages and to assess the impact of those forms on the future shape and direction of America's theatrical practices. To produce such an analysis in a book about American 'theatre' is fraught; one needs to be alive to the very real danger of reproducing and perpetuating the type of 'reading' of cultural practices that fed the colonial imagination. The communities of indigenous tribes, and Africans imported by colonial trade, within the Americas, were distinct from each other in terms economies, cultures and social organisations as well as distinct from the European construction of history within a linear trajectory.

To Europeans, history meant advance – a monolithic procession of progression. Such readings, which impose, territorially, a linear structure and schematic sense of progress/decline, consign non-linear cultural practices to the realm of the inexplicable or even obsolete. Randall T.

G. Hill cites the example of social scientist Elsie Parsons who, in 1930, 'authoritatively declare[d] the Laguna Pueblo culture dead' (1997: 112). Parsons based her assessment on her observations that there were no material signs of Laguna culture; however, Hill points out, 'history has demonstrated that she could not have been more authoritatively wrong' (ibid.). The lack of signs of cultural activity in the present should not lead, as Hill points out, to the assumption that therefore there will be no material signs of that cultural activity in the future. Linear organisations of enquiry and analysis are insufficient tools to explore the nuances of fluid and shifting cultural operations. Performance-based inquiry, though, according to Hill, usefully '"unfreezes" the synchronic moment of structural approaches' (ibid.). Thus performance-based methodologies are critically adept at 'reading' cultural operations, such as Native American strategies, which are 'under constant negotiation'. The performance-focused critique, argues Hill, 'allows scholars to examine the synchronic moment of a performance and the diachronic moments of cultural rehearsal through which a past is recounted in order to shape a future' (ibid.). Thus the mandate of performance-focused studies responds to Native American cultural operations, formed from non-empirical structures, and that consciously produce a consistently revalidated historical narrative founded on myth and ritual. A study of theatre, then, that is consciously performance-focused such as this, should explore performance as it occurs within the operation of social networks perpetuated through mnemonic dramas of myth and ritual.

Jeffrey Huntsman points out that, within Native American societies, 'there are many dramas, conceivably as many as there are cultures' (1983: 356). Another intervention for us to consider: the constituent parts of Native American 'cultures' have been informed repeatedly by imperialist doctrine homogenising an 'Indian' behaviour, caught in the boundary markers of liberalism/reactionary as noble/savage. Defining tribal structures is complicated by a colonial heritage that dates back over 500 years. This history incorporates the mass hysteria and might of Manifest Destiny, and continues in reservations.[3] Such institutionalised locations are troublingly ghettoised; at the same time, though, the reservation operates as a performance space for the perpetuation and reinvocation of ritual dramas. Reservations have had a positive impact in some instances, where, as Huntsman argues, 'native societies remain active and vital', but 'others are failing, their languages receding as the old die and the young lose interest in their bearings' (ibid.: 355). In his fears for the demise

of Native American cultural forms, Huntsman raises another important point, one that foregrounds the link between linguistic heritage and
dramatic performance: the development of an understanding of drama
amongst communities whose performance practices have been largely
oral is difficult indeed to societies whose practices have become largely
scripted.

European and early colonial American drama found a home in print as
well as performance – and frequently only in print. According to Frank
Pierce Hill's bibliography, *American Plays Printed 1714–1830* (1934) there
were 405 plays published in colonial American, a figure that suggests an
attention to the theatrical was very much a part of the colonial imaginary, and not necessarily through staged performance. Clearly, though,
as the 'print revolution' had already taken place as Europe headed to
the Americas, the concept of a non-print culture had become consigned
to the past, perhaps formative in the production of 'modern' culture,
but certainly not to be considered as contemporary and relevant or
aesthetically innovative. So native performance practices, over this same
period, are become obscured, or located as something 'savage', either to
be eradicated for the good of all or rendered as stereotypes such as the
'vanishing Indian' in early colonial plays. I hope to demonstrate, though,
that the variety of native performance strategies that were observed by
colonial settlers complicated dramatic substance and influenced what
was to develop from the importation of European theatrical entertainments to America.

Randall T. G. Hill argues that 'contemporary scholars now face
unlearning the history of the "invented Indian" to displace a cultural
hegemony. But unlearning is more destabilizing than learning and it leads
to radical revisions in critical practice"' (1997: 114). A key factor in that
process of 'unlearning' has been undertaken in anthropology and archaeology, exploring and reconsidering, as much as is feasible, pre-colonial
histories and traditions. Another strand in scholarship requires the strip-
ping away of the accreted layers of critical practice informed by ideologies of gender and sexuality, forged in the industrial, imperial era.

The position of women within Native American culture repeatedly
came under scrutiny by colonial powers, and frequently as a source
of contention. Bell cites the example of the decision by the Cherokee
nation, in the constitutional convention of 1827, to 'limit the privileges of
citizenship to "free" male citizens', which was made in order to 'effect a
public cultural and racial reconstruction of the Cherokee nation as Chris-

tian, literate and "civilised"' (2004: 315). The decision was not necessarily founded on a belief in or a desire to assimilate European gendered
ideology, but to assert citizenship in the face of a dominant colonial
power. But the net result has been that cultural critics, particularly in
the second wave of feminism, constructed and imposed a narrative of
subordination for Native American women within what was perceived
as a fundamentally patriarchal 'Indian' culture.

Understandings of sexuality within Native American cultures have
been similarly squashed. In traditional Native American social organisations, gender was not based on the duality of a masculine/feminine
binary – tribes operated through three and sometimes four versions of
gender that are variously associated with biology, but also 'demeanour,
dress, occupation, sexual object choice, talents, dreams, callings, expectations, and needs' (Kochems and Jacobs 1997: 260). The term 'berdache',
which according to the *Oxford English Dictionary* translates as 'a boy
kept for unnatural purposes', has come to stand for studies in Native
American attitudes towards homosexuality and transgenderism (cited
in Jacobs et al. 1997: 4). Somewhat understandably, Native American
cultural researchers have found the category of berdache 'derogatory
and insulting', arguing that 'two-spirit people' which is a direct translation from Native American languages, is the more appropriate term
(ibid.: 4–5).

Recent scholarship in Native American studies has demonstrated that
critical approaches to gender and sexuality require cultural contextu-
alisation to contribute effectively. Within tribal cultures, as Betty Bell
suggests, 'gender diversity – including but not necessarily paired with
sexual variance – is described as [...] a desirable and honoured social
construction in many North American tribal nations' (2004: 317). Such
investigations into gender and sexuality should not be confused with the
mutability of Native American performance characterisations – trickster, for example, takes on multiple identities of gender and sexuality in
performances that serve particular ritual functions. Trickster does not
cross-dress to perform a social role, trickster changes to become that
shape and function for the purposes of the drama. Shamans, also, as part
of their interpretation of tales in performance, will wear a variety of
dress associated with multiple genders and sexes; but this not a function
of a performative cross-dressing to produce a commentary on social
constructions of gender and sexuality – it is key to the performance itself
(Lang 1997: 151–60). A significant problem, therefore, for discussions of

Native American performance practices is the imposition of uninformed, if well-meaning, critical perspectives that construct gender and sexuality across a spectrum of cultural performance without heed to the history and function of those performative locations.

Critical practice in the past ten years has acknowledged the inaccuracies of its past dependency on discerning 'orality' as a one-story-fits-all, and the shift in methodological interpretation is key to reconceptualising the Native American as a diverse and dynamic figure in the history of Europe and America. This exploration of a performance history, and an overview of key performative strands in Native American cultural operations, hopes to demonstrate the ductility of theatre in America, in the face of a range of influences and factors and as the 'face' of American itself shifted.

We should keep in mind that the shapes of 'North' and 'South' America as specific regions with distinctive national identities are of recent history – and are specifically colonial. There are geographical distinctions that would have led to distinguishable empires, confederacies and chiefdoms; but the way we think about South America, Mexico, the United States and Canada came into being as a product of imperial possession and subsequent colonial wars. The Americas south of Mexico were the site of the earliest evidence of dramatic activity on the continent thus far. The South American subcontinent, which now consists of twelve independent countries, was home to a diverse range of Mesoamerican empires, including Olmec, Toltec, Aztec, Inca and Maya. Historical resources, based on the discovery of the Clovis site in New Mexico, have argued that somewhere between 5000 and 1200 BC nomadic tribes from Asia crossed the frozen waters of the Bering Strait. Travelling down the continent, they settled eventually in the regions of South America and established agrarian communities, based on the cultivation of corn. Recently, historians and archaeologists researching Native American culture and artefacts are beginning to challenge the concept of a monolithic 'Clovis' narrative of that early settlement in the Americas.[4] Origins notwithstanding, Olmec culture is regarded as the 'mother culture' of the southern subcontinent.

Significantly, Olmec civilisation is famous for the giant stone heads unearthed by archaeologists in the twentieth century. Carolyn Tate argues that the statues of La Venta, the centre of Olmec operations, offer an insight into the development of a pre-contact creation myth, and therefore a unique visual guide to an early performative culture. The monuments uncovered, Tate contends, 'in addition to their function as cosmic pillars', also served, potentially, 'to mark places for the staging of performances' (2008: 37). The site consists of statues, which operate as visual symbols of a particular creation narrative, but also incorporate columns across a platform, suggesting that this was a culture that built stages on which to act out that narrative of creation.

Olmec centres were beginning to fade by 200 BC and by AD 300 had disappeared altogether (although recent archaeology and performance-focused research is bringing that culture slowly back to life). Subsequent civilisations, such as the Mayans and the Aztecs, the latter standing as the dominant culture at the time the Spanish conquistadors arrived in the sixteenth century, have also left traces of performance strategies.

The north-eastern regions of the northern subcontinent were shaped, initially, by the Adena, in what is known as the early Woodland Period, from around 800–100 BC, overlapping with the Hopewell culture, which survived until AD 600. The Adena-Hopewell cultures shifted from nomadic hunters to semi-permanent communities, who took to an agrarian economy and culture, still moving occasionally in accordance with the seasons. Occupying the Ohio Valley, the Adena-Hopewell cultures have left evidence of social systems in earthworks, burial mounds and mercantile activities. The presence of goods made from a variety of materials that would have come from as far away as Lake Superior suggests an extensive trade network and interaction sphere. The Adena-Hopewell were famous for earth mounds, usually associated with burial grounds, shaped as animals and birds, indicating a cultural system in which ritual played a key role. However, little archaeological matter has been uncovered to develop our understanding of those practices. One of the most famous mounds in the region is the Serpent Mound which extends over 1,000ft, in a complex pattern of loops in the shape of a slithering snake, with an oval shape, either being consumed or regurgitated, at its mouth. The Serpent Mound has been variously associated with Adena, Hopewell and Fort Ancient tribal practices (which emerged in Ohio later than the Adena-Hopewell ancestry): traces of pottery from all tribes have been found at the site. Whatever its origins, the existence of the Mound, its geometry, its global positioning, and its aesthetic complexities determine that the peoples of the Americas in the North, prior to and at the time of contact, were socially and culturally dynamic.

Ephraim Squier and Edward Davies encountered the Serpent Mound in 1846, during their explorations on behalf of the Smithsonian. They began excavating it in 1848, at a time when archaeology was becoming a popular pastime across the United States, as part of an ideological mechanic constructing a 'history' for this new nation. The specific history established here is that of the 'Vanished Indian'. In 1888, Professor P. W. Putman, claimed as a seminal figure in anthropological studies in America, bought the land upon which the Serpent Mound resides. He produced the following account of his reaction to the location:

> Reclining on one of the huge folds of this gigantic serpent, as the last rays of the golden sun gleaming from the distant hilltops cast their long shadows over the valley, I mused on the probabilities of the past; and there seemed to come to be a picture as of a distant time, of a people with strange customs, and with it the demand for an interpretation of this mystery. The unknown must become known. (Cited in Randall 2003: 14)

Putman's comments are in line with the nineteenth-century nostalgia for an American 'past', inhabited by 'a people with strange customs', a mystical folk, whose very remains inspire a dream-like sensation in the man of science, taking his ease atop the sacred burial site. That tendency, to invent 'native' in non-Native terms, in terms of 'strangeness', though challenged, nevertheless has been perpetuated. One example can be found in Ross Hamilton's critical urge to link the Mound in the Ohio Valley with the 'religious heartland of the mystic East', conflating and exoticising belief systems of the 'past' in one sentence (2001: 6).[5]

The Hopewell system began to diminish around AD 400–500 in a graduated shift from Woodland to Mississippian structures. This structural modification continued into the colonial period, overlapping with the emergence of Fort Ancient culture, around 1400. The largest settlement of Mississippian culture was known as Cahokia and is situated in the floodplain of the Mississippi near the site of present-day St Louis. Timothy Pauketat and Thomas Emerson make reference to the 'large-scale labour projects (involving land levelling and monument construction), rectangular plazas, a palisade, elite burials and large residential areas' of Cahokia (1997: 5). Thus we can find evidence of complex cultural operations and conscious attention to spaces for the public display of performance in the city. Yet, Pauketat and Emerson point out that 'the Native Americans who lived in the area during initial contact with the immigrant Europeans knew nothing of Cahokia's prehistoric inhabitants is telling of Cahokia's ultimate demise' (ibid.: 6). Estimates of population in the region, although fluctuating, do seem to suggest that there would have been, subject to seasonal variation, around 10,000 at certain times and possibly up to 20,000, making Cahokia one of the largest cities in existence anywhere at that time.[6]

But, by the time the Europeans arrived in the region, there were no Native Americans resident in Cahokia. The city's structures, its politics and culture, seem to have vanished absolutely from the sphere of Native American operations, and also seem to be unmemorialised within subsequent cultural structures. The French monks that happened upon the remains of the city found that the Native American tribes in the region were uninformed as to its provenance, giving rise to a European myth that a more 'civilised' people had been in residence, of an entirely different 'race' to the current incumbents of the region. Recent scholars, however, have recognised that the demise may have been politically motivated. Around the latter days of Cahokia, the more egalitarian Oneota operations (as well as Fort Ancient) were emerging on the western regions of the Mississippian zones – around areas now known as Illinois, Iowa and the northern parts of Missouri. The Cahokian city was built on stringently hierarchical lines, with emphasis on elite rule, with non-elite groups paying tributes, and the city may have been deserted as a response to a shift in ideological operations.

Fort Ancient patterns emerged around 1400 in the northern reaches of Cahokian influence and, like Oneota operations, did not rely on the power of an elite. The looser confederacies of kinship groups and chiefdoms were constructed within the colonial imaginary as 'primitive', and percolated through narratives of 'savagery'. European attitudes towards the indigenous populations of the Americas, based on preconceptions about fluid social operations as 'primitive', would become, therefore, increasingly shaped by a drive to represent native peoples as they had always been represented within colonial narratives: either noble or brutal, the natives had to be 'savage', and the drama of encounter would become, as colonisation spread and the native population was deracinated, played out as a fraught and ultimately unconvincing act of civilisation versus savagery.

In the background, though, a diverse range of performance practices existed in the Americas, before, during, and after colonial momentum. It would be impossible to serve such a variety with any justice; yet, in order to appreciate the impact of cultural encounter in America, developing an understanding that such a range of performance material exists is crucial. It is not the purpose of this work to offer an extensive account of tribal dramas; but, rather, to explore the diverse and shifting performance strategies that contribute to the shape of Native American cultural output.

Native American Ritual Performance

There are clear distinctions to be made between tribal performance practices; but there are also key similarities, which are worth noting. Jeffrey Huntsman argues that 'despite the myriad [...] variety in Native American Drama, certain fundamental attitudes permeate all of it' (1983: 359). In distinction to concepts of temporal and spatial 'unities' that have permeated European drama since the writings of Aristotle, Native American cultural operations, argues Huntsman reside in 'the concept of non-linear time' and 'the concept of a dimensionless space' (ibid.). Both concepts express time and space as 'infinitely large, extending outward from the sacred event to include all creation, yet located around that event in a way that precisely fixes the position and assures the security of the participants' (ibid.). There is a structure, therefore, to the Native American world-view, one that fixes a central point – in ritual this would be the performance event – from which the cosmos is incorporated into that fixed point, creating a boundary, a loop, or hoop around that event.[7] Huntsman cites Joseph Epes Brown's explanation of the way in which the 'long house' symbolises that understanding, with its 'ritually defined centre' as an 'axis that pierces through a multiplicity of worlds [...] vertical ascent is impossible unless the starting point be the ritual centre' (ibid.). The defined centre, therefore, becomes a part of the dramatic enactment, crucial to the process of ritual; 'without such a centring in time and space', argues Huntsman, 'Native American dramas would be mere displays, robbed of their meaning' (ibid.: 360). Establishing a site for the enactment of the ritual, therefore, is foundational to the production of meaning. The sites of the Serpent Mound and Cahokia, therefore, take on distinct meaning for Native American ritual performances. Not all sites need to be so grandly dramatic, though, as these extensive ceremonial spaces: 'using ordinary living space', argues Huntsman, 'adds an extra dimension to the sacred ceremony, for it reaffirms the continuity between the parts of the cosmos that human beings conventionally inhabit and those in which their presence is charged with an unusual significance' (ibid.). The space for performance, then, can be grand ceremonial sites but can be also symbolised in the space for living.

Native American ritual performance, therefore, is not located as a cultural bolt-on, a commercial enterprise, but as a part of the organisa-tion of living. Richard Schechner draws attention to this very point in his consideration of the Arizona Yaqui Deer Dance, arguing that to the dancers, 'when the consumer audience comes in, the "spiritual power" departs' (1985: 6). Attempts to reclaim that 'spiritual power' of the ritual performance have been at the crux of much theatre theory and practice in Europe and American from the mid-twentieth century.[8]

Paula Gunn Allen argues that 'traditional American Indian literature is not similar to Western literature because the basic assumptions about the universe and, therefore, the basic reality experienced by tribal peoples and by Western peoples are not the same, even at the level of folklore' (2000: 51). To explore creative productions by Native Americans, one needs to reference, therefore, that whilst the enactments are distinct, and purposes varied, all ceremonial performances 'create and support the sense of community that is the bedrock of tribal life. This community is not made up only of members of the tribe but necessarily includes all beings that inhabit the tribe's universe' (ibid.: 57). Such intercon-nectivity feeds creative purpose. Western forms, Allen contends, are predicated on a system of poetic metaphors, where a symbol 'stands in' for something else. In Native American performance practices, symbols operate as a centre point for the demonstration of oneness. Symbols, therefore, are not understood as articulating an 'imagined reality [...] but that reality where thought and feeling are one, where speaker and listener are one, where sound and sense are one' (ibid.: 64). That which is symbolic is not separate or representative; it is part of the world from which interconnected spaces are available to be experienced.

Performance operates as such a central symbol for tribal organisa-tions. Those performances are, of course, not static; I focus here on a number of examples of Native American performance modes and characters, to illustrate fluidity and transformative possibilities, but this is by no means an exhaustive account of potential permutations.

Vine Deloria points out that 'Indian tribes, faithful to their tradi-tion, understand the origin of life on our planet as a creation' (1997: 212). Creation narratives are a recurrent dramatic ritual across Native American cultures, although the terms of its enactment are not consis-tent. There are some shared features: as Londré and Watermeier note, the congruence of social structure and nature operating jointly frequently recurs in the tales (2000: 31). Although some tribes have organised a scripting of their stories, creation narratives are a product of performance: spoken, acted, mimed in some instances, featuring shows about migration, integration of human and animal life forms, and transformation between physical forms. Creation narratives, argues Deloria, are not children's tales or spiritual accounts of human existence – as they have often been described by scholars – but are also constructs worthy of geological note (1997: 139). Deloria cites the example of the Chippewa narrative, which tells of sudden flooding due to melting ice, which can be dated to a time of rapid rise in the earth's temperature so noted by scientists (ibid.: 83). Creation narratives are performances that explore and express concerns about the wider context of human existence, where the material and spiritual do not need to be consciously brought into mutual contact; contact is part of the process of creation, and is embedded within the performance of that creation.

Duane Champagne explains that 'at the time of creation, many Native cultures received from the Great Spirit, often through intermediary spirits, the arts of culture, ceremonials, sometimes clan organisation, and political organisation' (2000: 5). The concept of creation, then, recognises no hierarchy between institutional and cultural codes. Creation tales tend to relate to place: 'ceremonials are held in these sacred places, and their performances recall the stories that define the meaning of the land and locations' (ibid.: 7). Colonial incursions, therefore, destabilised tribal cultures by destruction of the spaces that had been designated sacred at the moment of creation and had been recurrently asserted as sacred through performance.

Ceremonies of reciprocal exchange are considered to be significant performances of sacred cycles. That exchange took place within tribes, between tribes, or between groups within tribes, and between worlds – giving gifts to the dead as part of funeral rites was a major part of the ceremonial of reciprocity for some Native American tribes. The value of a gift is not measured in terms of commercial value, or material permanence – a song, poem or dance can be a gift between groups. Giving is not about commercial or value exchange between parties. This is not a commercial commodity-based market. The gift itself acquires prestige only in the act of giving – and prestige is an important measure of social status. But, argues McConachie, that prestige does not reside in ownership, in 'property or power' (1998: 115). Prestige is invested in the action of participation for the good of the social whole, not for individual glory. The performance, therefore, does not create an individual star to take centre stage: rather, reciprocity secures tribal survival.

One of the most famous forms of reciprocity is the ceremony of potlatch, performed by tribes in the north-western regions of the continent. James MacLynn Wilce argues that the reciprocity associated with potlatch has been critically denigrated as a 'purely material' form; 'introductory cultural anthropology texts', he argues, 'treat the potlatch in chapters with titles like "Economic Systems"' (2008: 199). The potlatch ceremonies represent distinct meanings in different tribes. Champagne notes that Tlingit tribes 'honoured clan ancestors, ended the period of mourning for a deceased relative, marked new ranks and titles, and paid off members of the opposite moiety for services rendered during a blood relative's funeral' (2000: 8). As such, argues Wilce, the giving of gifts to the dead is in payment, a form of tribute and recognition, a balancing of forces, and not to be understood as predicated on capitalist notions of exchange (2008: 199). For Kwakiutl structures, Champagne explains, 'the potlatch was associated with marriage, and noted the new wealth and status brought to the marriage by the bride's lineage' (2000: 8). The gift-giving here is also associated with balance, to ensure the affirmation of tribal structures; but it is done at a time of marriage, rather than as part of a funeral ritual. For Native American tribes, potlatch was a memorial for the departed and a celebration of continuance; European missionaries, however, regarded the concept as wasteful, as evidence of squandering and therefore anathema to Christianity and capitalism, both predicated on preservation of personal wealth and private acts of 'charity'. In Canada, ceremonies of reciprocity were banned in 1884; the United States followed suit early in the twentieth century. The ceremonial survived, however, and continues to be performed.

Huntsman suggests that, following the limitations placed on all aspects of Native American life and social operations, potlatch has shifted in emphasis from prestige to the 'ostentatious display and the demonstration of a hierarchy of wealth and privilege that puts, and intends to keep, all the members in their acknowledged positions' (1983: 367). Within some communities, also, concerns have been raised that the performance of potlatch ceremonials has become secularised. Sergei Kan cites the example of the 1975 Sitka Indian Education Program, through which Tlingit elder Charlie Joseph, Sr (Kaal.atk), was funded to teach traditional potlatch songs and dances to younger generations, whose knowledge of Tlingit culture had been limited by restrictions on tribal practices. According to Kan:

> Having mastered a number of traditional songs and dances, many of which are still performed in potlatches, the Sitka youngsters, known as Gajaa Héen Dancers, began taking part in various inter-tribal contests and festivals of native art and culture. They have also travelled to various places outside Alaska, performing for non-native audiences. While the children's success has received high praise from the elders, their ability to understand the deep meaning of what they perform and to empathise with those who are still moved to tears by the sad songs, have been called into question. Many elders say that without the command of the language and a good understanding of the traditional culture, the children will simply 'go through the motions.' (1990: 359)

Whilst recognising the validity of continued performance, tribes are contending with the concept of secularisation within communities and with an audience that does not participate in the sacred aspect of ritual.

Another shared feature of Native American performance dramas, argues Jeffrey Huntsman, resides with shamanism. Readings of shaman-istic activities tend to focus on direct contact with spirits, but, argues Huntsman, that is not necessary for the completion of shamanistic events. The display of context can be symbolic, in 'terms that represent true drama and does not depend on the immediate and direct manifesta-tion to the audience of the supernatural presence' (1983: 366). In other words, the shaman can draw on previous experiences of spirit visits and perform that concept of visitation, without compromising the validity of the exercise. For example, within curing rituals,

> on the psychological level, of course, what is crucial is the *belief* that the powers of the Shaman truly exist, and it is immaterial to the cure whether they are newly drawn at each cure or are, as it were, taken from stock.' (Ibid.)

Whilst shamanism might be 'dramatic', Huntsman further contends, it cannot be described as 'drama', for whilst 'the trappings of theatre may, arguable, be necessary [...] they are surely not sufficient' (ibid.). At the same time, though, the dramatic concept of the ritual brings it into the realm of structured performativity of the type that is associated with the theatrical format. Huntsman notes that while the shaman may

perform the concept of direct spiritual contact, it is not until the point
when 'the shaman begins to plan the ceremony in advance rather than
giving himself or herself over completely to the paranormal state' that it
becomes drama, in the sense of dramaturgical practice (ibid.).

Native American performance cultures all include a form of story-
telling that circles around the infamous trickster figure, whose physical
form varies between tribal narratives, but whose function is to bring
out 'death, illness, imbalance, and moral disorder' (Champagne 2000:
5). The trickster figure has been the subject of much critical debate, in
anthropological as well as theatrical studies. Paul Radin's 1956 study
locates the trickster as a constant figure in human narratives – a univer-
sally applicable 'type'. According to Radin, the trickster belongs to 'the
oldest expressions of mankind. Few other myths have persisted with their
fundamental content unchanged. The trickster myth is found in clearly
recognizable form among the simplest aboriginal tribes and among the
complex' (1956: ix). Inherent in Radin's assessment is a hierarchy of
cultural forms – he discusses the 'North American Indian' trickster as
one of the 'earliest and most archaic', of a 'type' that is to be found
generally in folk performances, and that figure is, therefore, 'primitive'
(ibid.: x). But, later critics, notably Franchot Ballinger, argue that the
trickster of Native American performances operates as 'a distinctive
dramatisation of the Native American view of life' (1991–2: 21). Tricksters, therefore, have emerged from distinct cultural and social forces.
The inherent performativity and absence of those fixed historical period-
isation that are integral faces of European and American epistemologies
mean that, as Ballinger suggests, 'we can see in the Native American
trickster an openness to life's multiplicity and paradoxes largely missing
in the modern Euro-American moral tradition' (ibid.). The trickster can
be, at any time and in any shape, good, evil, helpful, destructive and
malicious; the trickster operates between worlds and across worlds. The
mutability of the trickster figure, Jeanne Rosier Smith has argued, makes
the figure a 'vital actor' in the negotiation of social organisations and
understanding cultures and cultural shifts (1997: xii).

An important example of shifting performance practices can be
found, also, in the innovation of the Sun Dance, associated with the
hunter tribes of the Sioux nations.[9] This particular performance ritual is
a specific product of the eighteenth century. The performance is associated with Plains, Buffalo and hunting; but it was not until the arrival of
horses with Spanish conquests that the Lakota and Dakota tribes became

predominantly hunters. The performance is one that therefore grew
from a shift in social operations, as the hunting tribes became distinct
from the Pueblo agricultural locations. The Sun Dance has become
synonymous with famous Lakota chief Black Elk. The Lakota name,
Wiwanyag Wachipi, according to Brown's transcription of Black Elk's
testimony, translates directly as 'dance looking at the sun' (Black Elk
1989: 67) and requires the gift of flesh from the dancers who are bound
by leather thongs that are threaded through wounds made in their bodies.
The giving of the flesh is based on group dynamics: several of the tribespeople participate, including women, according to Black Elk (ibid.: 97).
No hierarchy emerges, and the participants are covered in rabbit skins,
to symbolise humility; this is a not a show of strength. The performative
drama resides in a display of endurance, as a form of ceremonial gift to
the sun, to demonstrate humility, to secure supplies of buffalo, and as a
method of entering multiple platforms of understanding with the transformation of the self through physical pain.

In the latter part of the nineteenth century, US government agents
began impeding the performance of the Sun Dance. The official rhetoric
was aimed at what was perceived as the 'barbarity' of the piercing of
flesh ritual. But, the performance had become feared by officials with
its ability to unite tribes and form common bonds across reservations.
Lakota tribes had been shifted into reservations since the 1850s, and
one of the main functions of this 'removal' policy was to 'break up the
community system among the Sioux; weaken and destroy their tribal
relations; individualize them by giving each a separate home and having
them subsist by industry'[10] (cited in Prucha 1984: 439). General John
Pope declared:

> The Indian, in truth, has no longer a country. His lands are every-
> where pervaded by white men; his means of subsistence and the
> homes of his tribe violently taken away from him; himself and his
> family reduced to starvation, or to the necessity of warring to the
> death upon the white man whose inevitable and destructive progress
> threatens the total extermination of his race. (Cited in Olson 1965: 3)

Following the Civil War, the process of 'Indian Removal' once again
gathered momentum. A key factor was the building of the Bozeman road
through Lakota lands, a project close to the economic heart of the United
States, and one that was resisted solidly by the tribal chiefs. General
Sherman, who had fought with the northern states against the south,

declared to the Lakota chiefs: 'the Great Father, who, out of love for you, withheld his soldiers, will let loose his young men, and you will be swept away'[11] (cited in Olson 1965: 78). The road, therefore, had become a symbol of the removal ideologies of Manifest Destiny: the 'Indian' had to give way for America to progress.

Another contributory factor was the discovery of gold in the Black Hills of Dakota, which had been designated Lakota territory in the 1868 Fort Laramie Treaty. Between 1874 and 1876, as miners discovered gold, Custer was sent in to remove Native Americans from the region, in an act of government-sanctioned contravention of the treaty. Although Custer was defeated – famously – in 1876, by 1877, troops had indeed 'removed' the Lakota from the region.

In the face of such attempts to destroy, literally and culturally, the tribespeople of the plains, the Sun Dance was, as Wilmer points out, 'reuniting the [Lakota] and in joining with other friendly tribes' (2002: 88). But the Sun Dance was, by the 1880s, coming increasingly under scrutiny by the authorities, who began to interfere with the performance of the ritual on reservations. In 1883,

> the commissioner of Indian Affairs issued a set of rules he hoped would stifle forever the 'demoralising and barbarous' customs of the Sioux. Henceforth it would be against the law to hold feasts and dances, and in particular, the Sun Dance. (Mails 1998: 3)

The suppression of the Sun Dance, though, produced another form of ritual performance. The Ghost Dance emerged at first within the Paiute tribes, under the auspices of prophet Wodziwob in 1870. Duane Champagne observes that in the immediate aftermath of the Civil War, Paiute peoples were 'in economic and social transition. Many worked for U.S farmers and ranchers as wage labourers, although they continued to live in their traditional lodges and hunted and gathered wild plants in the high desert' (2000: 35). The Dance was to bring about 'a great upheaval or earthquake' that 'would destroy the Euro-Americans and leave their houses and their wealth to the surviving Natives', and 'departed dead natives would be resurrected and live to claim the goods of the earth and the wealth of Euro-Americans' (ibid.). As Champagne points out, 'this revelation, in particular, was appealing since there had been great losses of life over the years' (ibid.). The prophet died, but the dance ritual was revived in the late 1880s, by prophet Wovoka, also Paiute, and this time with greater impact.

The Ghost Dance, assuming aspects from the Sun Dance within its configuration, took up the mantle of the prohibited ceremonial, reinvigorating and extending tribal unity in the face of government sanctions. The Ghost Dance, though, not only invoked the openness of the Sun Dance, it served a political purpose, reflecting the attitude of Native American tribes who refused to accept the Fort Laramie Treaty, and who had united to fight the treaty, electing Sitting Bull to be their chief. The Ghost Dance, then, operated as a very particular series of staged events in the history of America, circumventing US legislation by not only maintaining and developing tribal identities and structures but exploring and expressing communal methods of resistance to the imposition of law and culture by the government.

Inevitably, the popularity of the Ghost Dance, which attracted large gatherings of Native Americans in one place to participate in the performance, led to fears of antagonisms by the officers of the Indian Bureau who widely misunderstood the dance as symbolic of war. Although to the Lakota the Ghost Dance, Wilmer contends, ceremonially enacted the death of 'white settlers and to usher in a new independent nation in which the Indians would rule over a rich and plentiful land', the ritual was not a form of War Dance – to the Lakota, the Ghost Dance would eradicate white Americans through 'divine mediation', the summoning of 'a cyclone or whirlwind' (Kuwapi [Lakota], cited in Wilmer 2002: 87). The Dance, indeed, for other tribes, notably the Paiute, who signed the 1868 Fort Laramie treaty, was aimed more at co-existence. Although his message of the Lakota Ghost Dance was that of death to the white population, the Paiute prophet Wovoka had preached peace to the tribes. But the lack of interpretive initiative by white authorities expedited misunderstandings of the message of the Ghost Dance as a symbol of planned war. As DeMallie argues:

> For the Lakotas the dance was a symbol of religion, a ritual means to spiritual and physical betterment [...] For the whites, on the other hand, Indians dancing symbolized impending war [...] For the Lakotas, the ghost dance promised a reunion with the souls of their dead relations. For the whites it suggested that the Indians were expecting to die, caught up in a frenzy of reckless fatalism. (1982: 392)

The Ghost Dance, then, became infamous. The concerns of the authorities focused on Sitting Bull, regarded as the architect of the death of

Custer at Little Big Horn in 1876, who was believed to be a key participant in perpetuating the Dance.[12]

However, the only violence associated with the Dance came after the assassination of Sitting Bull; DeMallie argues:

> Sitting Bull's death was unrelated to the Ghost Dance. Agent McLaughlin had been clamouring for the old chief's arrest and removal from the reservation for some time, ever since Sitting Bull had refused to take up farming and be a model 'progressive' Indian. (Ibid.: 394)

Sitting Bull's death was one of a chain of events that led to the massacre of over 300 Native Americans at the end of December 1890 at Wounded Knee. But the Ghost Dancing continued, as Ostler points out, 'into the twentieth century, often interacting with other spiritual practices and undergoing significant modification' (2004: 363). DeMallie argues that by the end of the nineteenth century, 'whites assumed that Indian culture was stagnant and that the Indians could be transformed for the better only by the imposition of Western Civilisation' (1982: 390). However, what emerges, from an examination of performance history, is an understanding of how Native American cultures, under tremendous pressure to give way, were not only robustly maintained, but demonstrated dynamic creativity through the development of new performance strategies such as the Ghost Dance.

The ban on the Sun Dance was lifted in 1951 – inevitably, the Sun Dance had continued in various formats – but was now reinforced as a central performance of identity for the tribes. But, Clyde Holler warns, we should be wary of looking at the Sun Dance of the era prior to the ban as transiting into the contemporary version. Holler locates the former as the 'central religious ritual' and the latter as the 'central ritual' (1995: xx). As with the performance of Potlatch, Sun Dancing now faces the contingency of secularisation.

African American Forms

Erroll G. Hill and James V. Hatch makes reference to the 'unique conditions' (2003: 1) that brought about the cultural develop of a specific African American theatre: the slave trade, the trade in human flesh that funded the discovery and conquest of the New World. Portugal had early rifled the riches of Africa, and by the mid part of the fifteenth century, begun to traffic slaves to work in the Portuguese docks and fields. Hill and Hatch point out, 'there was no marked colour line' at this time and African and Portuguese 'mingled freely' (ibid.: 2). But, by the time of New World 'discovery' in 1492, racial distinctions began to be imposed. In earlier missions, Africans serving aboard ship were generally considered part of the crew; but by the 1500s, that situation had changed, and the mass operation of the slave trade had shifted into gear. Portugal was sanctioned by papal *Asiento* to carry slaves from Africa. Travellers to the New World took with them ships of slave workers for the sugar fields of Brazil, which, by 1532 had been claimed as Portuguese territory. Slavery in Brazil, we should note, was not abolished until the passing of the 'Golden Law' in May 1888.

Slavery brought with it resistance and, by the early years of the seventeenth century, escaped slaves were establishing a 'free' republic in the north-eastern regions of Brazil, variously, at this time, contested by Portuguese and Dutch forces. By the 1630s, this region, known as Palmares, established itself as an agricultural site, which traded with its colonial neighbours. Palmares was subject to attack from Portuguese forces, according to Ella Shohat and Robert Stam (1994), but managed to survive until the end of the seventeenth century. Errol G. Hill (1992) points out that a region known as Palmares remains in Brazil to this day. The inhabitants of Palmares came from all areas of Africa, and the social structure that grew up in the region was multiethnic, diverse and, to a point, tolerant, enabling cultural interaction, agrarian cooperation, governance and self-defence and, above all, strategic mechanisms to respond to conditions in the 'New World'.

Palmares, as a republic, was defeated by Portuguese forces in 1697; the story of Zumbi, the last king of this region, has become part of an ongoing theatrical narrative of the region. According to Arthur Ramos, the wars of Palmares were 'the first great epic of the African in this country' (1939: 42). In his collection of documents, entitled *Children of God's Fire*, addressing the history of slavery in Brazil from the fifteenth century to its abolition in 1888, Robert Edgar Conrad includes an article by Alfredo Brandão, which takes as its subject a performance festival that takes place in Alagôas, in the regions once occupied by the Palmares communities. The festival, according to Brandão, recalls 'one of the most important events in our history – the Palmares War' (1994: 378). As a performance strategy, the festival, contends Conrad, demonstrates 'healthy contempt for their ancestors' enemies [...] which, remarkably has survived for two and a half centuries', acting, thus, as evidence that 'the Palmares community were not totally eradicated in the late seventeenth century, as history would have it' (ibid.: 377). More substantial than the historical narratives of Palmares that stipulated an end point to that community, then, the theatrical tale of rebellion and resistance to slavery in the Americas is replayed, as a material sign of resistance to colonial power. National Black Consciousness Day, founded in 1978, is celebrated in Brazil on the day of the death of Zumbi – 20 November – and two key films as well as an experimental theatre group have revisited the events of the Palmares wars, Carlos Diegues's *Ganga Zumba* (1963) and *Quilombo* (1984).

The *Teatro Arena de São Paulo* emerged around 1953 as an experimental theatrical group, whose significant contribution to political theatre was Gianfrancesco Guarnieri and Augusto Boal's *Arena Conta Zumbi* (1965), which addressed the story of Palmares's conflict with the colonial forces in parallel with, as Margo Milleret argues, 'the Brazilian military dictators who imposed their rule after the 1964 coup' (1987: 25). Shohat and Stam argue that the Palmares Archaeological Project has uncovered evidence that the community also included 'Indians, mestiços, renegade whites, Jews, Muslims, and heretics, ultimately becoming a refuge for the persecuted of Brazilian society' (1994: 42). As a multicultural population that managed to forge a communal and inclusive social order, Palmarinos developed a syncretic language adapted from Africa and Brazil as well as a religious system that drew on both African and Catholic practices. Where conquistadors sought to eradicate indigenous practices through the accretion of Catholic rituals and systems, in Palmares, the polyphonic exchange between nations, cultures and languages was at the core of social being.

There is also evidence of concerted and significant ritual performance operations developed by the Maroon community, particularly those in and near Moore Town, Jamaica. These performances, which were strategic dramas of identity for a diverse, multilingual, multiracial social group, have become preserved as part of cultural memory. For those who were part of the Maroon culture, the concept of ancestry was central; a shared sense of belonging with ancestral voices forms part of the ritual of the Kromanti Play, setting out to affirm the oneness of Maroon peoples (Hill and Hatch 2003: 124). The play is derived from linguistic structures of Akan, in Ghana, from where most of the Jamaican slave population were abducted. The Kromanti Play involves dance, music, speeches and songs, within a strict structure. Werner Zips points out that Maroons 'are not free [...] to adjust ritual observance to conform to changing external factors' (1999: 172). Attempts to make changes would threaten the spiritual life of Maroons in the present time as well as that of their ancestors and therefore the very survival of Maroon culture. The Kromanti Play draws on African forms, but is not a specific re-enactment of any one performance mode; it is a product of a specific formation of a range of African voices, 'A new entity', Zips argues, 'for which their diverse African experiences were formative' (ibid.). The Kromanti Play is more than a response to slave conditions, therefore, it is a dynamic performance of traditions, albeit one with very specific parameters. The Kromanti Play is a memorial to a 'past', but also a distinct format for Black Jamaicans to conceptualise cultural operations.

It was highly unlikely that any non-Maroon would have attended to the performances in the colonial era, although the ceremony has become something of a tourist attraction since. Marcus Goffe argues:

> The Maroons have long complained of misappropriation of their knowledge. During the WIPO Fact Finding Mission to Jamaica in 1999, the Accompong Maroons complained that researchers from North America had gathered information and samples of Maroon plant genetic resources and subsequently published a book without providing any share of the benefits to the community. Cultural exploitation is also increasing, as government initiatives claim the Maroons as a national cultural and tourist attraction, and appropriate Maroon culture. (2009: 575)

The Kromanti performance has become both ritual drama of identity for contemporary Maroon culture, and theatrical entertainment for the tourist. But, in its eighteenth-century manifestation, the dramas of identity associated with the Kromanti Play were performed on behalf of and for the distinct bands of Maroon cultures, a form of performance endeavour developed in response to colonial conditions from the perspective of African and black residents and also those Native Americans who formed a part of the maroon groupings.[13]

One of the most infamous of performances emerging with African American communities in America is associated with Mardi Gras, a street performance that brings with it a plethora of tricky racial negotiations. The performers operate within an arena of racial indeterminacy that can be seen as both productive, as a challenge to hierarchies of identities in America, and problematic, in the assertion of an 'authentic Indian' identity. Joseph Roach quotes Allison 'Tootie' Montana (Yellow Pocahontas) who described one of the performers as looking 'just like an Indian' (1996: 193). There is no one 'authentic' account of the origin of Mardi Gras performance, Roach points out, but there is a 'tangle of creation narratives', that demonstrates a 'cultural politics of authenticity' (ibid.: 194). Some 'histories' are seen as damaging – for example, that the visits of Buffalo Bill's Wild West Show, the Creole Wilde West Show and the African Wild West Show inspired the performance. Such shows, though, are regarded as circumscribed by hierarchical discourses of racialised identities emanating from a dominantly 'white' political centre, and therefore 'deeply offensive' to the black Americans of the Mardi Gras performances (ibid.: 193).

Michael P. Smith argues, though, that the performers of the Mardi Gras theatricals should be considered as a product of Maroon ancestry. The performance operations fit the classic requirements of Maroon social and cultural structures, as 'renegade groups that maintain a year-round community dedicated largely to preserving their traditional African heritage' (1994: 45). Thus Smith situates the twentieth-century performers of Mardi Gras as descending, 'spiritually and culturally, and, according to oral history, by direct ancestry from those renegade, underclass groups in French and Spanish colonial New Orleans' (ibid.). The swamp lands around Louisiana were relatively supportive for runaway slaves, who formed links with Native Americans in the area, who were also, at this time, subject to enslavement by French and Spanish authorities. Slaves themselves in New Orleans prior to the Louisiana Purchase of 1803 were given some free time – generally to save their owners the cost of feeding them (ibid.: 46). Smith points out that:

> The Place des Negres (in later years known as Congo Square), located behind the old city, was a place where slaves, Maroons, and Indians gathered during their free time; it rapidly became one of the city's most important public markets. It may have existed as early as the late 1730s, but more likely became established in the late 1740s or 1750s, when the population of New Orleans was around two thousand. (Ibid.)

The square was also the meeting point for 'weekly processions [...] and legendary dance and drumming celebrations' (ibid.). Although the Louisiana Purchase effectively stifled the public demonstration of performance, the fundamental celebrations of African heritage continued (ibid.: 47). Roach points out that 'today's Mardi Gras Indians tend to sentimentalise the African-Amerindian encounter' (1996: 193). The reclamation of African heritage can be located, critically, as bearing troubling resemblance to the colonial American decision to cast its enmity to the Crown in the garb of Native identities. But, we should be wary of that direct comparison. The names of the Mardi Gras gangs are significant: all consciously acknowledge racial ambivalence: the 'Yellow Pocahontas', the 'Golden Star Hunters', the 'Spirit of Fi-Yi-Yi' suggest that the contentiousness of racial politics is a key part of the performance. Philip J. Deloria argues that whilst 'African-American Indian play – especially the carnivalesque revels of Mardi Gras – follow white practices to a degree', such practices should be considered from the perspective of 'a different history of Afro-Caribbean cultural hybridity' (1998: 8). Mardi Gras, then, operates as a performance type that consciously refers to and draws on the specific racial relations between African American and Native American, that grew out of slavery, conquest and the history of violence, that were imposed on both groups by colonial systems.

Jonkonnu is another form of public performance that developed in black American cultures. Whilst it has been located by some critics, notably Genevieve Fabre (Piersen 2002: 265), as an adaptation of the European mummers' play, anthropologist Martha Beckwith has suggested that the format can be assigned to an African lineage (ibid.: 266). John Canoe, also titled Jonkonnu and Jonkonoo, was a leading character in festivities practices by slave populations in North Carolina and Jamaica. The British government banned the performance in Jamaica in 1831, following a series of rebellions, but the practice continued. Jonkonnu, however, was permitted in North Carolina, being regarded as a way of maintaining order. In the manner of the carnival, the licence to conduct the masquerade was seen as an outlet for rebellious urges that might otherwise demonstrate themselves in slave uprisings. Unsurprisingly, though, slave uprisings were a constant feature of North Carolina, and the permitted freedom associated with the performance offered a resource for black slaves to find forms of unity against the slave state.

Traditions, then, in Jamaica and North Carolina, developed within distinct political frameworks. In Jamaica, the workforce in the nineteenth century was bolstered by importing labour from Britain's colonies in India and China, as well as from the regions of Sierra Leone, which is, according to Richards, where the performance originated (2002: 255).

The importation of labour from Africa, Richards argues, meant that the performance of Jonkonnu 'never lost contact with its African roots', whilst at the same time, 'specific black ethnic practices would syncretise within an "African" matrix and reflect contact with people from England, Scotland, Ireland and India' (ibid.: 257).

The character of Jonkonoo was appropriated by John Fawcett, in his pantomime of 1800, *Obi; or, Three-Finger'd Jack*, the story of a rebel Maroon, whose activities are finally thwarted by slaves loyal to the British owners. According to 'An Accurate Description' appended to the 1801 publication of William Burdett's *The Life and Exploits of Three-finger'd Jack*, the pantomime concludes with a fight scene followed by a ball, to celebrate the death of Jack. The ball is presided over by Jonkonoo, described as 'a grotesque personage, with a ludicrous false head, and head-dress, presiding as master-of-the-ceremonies at Negro balls' (1801: 55). Such an invocation of Jonkonoo inscribes meaning onto the figure: Jonkonoo is 'grotesque' and 'ludicrous'. Ideologically, the figure of Jonkonoo is inscribed by English concepts of performance, and becomes a festive master of revels for the slave population of Jamaica, a mimicry therefore of English forms of performance and thus disconnected from its cultural function amongst the slave communities.

But for communities informed by African cultural belief systems, the wearing of an animal mask was loaded with symbolic meaning. Errol Hill notes that 'Africans invested all things, animate and inanimate with a resident spirit that they were wont to placate through imitation and various other rituals' (1992: 231). The sporting of the bull-mask, for example, that was mocked in Fawcett's pantomime, to African cultures, demonstrates a symbolic 'reverence for the elements of nature that make man an equal partner with, rather than exploiter of, earth's riches' (ibid.). Jonkonnu, therefore, performed a very significant role for African cultures.

Hill makes reference to the journal of Michael Scott, resident in Kingston during the early nineteenth century, which records that the figure of Jonkonnu had begun to appear in 'an old blue artillery uniform [...] and three tarnished epaulettes, one on each shoulder and [...] the biggest stuck on his rump, the *point d'appui* for a sheep's tail' (Hill 1992: 232). The unrest of the late eighteenth and early nineteenth centuries, as Hill points out, had led to an increased military presence in Kingston; thus 'it it entirely possible that discarded uniforms would make their way into the Jonkonnu' (ibid.). The location of one of the epaulettes, at the joint of the rump and the sheep's tail, is more than decorous; rather, such a significantly irreverent costuming points to a radical dynamism in the political manifestations of the performance. *Obi; or, Three-Finger'd Jack* had tried to decentre Jonkonoo's power; but in Jamaica, the figure maintained both power and presence for African and black Americans. Indeed, the colonial forces understood fully the power of the masquerading figure of Jonkonnu, which caused sufficient discomfort to the political hierarchy for them to pass a ban in Kingston in 1831. The performance continued outside of the major colonial centres, though, regardless of legislation, and in the 1950s, Jamaican newspaper, *The Gleaner*, orchestrated a revival (Richards 2002: 254).

In *Incidents in the Life of a Slave Girl Written by Herself*, Harriet Jacobs records the function of the North Carolinian version of Jonkonnu:

> Every child rises early on Christmas morning to see the Johnkannaus. Without them, Christmas would be shorn of its greatest attraction. They consist of companies of slaves from the plantations, generally of the lower class. Two athletic men, in calico wrappers, have a net thrown over them, covered with all manner of bright-colored stripes. Cows' tails are fastened to their backs, and their heads are decorated with horns. A box, covered with sheepskin, is called the gumbo box. A dozen beat on this, while other strike triangles and jawbones, to which bands of dancers keep time. For a month previous they are composing songs, which are sung on this occasion. These companies, of a hundred each, turn out early in the morning, and are allowed to go round till twelve o'clock, begging for contributions. Not a door is left unvisited where there is the least chance of obtaining a penny or a glass of rum. They do not drink while they are out, but carry the rum home in jugs, to have a carousal. These Christmas donations frequently amount to twenty or thirty dollars. (1861: 179–80)

For the slave owner to supply rum or small funds was part of the act of sanctioning that momentary escape from drudgery for their slaves, a method, as I have said, of maintaining overall order on the plantations. The concept of the festivity, for Frederick Douglass, was also tied in with that sense of escape from the brutalities of the everyday life of slavery. Slaves, he points out, were encouraged to drink, to celebrate: 'it was deemed a disgrace not to get drunk at Christmas' (2007: 87). Douglass's dismay at the drunkenness is framed by the ideologies of the abolitionist movement, liberally laced with temperance and a Quaker disapproval of dissipated leisure. But his account tallies with a sense that Christmas festivities were permitted by slave owners as a momentary break for slaves from 'the system'. Peter Reed argues, though, that no matter how 'fleeting' such moment of liberty were, in material terms, the Johnkanaus of North Carolina, like the Jonkonnu of Jamaica, evoked a 'ritual power inversion' that would have a lasting impact across America (2007: 83). The evolving ritual of freedom that persisted in one of the most virulently policed of slave states offered an insight into a world without slavery – for slave owner and slave alike.

In this chapter, I have considered the implication of diverse performance practices across America that came into being from the framework of cultural perspectives and practices. Native American performance structures fall into a variety of categories, but demonstrate a shared concern with centring tribal identity, support and connectivity. In the late twentieth century, tribal groups were consciously reclaiming performance from the doldrums of colonial histories, making an effort to 'restore and extend cultural traditions and communities' (Champagne 2000: 46). The endeavours of Native American theatre groups have contributed to that task significantly, notably through the auspices of Project HOOP (Honoring Our Origins and Peoples through Native American Theater, Education and Community Development), individual theatre companies, such as Spiderwoman Theatre, and playwrights such as Rollo Lynn Riggs, Hanay Geiogamah, Judy Lee Olivia and Diane Glancy. Huntsman suggests that the Native American playwrights of the late twentieth century had continued 'to show the strength of the traditional aesthetics and metaphysics', associated with tribal cultural operations (1983: 370). From pre-colonial performance operations, then, through to contemporary theatrical productions, what has emerged is 'a sometimes battered but unbroken line of traditional dramatic art' (ibid.: 371).

Black American theatre has also looked to reclaim a sense of non-colonial identity. The system of performances that emerge within black American cultural operations focus on ancestry as memorial and as insistent presence required to maintain social stability and enable survival. In theatrical endeavours, also, the concept of memory and re-encountering the past has been incorporated into dramatic productions. Harlem Renaissance writer Marita Bonner, argues Annemarie Bean, is one of a group of Harlem renaissance artists who meshed 'pageant, folk, social issue and history', responding to 'W. E. B. DuBois' call to create "art of the black folk"' (2007: 91). The Black Arts Movement (albeit short-lived in its material form) and the New Federal Theatre picked up the mantle of the Harlem renaissance, and have contributed to a reshaping of theatre across the United States. More recently, groups such as Pomo Afro Homos and playwrights Anna Deavere Smith, Susan Lori Parks and Tyler Perry have been exploring concepts of racialised identities through experimental dramas examining the constructs of history and memory.

In subsequent chapters, I examine the development of theatrical practices as framed by a consistently shifting network from the seventeenth century to the present day. I start with an investigation into American theatre in the colonial era, from the arrival of the Spanish in the late fifteenth century, assessing the impact of colonisation on the production of theatre in America. As the colonials landed on America's shores, they were faced with a variety of social systems, some permanently located, others subject to seasonal shifts in location. Yet, with the arrival of Columbus, the myth of the one-size-fits-all 'savage' put into circulation by early explorers and travellers perpetuated. But the dramatic structures that we see emerging in the early colonial period suggest a far more complex exchange between local populations and settlers, as each began to assess and evaluate the other. Colonial exchanges, then, produced a complex series of encounter dramatics.

CHAPTER 2

European Forms

This chapter addresses two areas of concern for American theatre history: colonisation and diversification. Across America, the colonial presence was not a static or consistent force in and of itself. Theatre and dramatic performances were regarded as crucial, by Spanish colonisers, to conversion, conquest, repression and, therefore, control of tribal populations. French colonial settlers made use of theatre to assimilate Native Americans into the colonial project and ideologies. English colonisers regarded theatre as a form of devil worship and political protest, working to ban all theatrical activity. At the same time, though, religious leaders incorporated dramatic practices into preaching dogma. In this chapter, therefore, I delve further into the exchanges that took place between colonial settlers, English, French, Spanish, with brief reference to Portuguese, the earliest African populations and indigenous nations, and consider the relationship between religion, tradition and performance.

Early Exchanges: Spain

Antonin Artaud declared that his intended production titled *The Conquest of Mexico* would be 'The first spectacle of the Theatre of Cruelty', emphasising the significance of Spanish occupation to the development of European theatre history, as well as American (1958: 126). Spanish and Portuguese forces patrolled and dominated the Americas, almost unopposed, for two centuries following 'discovery' and the Treaty of Tordesillas in 1494 divided the southern subcontinent between them. One of the earliest of the Spanish invasions, in 1519, which conquered Mexico's chief city Tenochtitlán, was led by Hernando Cortés. The Spanish leader, adept at conquest, was also, as Castillo notes, 'an experienced adaptor of political theatre and dramatic gestures [...] not a stranger to the tactical use of performance' (2006: 29). Cortés requested that Franciscan monks be sent to the colony to organise the conversions to Catholicism required by Isabella and Ferdinand, Spain's royal 'Catholic Couple'. Cortés's request suggests, as Castillo notes, two issues: Franciscan monks must take a vow of poverty on entering the order, and would therefore be unlikely to cause political instability through greed; and their experiences at conversion in Grenada had taught them the values of performance and theatrical devices in the conversion of populations with vastly different linguistic and cultural structures (ibid.). Outright oppression would rob and indeed had robbed the Spanish settlers of their workforce in their unceasing search for gold. But performance could achieve what brute force could not: the conversion of the workforce, therefore the enabling of the work. The Spanish missionaries focused on the conversion of local children who became a rich source of information about traditional rituals and practices, ensuring that the Franciscans could match Catholic and Native liturgical dramas.

That the Spanish conquerors and religious missionaries, Franciscan, Dominican and Jesuit, found their way to communicating Catholicism through interaction with the Aztec social order on the level of theatrical performance should lead us to think more carefully about how we define the structures, function and purpose of theatre. For example, a play that is still performed in Guatemala is the *Deer Dance*, a traditional drama that was transcribed by Franciscan monks uniting hunting rituals with church authority to emphasise the 'benefits' of conversion. The *Dance* consciously celebrates the Guatemalan population's acceptance of Catholic orthodoxy, and Spanish military presence. The transcription of the play by Catholic monks elides pre-colonial history and culture as Guatemalan life begins in the *Dance* with the Spanish presence. What was produced in performance, however, was a dialogue between tradition and Christianity rather than an overwriting of those traditional practices. The appeal of Native performance practices, which incorporated vivid masks, cross-dressing and pantomimic gesture, came to be as important as, if not more so than, Catholic dogma.

In 1544, Juan de Zumárraga, Archbishop of Mexico, declared, 'it is disrespectful and shameful that in the presence of the Holy Sacrament men go about wearing masks and women's clothing, dancing and cavorting with immodest and lascivious gestures, making noise and drowning out the church hymns' (cited in Londré and Watermeier 2000: 46). The equivalence of performance with transgression was therefore assumed by the earliest colonial authorities in the New World. Throughout the latter part of the sixteenth century, the immense pageants of early coloni-

sation staged by Spanish missionaries were toned down in an attempt to
control and suppress the transgression that was rooted in multicultural
performance.

That policy, of staging smaller-scale productions under careful
monitoring and control, though, was no more successful in curbing
dialogic performance than the grand attempts of early strategies,
which saw flamboyant Catholic scenes drawn to a conclusion with
mass baptisms of the native populations. Another key example of those
later performance strategies organised by the Franciscans was uncovered, in 1996, by Louise M. Burkhart. A key text, published as *Holy
Wednesday: A Nahua Drama from Early Colonial Mexico*, is based on a
Spanish drama by Izquierdo Zebrero (1582) which was translated into
Nahuatl and performed as part of the Catholic calendar of events. *Holy
Wednesday* is based on the story of how Christ informs his mother that
he is to go to Jerusalem, where he will be crucified. She exclaims against
hisintentions, but is persuaded by letters from Old Testament prophets
that this is the path for her son. The play evokes audience empathy for
Mary, a mother about to lose her son, as well as informing the uniniti-
ated of the divinity of Christ. In Catholic Spain, the play was received
as part of the ritual of religious worship. In the New World, when translated into Nahuatl, argues Burkhart, the play was rendered 'culturally
ambivalent' (1996: 4). The act of translation, according to Burkhart,
does not merely reproduce the dogma of Catholic Spain, but stretches
the interpretation into 'a cultural critique of the Spanish model' (ibid.:
5). In order to interpret the play for a Nahua audience, the translation
shifts the emphasis of the dramatic interplay: for example, in the Spanish
version, Christ ponders his fate, toying with the concept of free will;
in the Nahuatl version, argues Burkhart, 'Christ has no choice' (ibid.:
91). Dominican Friar Diego Durán, paraphrased by Londré and Watermeier, noted the preservation of 'hidden meanings in performance'
(2000: 16) – that the strategies employed by the Nahuatl actors extended
the play's frame of reference. Beyond the textual distinctiveness, then, of
the Nahuatl script, we can also surmise that the performance of the play
would have conveyed a particular message to a Nahuatl culture aware
of the intrinsic meanings of dance and gesture that would not be available to a Spanish conquistador. Thus the imperatives of Nahua cultural
order intervene in the display of Christian performance, forming a type
of intercultural dialogue that is so significant a feature of theatricality in
America.

Colonial theatre, therefore, did not necessarily entirely overwrite or subsume local performance strategies. Whilst the Catholic missionaries attempted to reassemble elements of local dramas into the shape of Catholic tales, performance styles retained the mark of the traditional mould. Another play recently retranslated and republished is *Rabinal Achi*, a major drama from the pre-Columbian era, based on historical events that pre-date colonial contact. The drama has been handed down through generations, with signs of performance dating back to the thirteenth century, according to Londré and Watermeier, but also demonstrates a symbolism, argues Dennis Tedlock (2003), which relates to the Quiché royal social order of the fourth to the ten centuries in Guatemala. *Rabinal Achi* charts the conflict between the Man of Rabinal and Cawek, a Quiché warrior who has, without the authority of his ruler, invaded Rabinal territory. Read symbolically, the conflict between the two rival warriors can be read as representing the breaking up of the confederation of the Quiché and Rabinal nations, prior to the arrival of the Spanish in the early sixteenth century. The play, albeit founded on key characters and a particularly Mesoamerican dramatic conflict between rival tribes, assimilated a range of material following the arrival of the Spanish colonisers. Such a shift was forced, in part, as the play was rescripted for Christian propaganda. The story was analogous, Tedlock points out, with the life of the Apostle Paul that formed the subject matter of one of the miracle plays performed across medieval Spain, which became known as *Nima Xajoj* (*Principal Dance*). The plays also share focus on a soldier hero whose military career has finished and who will be decapitated in the finale of the performance (Tedlock 2003: 188). *Nima Xajoj* became the sequel to *Rabinal Achi*, clearly grafting Christian onto Mesoamerican symbolism, but at the same time ensuring the survival of a dramatic text relating to productions that pre-date colonial encounter.

We should bear in mind, though, that our scripted sources for *Rabinal Achi* come from European hands and from recent history, which may lead us to question, or to be suspicious of, the ideological weight in the hand of the coloniser that scribed the 'native' text. Charles Étienne Brasseur de Bourbourg, either from a manuscript or from the personal account of Rabinal inhabitant, Bartolo Sis – or both – produced a French edition in 1862. Any manuscript that may have been the originating source for Brasseur's text is no longer extant, but, argues Tedlock, the cultural act of memory in Guatemala makes the role of the script somewhat redundant, plays being transmitted from memory rather than manuscript (ibid.: 207–14). Although Brasseur, an agent of church and imperial centre, transcribed the play, he did so in the presence and under the supervision of Rabinal resident Sis. Rather than regarding the current version as tainted by colonial encounter, then, we can locate the text as a 'polyphonic' source of material within which the drama of encounter interacts within this narrative of Mesoamerican theatre.

In Spain, the New World provided dramatic material for theatrical production. Michael de Carvajal's *Complaint of the Indians in the Court of Death* was first published in Spain in 1557. Whether the play found its way onto the stage is debatable, although the structure, as Carlos A. Jáuregui argues, indicates that live performance was part of the writer's intention (2008: 4). The structure of the play is that of 'The Dance of Death', a motif popular with artists from all disciplines across medieval Europe and into the Renaissance era,[14] and therefore was framed by an aesthetic that would be familiar to audiences in old Spain. The subject matter, however, was informed by a very contemporary debate: colonial engagement, a dramatisation of the brutality of Spanish conquistadors on the Native populations. The Spanish imperial mission was framed by violence; as Patricia Seed notes, land was taken by force under the authority of the Requirement, which set the tone for subjugation, repression and 'an ultimatum for Indians to acknowledge the superiority of Christianity or be warred upon' (1995: 70). It is with a nuanced irony that, in scene xiv of the *Complaint of the Indians in the Court of Death*, the chieftain come to represent the grievances of the New World populations should say:

> Before we were Christians
> And still worshipped the silent gods,
>
> Crude, bestial, and false,
> Of the men who year after year
> Traveled through our lands,
> Not one came to kill or rob us,
> Or wage cruel warfare upon us.
> Now that we have seen the light
> And should by rights enjoy
> Even more pleasant life
> As the rewards justly due
> To those whose life is now pious,
> It seems that, wretched, instead

> We get injustice, murder and fire,
> Fierce and terrible events upon our heads.
>   (Jáuregui 2008: xiv, 28–43)

Jáuregui, in his introduction, points out that the ritualised Dance of Death, in Europe, forms an expression of anxieties produced by the 'frequent and catastrophic epidemics' of the fourteenth and fifteenth centuries in Europe (2008: 5). In Mexico, disease, as well as violent conquest, likewise took its toll, as much on European settlers as indigenous populations and the play engages with that issue; but it is specifically from a Spanish perspective. This play was written in Spanish, for Spanish consumption – a dramatisation of colonisation from the perspective of the coloniser and imposed on the body of the colonised. The chieftain speaks, as if a representative from the peoples of the Americas, but appeals to a specifically Catholic mantra of conversion to demonstrate the brutality of colonisation, framed by the requirements of Spanish ideologues – and authorities: without that framing concept, such a play would have been repressed by the Inquisition. The play, then, forms an investigation into what has gone wrong with the conquest of the Americas, and not an interrogation of colonisation as a legal right of Spain.

What has corrupted the process, the play argues, is gold, described by the 'Indian' chieftain as: 'the cursed wealth within our land' (ibid.: xiv, 46). Death responds to the plight of the 'Indians': 'Believe me when I say He'll [God] save you / From these marauding wolves' (ibid.: xiv, 339–40). Death is accompanied in the court by Saints Augustine, Francis and Dominic, representing the Mendicant orders, involved in the missionary conquests of the New World. Although the saints condemn colonial greed, one telling speech by St Dominic situates the New World as the harbinger of its own ills:

> Oh Indies why did you show
> Europe those treacherous metals
> That drew her with their false lure,
> Only to send her back home
> Loaded with so many evils? (Ibid.: xiv, 391–6)

And later in the same passage:

> O Indies, who opened the door
> To those miserable mortals
> Only to bring brawling and sorrow!

Indies who hold wide open
The very jaws of damnation!
Indies abyss of sinfulness,
Indies, wealthy with evil,
Indies, home for unfortunates!
Indies, that with gold pieces
Paved the pathway of sin! (Ibid.: xiv, 401–10)

The above passages damn the 'Indies' as a site of temptation too much for 'mortals' to contemplate. Reassuring the Inquisition, these passages note the trials of the occupants of the New World, but at the same time eroticise the 'lure' of base metals. Subsequent speeches shift focus from the plight of the indigenous natives of the Americas to the evil born of greed, the corruption of the Spanish themselves: in the speech of 'Flesh', we are told of 'every pauper dreaming / of dressing like the king' (ibid.: xiv, 424–5), sending social structures into disarray. Gold, thus, disrupts order, a challenge to class-based systems in which paupers can become kings. The 'evil' of the Indies' wealth, therefore, is radical in its capacity to overturn the order of Old Spain.

I suggested above that the play was a dramatisation of specifically Spanish issues, within the framework of an established performance framework, one that audiences of Spain would comprehend; at the same time, though, we can see that the reading of the colonial space has transformed the shape of the colonial centre irrevocably: the moral lessons of this (New) Spanish drama are shaped substantially by the conquest of the New World.

So, not only in dramas performed in the Americas do we see polyphony work to temper ideological poles. Spain's first 'Golden Age' playwright, Juan Ruíz de Alarcón, was born in the New World, in Mexico, and attended university there, before establishing himself in Madrid around 1613. Londré and Watermeier argue that his most famous play, *The Truth Suspected* (*La Verdad Sospecha*), written in 1619, demonstrates an 'elaborate courtesy typical of New World manners as influenced by the natives, sharp views expressed with brevity, more logical and reflective action than in Spanish *comedias*' (2000: 50). If Alarcón was indeed writing drama influenced by local behaviours in Mexico, then we should note Angel Flores's introduction to his translation of *La Verdad Sospecha*, which claims that the New World writer's 'style found imitators in other countries, such as Corneille, Molière, Goldoni, Schiller, and Victor Hugo' (1991: 136). That the work of a *Criollo* should be considered such an extensive influence on important European dramatists illustrates the tangled cultural reach of New World encounters.

Spanish strongholds were predominantly in the southern regions of the Americas, but several incursions northwards produced permanent settlements. The earliest of the colonial incursion into 'north' America established Spanish rule in St Augustine, Florida in 1565. By the late seventeenth century, New Spain stretched from the southern reaches of the continent through to the forty-second parallel, and incorporated regions now known as California, Texas and New Mexico. The population of New Spain increased exponentially – Londré and Watermeier record an increase in of Spanish settlers from 3,000 in 1574 to over 1 million by 1810 (2000: 50). Such an increase in population manifested itself, culturally and politically in a variety of works produced by *Criollos* as well as Spanish-born dramatists.

The shifting landscape of the American nation at the time of the colonial conflicts and wars can lead us to overlook some significant facts: for example, that in the years AD 300–900, Mexico had become an agricultural society, one in which performance rituals played a key part, developing special courts for ceremonial games; that by 1519, Mexico was a powerful nation, governed by Aztec Emperor Montezuma II, with a population of at least 5 million, with some estimates reckoning closer to 20 million, at a time when the population of London was in the region of 80,000; that the Inca empire, at the time of Spain's invasion, spanned the thousands of miles from Ecuador to Chile, operating from a tightly controlled centre and organised through a complex system of roads; and that, above all, the diverse cultural operations of pre-Columbian America and the repercussions of colonial contact should refresh critical thinking about theatre.

Playhouses, in the Spanish style, had been built in Mexican regions since the arrival of the Spanish in the sixteenth century, made from wood, and subject to the vagaries of the climate. Londré and Watermeier suggest that a wooden playhouse 'existed in Puebla de los Angeles as early as the 1550s' (2000: 53). Throughout the sixteenth and seventeenth centuries, New Spain produced a plethora of dramatic texts, theatre houses and performance strategies; from *autos* to secular drama, the dramatic productivity of New Spain was unrivalled.

French Colonies

Spanish and Portuguese dominance in the Americas was eventually challenged by France, Holland and England, and colonial regions with distinct flavours emerged. French colonial forces focused attention to the south initially, and then to the north, to the regions that would become known as Canada. In France, theatre had been managed by both monarch and church. At the time of colonial exploration, though, religious dramas were coming under the eye of the *Parlement*, and, in 1548, for the first time, the licence to produce drama in the Hôtel de Bourgogne was done so under the proviso that there would be no religious performances, marking a shift in the official state theatre of France from sacred to secular drama. Colonial excursions, then, coincided with a change in approach and attitude towards the concept of dramatic performance in France. According to Roaten, there was a 'tenacious conviction that the sixteenth-century French theatre is nothing more than a period of preparation for something better that made its appearance in the seventeenth century' (1960: 18). Such a preconception has been broken down, not least by an examination of theatre in France in the sixteenth century. The 1540s, argues Marvin A. Carlson, were 'the watershed years of the French Renaissance' (1993: 68). Earlier in the century, French humanists had been formulating a body of theatre criticism, with the publication of Reginaud de Queux's *Instructif de la Seconde Rhétorique* in 1501 and Lazare de Baïf's translation of Sophocles's *Electra* in 1537 bringing classical Greek structures into communion with the increasingly secularised performances of the sixteenth century.

The conflict between religious factions in France also fed into the attitude of explorers in the New World. Huguenot missionary Jean de Léry was sent to Brazil in 1556, having been trained by the Calvinist Genevan church. His record of that visit, *Histoire d'un Voyage Faict en la Terre du Brésil* (1578), was written in part, argues Castillo, as a riposte to André de Thevet's *Cosmologie Universelle* (1575), which had blamed the Huguenots for the failure of the French colony in the region: the Portuguese had taken that territory by 1560. Léry's *Histoire* constitutes a record of emerging religious divisions within European nations, as papal control stuttered and Protestant reformism spread. The New World became the stage for encounters not only between settlers and incumbent populations but also between European religious dogmas and codes. Catholic missionaries, mainly Franciscan, Dominican and Jesuit friars, found the theatrical practices of liturgy suited their purposes. But their Protestant counterparts, suspicious of the iconography of performance as representation, Castillo contends, 'were reluctant to resort to dramatic performances as a tactic for spreading the Faith' (2006: 51).

Prior to Léry's voyage in Brazil, the French King, Henry II, had been treated to a fine display of Brazilian 'life'. Janet Whatley in her translation of the *Histoire* notes that, in 1550, in Rouen, a 'spectacle' was put together to greet the new king: a 'mock Brazilian village, where fifty real Tupinambá Indians, joined by two hundred and fifty sailors in savage guise (naked and painted black and red), hunted, cut Brazilwood, fought amongst the trees, swarming with parrots and monkeys' (Léry 1990: xxiv–xxv). The Brazilian extravaganza was part of the Royal Entry festival, a ritual dating back into medieval France. As Michael Wintroub points out, what had been a 'relatively simple affair', had 'by the end of the fifteenth century [...] become an elaborately constructed ritual drama, with richly produced pageants marking the various stages of the king's itinerary' (1998: 465). Even by contemporary scales, though, the entry of Henry II into Rouen was extraordinary, being amongst the 'most spectacular and elaborate entries ever staged' (ibid.: 466). And the most exotic of spectacles 'extended from Old World to the New, for there, before [the king], on a small strip of land two hundred paces along and thirty-five wide, was a Brazilian village' (ibid.). Janet Whatley suggests that Brazil had thus become a 'consumer item', for French colonisers, performing as signs of savagery and exoticism for the imperial gaze. Indeed the construction of 'Brazil' in Rouen does conform to and confirm the brutal ideologies of non-Christian 'savagery'; at the same time, though, encounters in the New World had brought a new imaginary to France, in a renewed and invigorated range of pageantry and performance. The Tupinambá also visited Rouen in 1562, meeting with King Charles IX and, more famously, Michel Eyquem de Montaigne, whose essay 'Of Cannibals' has long been regarded as seminal in the study of Renaissance Europe. The French presence in Brazil was aborted by the Portuguese in 1560, and it was not until the beginning of the seventeenth century that France again focused on settling the New World, this time much further north in Acadia, and with much more impact.

In the early years of the seventeenth century, a variety of settlements sprang up in Acadia/Nova Scotia, including Port Royal, scene for the 1606 performance of *Le Théâtre de Neptune en la Nouvelle France* (*The Theatre of Neptune in New France*). The play was written by Marc Lescarbot in honour of the settlement's leader, Baron Jean de Biencourt de Poutrin-court, as a method of yoking potentially destabilising elements within the colony. In his *History of New France* (1609), Lescarbot describes the status of the colony as 'in danger of mutiny' suggesting, indeed, the need for a distraction (1907: 341). Lescarbot's 'jovial spectacle' *The Theatre of Neptune in New France* performed that role, harnessing the energies of a potentially mutinous colony and reinvoking the power of the returning leader (ibid.). Although, in reality, Poutrincourt was returning from a failed exploration, which had put both colony and travellers in danger, the enactment of *The Theatre of Neptune* was predicated on his triumphal procession into Port Royal and on to Fort Royal for a celebration feast. Hannah Fournier argues that the spectacle is therefore a form of the Royal Entry ceremonial, in which the principal figure was:

Welcomed by the more important residents and escorted to his destination where he was offered a feast [...] he was also offered reassurances of their loyalty by representatives of the various orders of inhabitants. The entry was a visible sign of a contract between ruler and subject town [...] the ordered form of entry expressed symbolically the relationship between the entering dignitary and the townspeople, as well as providing an opportunity for communal rejoicing and solidarity. (1981: 3)

The term 'ceremony' is significant here. Patricia Seed argues that in French, unlike other European languages, 'ceremony' frames a set of meanings, one of which is 'complex' – as opposed to simple, and, also, 'ceremony, in French alone, signified order. To do something ceremoniously was to do it according to the rules' (1995: 49). Lescarbot, the French intellectual, with knowledge of the forms of such ceremonies in France, produced a spectacle that was tailored in accordance with a specific set of regulations for the processional Royal Entry. Nautical motifs featured in such ceremonies as they did in *The Theatre of Neptune*. As Margaret McGowan points out, on Henri II's entry into Rouen, following a successful campaign against the English, he was greeted by Neptune, 'offering him dominion over the waves' (1968: 222) in a manner we see very clearly resonating in Lescarbot's play.

A further structural echo can be found in the stage effects set up for the performance. In his *History*, Lescarbot describes how, 'to give the greater honour' to Poutrincourt on his return, the colony has 'set up above the gate of our fort the arms of France, encircled with crowns of laurel [...] and with the King's motto, "*Duo protegit unus*"' (1907: 341).

Effectively, then, the staging invoked the power and majesty of the ruling order of France. The spectacle thus elevated the returning leader Poutrincourt to the league of kingship in the theatre of the New World. As a political tool, the play served a dual purpose: holding the colony together in the absence of the leader, and ensuring that the position of the leader was secured as an intrinsic part of the spectacle.

At the outset of the performance, Neptune greets Poutrincourt:

> I will always send you good winds to fill your sail.
> The day will never dawn when your splendid plans shall fail.
> Fine courage you have had, that has led you to explore
> With a bold constancy this strange and fog-bound shore,
> That you may here establish a wide realm for France
> And carefully may guard my laws from all mischance.
> By my sacred trident, by my sceptre, I now swear
> That to favour this high project shall be my happy care!
> Even though you override me I shall never take my rest

And continues:

> I forsee the day
> When a prosperous domain you will prepare for France
> In this fair, new world and future you will enhance
> The glory of de Monts, so too, your name shall ring
> Immortal reign of Henry – your great king. (Lescarbot 2006: 62–3)

There is little subtlety in this rhetorical strategy; it is a consciously wrought ceremony of triumphalism, of order and of possession.

A notable feature of the production was a scene with Mi'kmaq hunters bringing gifts to Poutrincourt. There has been speculation that the Mi'kmaq figures were performed by French colonists in costume – 'playing Indian', to borrow Rayna Green's expression (1988: 30). The 'Indians' brought gifts, of deer meat, beaver skins, a scarf and bracelets, to this royal representative from France, to demonstrate their allegiance to his rule in the region. The bringer of deer meat concludes his speech with a desire 'to live forever in your grace / is all our wish, our whole desire' (Lescarbot 2006: 66). The giver of the scarf and bracelets declares ''Tis not alone in France / That Cupidon commands / Throughout this young new France / As in your world he stands' (ibid.: 67). A fourth figure is empty-handed despite his best efforts to harpoon a fish, but declares that he will 'try / my luck upon this rocky coast. / Perchance upon this shore will lie / Something for your cook to roast' (ibid.: 67–8). The tribespeople, therefore, promise to ally with the French for the present, a promise made manifest in the gifts and words of the first three 'Indians', but also for the future, in the shape of the empty-handed harpooner's pledge to continue his hunt on behalf of the colonisers. The offering of gifts by the 'Indians' would seem to confirm, as Susan Castillo points out, 'subservience to the designs of French Imperial policy' (2006: 164). *The Theatre of Neptune*, therefore, was a consciously constructed celebration of French colonisation – an imperial drama staging a specifi-cally political spectacle.

The play also incorporated local language forms: for example, the Mi'kmaq term for leader, 'Sagamos', is repeated throughout, addressed to Poutrincourt, made 'chief' of colonials and colonised alike. Further, the audience for the performance consisted of the French settlers and members of the local Mi'kmaq communities. Therefore, the imperial message grafted explicitly into the performance was to be carried to coloniser and colonised alike. Alan Filewod suggests:

> In this moment of racial impersonation and colonial masquerade, Lescarbot had claimed the new world in a new way by enlisting the spectating bodies and appropriated voices of its inhabitants in his imagined theatre, and he had established the principle that the colonialism of spectacle is the necessary precondition of imperial invasion. (2002: xiv–xv)

And Rick Bowers concludes that *The Theatre of Neptune in New France* is:

> An accompaniment for a new world perceived as untamed and hostile, but also one in which the French now consider themselves resident. The mythic and the realistic have been merged to produce the cultural material of the script through an image of hegemonic interaction in which the Europeans predominate. The play thus encodes sweeping and unprecedented social energy: new-world exploration and endur-ance, European/Native acculturation, cultural hegemony through assertion of the dominant myth. Its author has both a practical and metaphorical purpose in mind. (1989: 48–9)

Thus, one of the founding moments in the history of Euro-American theatre is also one of the founding moments in the determination of cultural hegemony, and colonial control.

Susan Castillo points out the practical difficulties of the performance and in the process makes reference to a key aspect of performance strategies: 'the audience of colonists would have been at some distance, and would not have been able to hear the words of the actors', although they would have been able to 'enjoy the colour of the costumes and sounds of the trumpet fanfares and cannons' (2006: 166). The issue of audience and performances is complex, and a traditional performance transported to a unique location inevitably encounters a shift in structure, atmosphere and reception. Lescarbot locates his spectacle as 'a ceremony absolutely new on that side of the ocean' (ibid.: 341). Indeed, this ceremony, albeit drawing on the established conventions of the Royal Entry format, becomes a 'new' performance type within this New World space, fashioned at the Land's End of the Acadian colony. Lescarbot seems to suggest that the newness of this ceremonial relies on its location: the scene is what has changed, rather than the performance type. But there is a shift in spectator as well as spectacle. The 'newness' of the performance resides also in its being brought to a new audience. The Mi'kmaq spectators, no doubt, were familiar with the concept of ritual demonstrations of power, but the format of this display would have been alien. Alan Filewod points out: 'For [the aboriginals] this was a spectacle of the new and was likely incomprehensible as a performance [...] two sets of eyes saw two very different events' (2002: xiv).

As discussed in the introduction to this book, Richard Schechner's detailed studies in theatre theory have stipulated several key points about the concept of performance, and the role of the audience. To Schechner, the performance itself, the manifestation of the spectacle, is 'the domain of the audience' (1988: 70). Audience, however, is not monolithic or homogeneous; a range of interpretations are possible within one audience. History also makes a distinction to audience reception: at the time of its performance, *The Theatre of Neptune*, we have seen, is a product of the Royal Entry ceremony, which was understood in very specific ways by the colonial population of Port Royal, who were aware that their leader had returned and their fealty was to be sworn. Jerry Wasserman's 400th-anniversary edition of the script, published also in 2006, notes that *The Theatre of Neptune* is 'paradigmatic of a kind of performance that was more than just art or entertainment [...] that engaged political and cultural issues that were specific to North American colonial history but that remain current' (Lescarbot 2006: 9). The play's currency is demonstrated by the *Sinking Neptune* project currently underway, which was initiated as a challenge to an attempt by the Nova Scotia theatre company to stage a production of the play on its anniversary, *in situ* at Fort Royal. That proposed performance did not take place – there was no funding granted. But the opposition group, Optative Theatrical Laboratories, went ahead with *Sinking Neptune*, and a script of their performance is available at their website.[15] The caption on the cover reads 'this is a play about cultural genocide'. Although, as noted previously, we cannot know what the spectacle would have meant to indigenous spectators at the time, we are clear about what it symbolises for First Nation people now, in the context of the history of colonisation.

The distinction between audiences' receptions is also informed by the concept of performance as it was emerging across Europe and performance strategies as they were practised in tribal communities. By the seventeenth century, European models of performance had become recognisably shifted along Schechner's dyad of efficacy and entertainment towards the leisured end of the spectrum. The invention of the printing press enabled the flow not only of religious documents but also of secular accounts of classical staging effects. Acting was a profession in European nations – only just, perhaps, but nevertheless, there were members of the populace who took it upon themselves to act for a living. And audiences went to be entertained. As Jean-Christophe Agnew argues, 'not withstanding the many ceremonial [...] residues to be found in renaissance drama, people streamed to the [...] theatres in order to watch a professional presentation of an entertainment' (1986: 103). At the time *The Theatre of Neptune* was performed, then, a gap was emerging between sets of spectators growing accustomed to entertainment, and groups who predicated their performance strategies on efficacy: although both were a feature of this production. As I noted earlier, the French colonists would have enjoyed the spectacle as an entertainment, whether they would have heard the speeches or not – with trumpets, canons and merry costumes, there was enough to occupy their attention. The performance, though, would also have been recognised as a ceremony within which Poutrincourt took his place at the head of the colony: a ritual display of power and control.

However, in the enactment of ritual forms across the tribes of the North American continent, the event, as Jeffrey Huntsman argues 'establishes and maintains (even when the details of the event are all known in advance) that extends to all participants, "performers" and "audience" alike' (1983: 367). We have no evidence of the Mi'kmaq audience's appreciation, or lack thereof, for the sight assembled before them, or that the symbolic power of empire was communicated at all. Perhaps, though, we could speculate on other ways of thinking through this ceremonial spectacle. We have seen that the piece echoes the format of the Royal Entry pageant, a ritual event specific to France in the era of the Ancient Regime. The format suggests a celebration of royal order, where a respectful populace greet their king with gifts and promises of fealty. Michael Wintroub argues that the concept of the procedure resided in a 'reciprocal contract between the king and the people' (2006: 22). Wintroub cites Nicolas de Montand's *The Mirror of the French* (*Le Miroir des François*, 1589) as evidence for this claim, which states that 'when the king enters into any city or province, he is held to confirm its privileges, and to swear that he will maintain its laws and customs' (ibid.: 95). In the existing script for Lescarbot's version of the Royal Entry, we find no references to Poutrincourt's responses to the speeches of the performance, other than the odd note in the script detailing that he 'thanked' Neptune and 'the Indians were also thanked for their good wishes and devotion, and they were invited to come to Fort Royal and to take bread' (2006: 68). Perhaps in this suggestion of hospitality, we find some seeds of the 'reciprocal contract' of the Royal Entry. We learn, from Lescarbot's *History* that Poutrincourt established the Order of Good Cheer, to ensure the health of the colony, following his return; individuals were, by rota, made responsible for delivering supplements to everyday fare, through hunting, fishing or trapping. We also find that the Mi'kmaq chief and tribespeople were frequent guests – and no doubt at times suppliers – of the assemblies that resulted from the establishment of the Order. Generally speaking, French colonists were less directly antagonistic to indigenous populations than their Puritan counterparts further down the coast. Their numbers were smaller and the approach to colonisation focused more on dialogue, diplomacy and mediation: though that mediation did involve shooting the tribal enemies of those communities with whom they had forged alliances. Indeed, just two years after the performance of *The Theatre of Neptune*, Lescarbot records in his *Histoire* how explorer Samuel de Champlain, who had been instrumental in establishing the Port Royal colony, joined with a group of Huron and Algonquin natives and opened fire on their enemies, the Iroquois, with an outcome of lasting hostility between the French and Iroquois nations. The Port Royal community, though, seems to have maintained a stability and peace between Mi'kmaq and French colonists.

The history of the relations set out here is tricky, in that it is framed by Lescarbot's version and we are not privy to alternative accounts. But, perhaps, within the enactment of *The Theatre of Neptune*, and its aftermath, although the work of colonial hegemony was achieved, one might unveil another interpretation, related more to audience perception of the drama through its performance. If indeed, as Lescarbot claims, a mutinous cloud hung over the colony in Poutrincourt's absence, and fractures were appearing in the colonial body politic, tensions would have been visible to all living in the region. The rapidity of colonial spread through violence, and the potential threat therefore to the Mi'kmaq nation in the surrounding areas, would have been evident to Chief Membertou. The volatility of the colonial presence, with enmity between French colonists and Algonquin tribespeople, may have suggested to Membertou that the most secure future for his tribes resided in the continued leadership of Poutrincourt. *The Theatre of Neptune*, then, may have communicated a sense that Membertou had, at this point, no need to prepare for the type of colonial war that would eventually become a feature of the entire continent. In the short term, at least, *The Theatre of Neptune* may have operated, for Chief Membertou, as a dramatisation of future stability rather than a symbol of future colonial violence and usurpation, though that would come soon enough.

I am not suggesting that the situation here was some sort of Utopia, or an idyll, or a representation of a symbiotic cultural relationship, but that the tribes were managing the situation carefully, to ensure minimum confrontation with a potentially lethal force in possession of an array of combustive weaponry. Membertou died in 1611 from dysentery (of course, a European disease), but good relations between the tribes and French settlers continued. When violent confrontation did reach Port Royal, it was at the hands of English sailor, Sir Samuel Argall, who had been commissioned by the council of the Virginia Company to destroy all French settlements south of the 46th parallel. Port Royal, therefore, fell to the English in 1614 and the managed diplomacy of Chief Membertou was finally over.

Londré and Watermeier note that, in terms of documentary evidence, 'a thirty-four year hiatus follows *The Theatre of Neptune*' although it is likely that further performances took place' (2000: 77). One of the problems of finding records of performance history in New France is the lack of settled communities. The charter governing the region dictated that only French Catholics could colonise the region, so the populations remained small and feudal – Catholic – in structure. The role of religion in the affairs of New France cannot be overlooked. Port Royal was, in the first instance, funded by merchants, and therefore its politics were linked to its economics. Later, as Jesuits became financial backers of French colonisation, Catholicism was embedded firmly in the structure of social organisation. Jesuits in New France, like New Spain, were thirsty for conversions. In 1640, Governor Montmagny of Quebec, in celebration of the birth of the dauphin (to be Louis XIV), organised a performance of a mystery play by the Jesuit missionaries. The 'entertainment' turned inevitably into a political and colonial affair. According to later Jesuit records, 'we had the soul of an unbeliever pursued by two demons, who finally hurled it into a hell that vomited forth flames', and those 'demons', spoke 'in the Algonquin tongue' (cited in Londré and Watermeier 2000: 77). Thus the performance ensured the transmission of a specific message, 'so that those Indians present', declares Elaine Nardocchio, 'might understand the moral significance of the play and realise the fate of the unfaithful' (1986: 4). Another available interpretation is, of course, more literal: to the French colonisers, Algonquin tribespeople were demons. The dominance of Catholicism on the politics of New France overthrew the diplomatic complexity that can be seen in *The Theatre of Neptune* and its reception.

In terms of the development of theatrical performance across the American continent, the Jesuit presence twined performance with an urge to control and convert local tribal populations. In Quebec, students from the Catholic seminaries were responsible for the majority of productions. The tragedies of Corneilles were popular, particularly *Le Cid*, perhaps unsurprising given that Corneilles's drama is based on the demonstration of heroism by Spanish nobility defeating 'Moorish' invaders, a symbolic evocation of the relations between Spanish colonials and colonised populations. The Royal Entry format that we witness in *The Theatre of Neptune* was also a recurrent feature of early theatricals within the Jesuit and Ursuline colonial groups. In 1658, as recorded in Luc Lacourcière's *Anthologie Poétique de la Nouvelle France*, 'a little play in French, Huron and Algonquin' took place (cited in Castillo 2006: 169). The performance of 'The Universal Spirit of New France Presents all the nations of Canada to the Governor', took place in the garden of the Jesuit school, with enough seating for all of Quebec's population of around two thousand. Londré and Watermeier note that the performers 'spoke in four different native dialects', which were translated for the French audience by a character named 'the Universal Genius of New France' (2000: 78). The performance pays tribute to the newly arrived Lord Governor, Viscount d'Argenson, and, more specifically, to the French Jesuits as 'saviours' of Huron and Algonquin tribes against the Iroquois. The 'native' roles were played by French performers – in this instance, children from the Jesuit school. The performance dramatises what was specific and distinct in French colonisation in the New World: colonisation through negotiation and alliance.

As Castillo notes, curiously, whilst there is no record of authorship for the performance, the names of the cast have survived. Nor, in any account I have read, has there been mention of Algonquin or Huron peoples present at the performance. The Royal Entry pageantry of *The Theatre of Neptune* was a dramatisation of colonial power, as we have seen, but it also demonstrated the nuances and complexities of that power, performed in the shared social and economic space of the port, and before a diverse audience. This later version, however, is performed in the enclosed space of the Jesuit school garden, in 'the sight of all the people of Quebec' (Lacourcière, cited in Castillo 2006: 169), more specifically, all the French colonials in the region. Therefore, the format of the Royal Entry drama, framed by the political dynamics of the Jesuits, has shifted emphasis from the power of diplomacy to the controls of conversion. For the remainder of French colonisation of the northern regions, Catholicism would control and censure theatrical output, a situation which came to a head in 1694, as a proposed performance of Molière's irreverent comedy *Tartuffe* was planned. The Bishop of Quebec, Jean de la Croix-Chevrière de Saint-Vallier, who had spent several years protesting against entertainments as damaging and licentious, succeeded in cancelling the performance. It would be another century, almost, before plays would be staged again in Quebec, and then, it was as a response to the fall of New France to English forces, in 1760.

New England and the West Indies

For the English, the battle for power in the Americas was initially profiteering, founded in prize-taking – or pirating – Spanish ships laden with goods for trade, and raiding coastal settlements. Francis Drake, prior to his knighthood, spent three years between 1577 and 1580 looting territory from California to Peru. England's emergence as a superior sea power

set the stage for a more concerted and organised set of colonising strategies. Settlements were formed in Newfoundland and North Carolina
in the 1580s; they did not survive for any extended period. It was not
until the establishment of Jamestown that England could declare itself a
colonial presence in the region.

During the sixteenth century, England's attempts in the New World
were limited by the internecine strife of the Reformation. Richard
Hakluyt wrote *A Discourse of Western Planting* in 1584, for Queen
Elizabeth I, in which he argued that England required colonies in the
Americas as an extension of reformist worship, for trade and commerce,
and to offload unwanted surplus labour from its own shores. Sir Walter
Raleigh's half-brother, Sir Humphrey Gilbert, was granted a royal patent
to organise New World settlement. Gilbert initially did so in Newfound-
land, although he was lost in a shipwreck on his journey home. Raleigh,
with the approval of the Queen, established a colony in North Carolina.
The settlement, though, when Raleigh returned to it in 1590, was gone.
'Roanoke', England's 'Lost Colony', marks the fragile relevance of
England in the colonisation of the New World in the sixteenth century.
When settlers from England finally began to establish permanent sites
in the Americas, it was as economic developers and as religious exiles.
James I contracted the Virginia Company in 1606, which consisted of the
London and Plymouth Colonial groups, who were directed to occupy
and explore locations on the east coast, looking for the riches found by
Spain in the southern hemisphere. The Native American nations of the
east-coast regions were Algonquin-speaking members of the Powhatan
confederacy and were themselves agrarian, raising crops of corn.

One of the most infamous dramas of Anglo-American history stems
from the settling of Jamestown. The story of Pocahontas has been the
subject of many spectacular texts and performances, the first being
Captain John Smith's own account in his *Generall Historie of Virginia,
New England & the Summer Isles*. Smith's account of Pocahontas
appeared in his *Historie*, which was published in 1624, thus following his
reunion with Pocahontas – by then married to John Rolfe – in London.
His first account of his sojourn in the New World, published as *True
Relations* in 1608, some sixteen years earlier, makes no mention at all
of the Powhatan princess. Cynics have suggested the thrilling story of
rescue was a product of Smith's imagination, drawing on the popularity
of Pocahontas with the royal court. In this analysis, Smith, who was at
that time experiencing a downturn in his own fortunes at court, chose

to write Pocahontas into his memoirs. Smith seems to have been well practised in recounting stories of personal peril and romantic rescue – he tells a similar tale about the aid of a 'lady' from his captivity in Turkey. In this instance, it was the 'beauteous Lady *Tragabigʒanda*, when I was a slaue to the *Turkes*', who 'did all she could to secure me'. (*Generall Historie*). However, the preface to *True Relations* (1608) points out that Smith excluded several other key events, as well as his encounter with Pocahontas, that would later appear in the *Generall Historie*. Whether the event happened quite as Smith describes it is debatable. But Smith's account has lingered in the popular imagination and certainly constitutes a clear example of performative textuality.

The story of Pocahontas, John Smith and John Rolfe has been retold many times. One of the earliest playscripts was written by James Nelson Barker in 1808. Titled *The Indian Princess*, Barker's adaptation inaugurated a series of what would become known as 'Indian Plays', popular with audiences in the early part of the nineteenth century. Other versions include John Augustus Stone's *Pocahontas* (1830) and John Brougham's spoof *Po-ca-hon-tas* (1855). The catalyst of the drama, in all instances, is that infamous image of Pocahontas's rescue of Smith, laying her head and arms across him, as he is about to be brained. That momentous event in and of itself is performance – a piece of theatre, a staging of Native American power and supremacy. As Tindall and Shi suggest, this consistently retold scene constitutes 'the climax to a ritual threat of execution – that is, a bit of playacting to impress Smith with Powhatan's authority' (1999: 58). Smith's *Historie* is littered with references to a 'seeming' attack that turns into dialogue and diplomacy, part of a ritual of trading. The danger though, of Smith's recounting, is thrilling: potential execution; the heroine bounding on stage, physically protecting Smith from the enactment of punishment, willing to sacrifice herself to save the life of a man to whom she had, at the very least, taken a fancy, this is drama tailored to agitate the most exquisitely trembling of sensations.

There is a particularly evocative engraving that accompanies the story in Smith's *Historie*, which adds to that sense of the theatrical. The audience sit across two sides within an enclosed arena – almost an auditorium – looking down on Smith, Pocahontas and the potential executioners, who take position on the main 'stage'. Powhatan sits, larger than life, at the edge of the stage, dominating the scene. The audience, positioned in rows, rise from front to back and form a full house, appreciating the drama of the encounter. Chief Powhatan stages an elaborate piece of theatre to impress Smith; then Smith enhances the drama in his retelling – a theatricality of language that is rearticulated in the meta-theatrical illustration. The dialogic chain between cultural encounter, dramatic structure, textual strategy and performance technique, the event – and the consistent retelling and re-enacting of the event – operates as a telling polyphony of American theatre history.

The English presence in the American colonies was initially motivated by commerce: the inaugural populace of Jamestown were not religious exiles, but representatives of the commercial classes. Their encounters with Native American tribes were modelled on recent colonial activities in Ireland: governing by subjugation and plantation (Takaki 1992). From a practical perspective, whereas the Spanish in the south had encountered settled civilisations and the enchantment of gold and silver, in the north, the English settlers found a more sparsely occupied region, where Native American tribes operated within the more loosely woven Powhatan confederacy. The initial stance of the confederacy was one of support, but that changed rapidly to defence, with their realisation of impending conflict, as the settlers moved to take land and enslave the native population.

The early endeavours of this English colony formed an intrinsic part of the drama of encounter through the story of John Smith and his participation in Powhatan's theatrical show of power, but also through the shipwrecking of Sir Thomas Gates on Bermuda in 1609. Gates had been sent to reinforce the Jamestown colony, and found himself stranded on Bermuda and rendered by Shakespeare's *The Tempest*, for the colonial imagination.[16] The Jamestown colony, in its early years, foundered and was for a time abandoned, as a new colony, Henrico (which would become Richmond), was established and its future secured by John Rolfe's experiments with tobacco farming and his marriage to Pocahontas. Living conditions in the harsh landscape of the Delaware regions produced melodramatic actions: and in order to exhort corn from the local tribespeople, the settlers had kidnapped Pocahontas. To settle the crisis, Rolfe married the captive princess. She was taken to England by Rolfe and died shortly afterwards.

In the meantime, the tobacco experiments had worked; and the need for further land to cultivate the crop was exacerbated by an increase in population, with the arrival of more settlers, including wives for sale and African slaves. Between 1618 and 1623, as Ronald Takaki points out, the settler population increased from 400 to 4,500 (1992: 903). War was the inevitable result of land acquisition, and the colonists set about the destruction of the local power base, culminating in treaty talks between the tribes and colonisers, orchestrated by Captain William Tucker in 1623. Later in the seventeenth century, the signing of treaties would become part of a theatrical ritual, as Constance Rourke argues, a series of 'chronicle plays – recording what was said in the parleys, including bits of action, the exchange of gifts, of wampum, the smoking of pipes, the many ceremonials with dances, cries and choral songs' (1942: 62). This prototypical ceremonial drama, however, was an act of duplicity and trickery. Takaki notes that as part of the treaty ceremonial, the tribespeople were encouraged to drink a toast to the negotiated peace. However, they were served with 'poisoned wine. An estimated two hundred Indians died instantly; Tucker's soldiers then killed another fifty and "brought home part of their heads"' (1992: 903). The war between the Virginian colonisers and the tribes lasted from 1622 to 1625.

Louis B. Wright points out that 'among the first settlers who landed in Jamestown in 1607 were some who undoubtedly had frequented the London Theatres' (1962: 176). But theatre was not transported by these travellers to Virginia. Perhaps, as Wright speculates, there was 'drama enough in their fight for survival', though certainly there are accounts of the Native American tribes, in the early years, providing a source of theatricality for the colonials, as can be seen in chronicles of the early colonial era.[17] Also, we should note that one of the early Governors of Virginia, Sir William Berkeley, had been involved with dramatic writing, producing a play titled *The Lost Lady*. The play, written in 1637, was a product of Berkeley's duration in English court life, though, not of his direct association with the colonies. Berkeley was also a Royalist and an anti-Puritan. So, the early years of Jamestown cannot be regarded as indoctrinated against theatre, as we might suggest were the occupiers of Maine.

Whilst the Virginia Company of Jamestown were, in the main, traders with an eye on economics, those who settled further north, in Plymouth and the surrounding regions, were driven by religion. The groups that began to settle in the New England regions are grouped together as Puritans; we should acknowledge here the complexities associated with that term. Even a cursory glance at the demographics of the colonial towns in New England illustrates the range and diversity of socio-economic groups and cultural structures. The immigrant population featured merchants and farmhands, labourers and aristocrats. The common bond was a belief in the need to 'purify' the Anglican Church. Common critical practice has led to a somewhat vexed argument that the moral code and value system that contributed to the demise of theatres in Commonwealth England under Puritan rule were transplanted, more or less intact, to Plymouth Rock. Elders, we understand, frowned collectively and absolutely on the concept of performance and entertainment.

But Puritan anti-theatricality was itself a multifaceted series of ideological perspectives. We should note that performances and entertainments were a feature of colonial life in New England. One event that has passed into the popular theatrical imaginary, one of the most historically recounted, was the desire of those early Puritan settlers to celebrate a good harvest with festivities and fun, an event looked to as the foundation for Thanksgiving. In the *Chronicles of the Pilgrim Fathers of the Colony of Plymouth: from 1602–1625*, Edward Winslow, in a letter to a friend in England, tells us, 'amongst other recreations, we exercised our arms, many of the Indians coming amongst us, and among the rest their greatest king, Massassoyt, with some ninety men, whom for three days we entertained and feasted' (Young 1841: 231). Each party contributed to the feast with provender and also with dramatic action. Scenes of hunting were enacted for the entertainment of each other. The Native Americans demonstrated their prowess as archers, whilst the power of the smoking guns portrayed by the Puritans equally impressed their neighbours.

I should point out that whilst the concept of this inaugural version of Thanksgiving has taken hold as recurrent symbol of national identity, ritualised on the fourth Thursday of November, its origins have been located in many and varied festivities in colonial American history. Ultimately, as Melanie Wallendorf and Eric J. Arnould argue, Thanksgiving has become a 'collective ritual that celebrates material abundance enacted through feasting' (1991: 13) – a festival celebrating plenty as an event, the festivity owing a debt to the harvest festival, perhaps even the ritual worship of the corn gods of agrarian tribespeople. But that popular image of the inaugural feast, perpetuated in recurrent narratives and performances of the Pilgrims sharing their bounty with their native neighbours, has retained veracity in the imaginary of America; this image dates back to the 1621 event that saw Puritan and Native American enact friendship and reciprocity.

The anti-theatre dogma associated with Puritan settlers, and indeed Puritanism, is expressed most completely in William Prynne's *Histriomastix*, published in 1633. Prynne spent many years researching for this book, which is exhaustively founded on 'examples' to 'prove' his argument. Prynne's extensive title summarises the content of the book:

> The players scourge, or, actors tragædie, divided into two parts.
>
> Wherein it is largely evidenced, by divers arguments, by the concurring authorities and resolutions of sundry texts of Scripture, That popular stage-plays are sinfull, heathenish, lewde, ungodly spectacles, and most pernicious corruptions; condemned in all ages, as intolerable mischiefes to churches, to republickes, to the manners, mindes, and soules of men.
>
> And that the profession of play-poets, of stage-players; together with the penning, acting, and frequenting of stage-plays, are unlaw-full, infamous and misbeseeming Christians. All pretences to the contrary are here likewise fully answered; and the unlawfulnes of acting, of beholding academicall enterludes, briefly discussed; besides sundry other particulars concerning dancing, dicing, health-drinking, &c. of which the table will informe you. (1974)

Prynne's text, written at the front end of Puritan agitation, but during the rule of Charles I, conforms politically to an anti-theatrical, anti-enter-tainment, anti-aesthetics agenda. At one point, Prynne rails against the scandalous printing of Shakespearean texts on finer paper than that used for the bible. Prynne found himself in serious trouble with the Royalist regime: the publication of *Histriomastix* coincided with a performance of *The Shepherd's Pastoral* (William Montague), with Queen Henrietta Maria in one of the starring roles, and, at his trial in the Star Chamber, an entry from the index to the book which lists: '"Women actors," notorious whores', was used as evidence of insult to the Queen; at a second trial several years later, Prynne was infamously branded with the letter SL (Seditious Libeller) on his cheeks, and lost what little was left of his ears, which had been cropped after his first trial. Prynne was later released by the Long Parliament and continued to agitate for strict, uncompromising Puritan morals and order. The tone of the *Histriomastix* is ranting and the level of scholarship debatable; that Prynne could possibly have been able to consult all documents claimed in the work is implausible. The wider impact of the book itself on political motivations that did lead to the banning of theatre in the Commonwealth is also subject to critical slippage: nevertheless, Prynne's *Histriomastix* offers a key account of the most indignant of anti-theatrical ideologues at this time.

In the Protestant mind, as Peter A. Davis notes, 'the Jesuits spread

Catholicism throughout central Europe with their well-funded and professional staged productions' (1998: 221), therefore linking theatre with the threat of pervasive Catholicism. But received understandings of Puritan antipathy to theatre are worth investigating more thoroughly. Margot Heinemann argues that 'it has been customary to regard Puritan doctrinal objection as the primary reason for opposition' to the theatre (1980: 35); however, many of the anti-theatre writers of the pre-Civil War decades were not 'Puritans in a theological or doctrinal sense' (1980: 28). The opposition to theatre, for Puritan leaders, was not just, or even necessarily, all about doctrine: it was as much about political power and controlling a shifting and unstable urban population. The Jacobean court that succeeded the Tudors on the death of Elizabeth had already put censorship of political issues in place, as Wickham points out:

> The most topical of all subject matter, the relationship between Church, State and the individual human being – the topic which had kept English drama so very much in touch with life in the Tudor era – was the very material which the whole machinery of censorship and control had been devised to suppress. (1963: 94)

London in the late sixteenth, early seventeenth centuries was a place where one could, if one needed to, become invisible, could assume a new guise, performing in 'character' as a method of concealment. The spread of the enclosing and cloaking city space led to a set of fears and anxieties about the character of that space, and its destructive 'plague, riots and traffic jams' (Heinemann 1980: 35). More specifically, according to Davis, theatre, in sixteenth-century London, had become a meeting place for Royalists (1998: 221). The minds of the economic elite, following on from Royal mandate under James I, were as much alive to the relationship between theatre and plague as Antonin Artaud could be: social unrest spread through staging, invidious diseases through the medium of drama, infecting the body politic.[18] The threat of a transgressive theatre space was thus made manifest to Puritans, as their 'enemies' made playhouses their home.

Anti-theatrical ideologies headed across the seas, with the Pilgrims who landed at Plymouth Rock. Tindall and Shi describe these settlers as 'the most uncompromising sect of Puritans' (1999: 65). And certainly, no public theatres flourished in Puritan-governed regions of the North American subcontinent until the very end of the eighteenth century. The first legitimate theatre in Boston, that 'City on a Hill', was not opened until 1792. Jean-Christophe Agnew argues that the economic conditions of the New World meant that 'theatre did not and indeed could not operate as it had in England' (1986: 150). Theatre practice during the reigns of Elizabeth I and James I had become a 'collective public dreamwork', one that could not be sustained in a 'colonial society' that was 'too young' with an 'authority too brittle' (ibid.: 151). The forces of economics in the colonies disadvantaged the English system of strolling players, and combined with the urge to assert authority and garner political power in new worlds, operated to disable any wholesale transatlantic crossing of English theatre at this time.

So, the opportunities for staged entertainment, as they were performed in old England, were few and far between. For obvious reasons, theatre professionals would not have found a welcome in the Separatist communities of New England and did not form part of the earliest settlers in the region. Not that all the travellers to the New World on this voyage were of the Puritan factions: the immigrants had various reasons for travelling. William Bradford's 'Model of Christian Charity' (1630), composed and delivered aboard the *Mayflower*, was designed to quell potential rebellion from the disparate group of travellers. That such a sermon on the subject of obedience, patience and community was considered necessary illustrates the existence of a divergent range of opinion and intention aboard the vessel of immigrants. Quoting from Bradford and Edward Winslow's *Mourt's Relation: A Journal of the Pilgrims of Plymouth* (1622), Mark L. Sargent acknowledges that a key site of anxiety, for the new governors of the colony, was 'to squelch "faction" and to insure "unity and concord"' amongst the colonists (1988: 236). The fear of civil disorder, then, carried from England, with its developing censorship of theatre, shaped cultural operations to absent performance arenas, except for the levels of performance inherent in the operations of the factional church.

The annals of the settlers provide a wealth of information about colonial life, providing an insight into the frequency of attempts to stage performance events – generally through a tone of disapproval. Antipathy towards 'playing' in the new colony is made very clear in William Bradford's *Of Plymouth Plantation* (written between 1606 and 1646), particularly in a passage concerning one, now infamous, Thomas Morton, who arrived in one of the newly developing satellite sites, of Mount-Wollaston, Massachusetts:

And Morton became lord of misrule, and maintained (as it were) a school of Athisme. And after they had gott some good into their hands, and gott much by trading with the Indeans, they spent it as vainly, in quaffing and drinking both wine and strong waters in great exsess and as some reported, 1oli. worth in a morning. They also set up a May-pole, drinking and dancing about it many days togeather, inviting the Indean women, for their consorts, dancing and frisking togither, (like so many fairies, or furies rather,) and worse practises- As if they had anew revived and celebrated the feasts of the Roman Goddes Flora, or the beasly practieses of the madd Bacchinalians. Morton likwise (to spew his poetrie) composed sundry rimes and verses, some tending to lasciviousnes, and others to the detraction and standall of some persons; which he affixed to this idle or idoll May-polls. They changed also the name of their place, and in stead of calling it Mount Wollaston, they call it Meriemounte, as if this joylity would have lasted ever. (1908: 412)

Morton's 'crime' is significant: performing the Lord of Misrule, of Bacchanalian festivity; in short, guilty of framing theatricality in the New World. Bradford also accuses Morton of trading guns with the local tribespeople, which 'was a terrour unto them, who lived straglingly, and were of no strength in any place' (ibid.). The sight of natives, armed as the colonials themselves would be armed, was a frightening prospect: but it was Morton's facility for frolics that posed more of a threat:

all the scume of the countrie, or any discontents, would flock to him from all places, if this nest was not broken; and they should stand in more fear of their lives and goods (in short time) from this wicked and debostetrue, then from the salvages them selves. (Ibid.: 415)

Therefore the:

Sundrie of the cheefe of the stragling plantations, meeting togither, agreed by mutuall consente to sollissite those of Plimoth (who were then of more strength then them all) to joyne with them, to prevente the further grouth of this mischeefe, and suppress Morton and his consortes before they grewe to further head and strength. (Ibid.)

There were not, as such, specifically colonial laws against either the 'Maypole of Merrymount' (as Nathaniel Hawthorne's story of 1836, commemorating Morton's escapades, would be titled). Indeed, the events of Merrymount took place in 1628, prior to the ban on theatre enacted by the Commonwealth in 1642. Nor was the selling of guns to tribes prohibited by law at this time. But Bradford makes clear that it was the setting up of an arena of merriment and performance-based entertainment that was the greatest threat to the colonial communities. Armed Native Americans were a secondary anxiety to the fear of transgression embedded in the transformative possibilities of performance.

In the English colonies of the West Indies, the restriction on theatre practice was also felt. Jamaica had been under Spanish rule from 1494 until the English capture of 1655, but did not feature any theatrical space, unlike mainland Spanish America, which made use of pre-Hispanic performance venues of the Aztec and Mayan nations, and also brought into theatrical usage the large courtyards or open chapels that were a feature of New World Church structures (Londré and Watermeier 2000: 43–4). The population was scant and no records of specific cultural activities are in circulation. The English conquest of Jamaica brought with it the official ban on theatre that was the hallmark of Cromwell's Commonwealth. That ban ended with the return of monarchy to England in 1660. The first evidence historians have found for theatrical activity in Jamaica is in Francis Hanson's account of *The Island and Government Thereof*, appended to *The laws of Jamaica: passed by the Assembly, and confirmed by His Majesty in Council, Feb. 23. 1683*. Hanson records: 'recreations (as Horse-Races, Bowls, Dancing, Musick, Plays at a publick Theatre, &c.) sufficiently demonstrate the flourishing condition of the Island' (cited in Hill 1992: 19–20). The exact location of this theatre, which Hanson did not specify, has been subject to debate, but Errol Hill suggests that the most likely spot would have been Spanish Town, which was the location of the intellectual elite, for whom an indoor theatre space would have been an attraction. Hill also notes, however, that Port Royal, with its 'reputation for extravagant living would have attracted performers of all types' (ibid.: 20). Performance, then, in Jamaica, was not necessarily associated with theatre spaces, or intellectual appetites, although scant records remain to enable more detailed discussion of this supposition.

I have offered some readings of the early colonial histories of New Spain, New France and New England, in addition to assessing the early performance endeavours of Africans in the southern regions of the Americas, in order to demonstrate that the history of theatre in the region is tangled. Students of theatre in America, be it of the United States, or Canada, or Hispanic zones, should make themselves aware of the lack of pattern and coherence in 'American theatre'. Theatre histories of the southern- and northern-most reaches of the Americas warrant book-length studies on their own right – it would be impossible to do justice to the range and specificities of contexts and cultural outputs in this book. Subsequent chapters, therefore, focus on the colonial formation that would soon become the United States, and what that meant, given the strange cultural heritage of multiple languages, cultures and encounter narratives, for the theatre that came to be performed in that space.

I have discussed, in this chapter, the impact of colonisation on the shape and form of performances within colonial sites, as part of a series of conquest, settlement and containment. As I have been considering early colonial endeavours, and the distinctions between the performance forms that developed within specific colonial and encounter narratives, I have, as yet, made no distinction between North and South American territories; but as the eighteenth century wore on, that distinction emerged – at least between European powers and colonial zones. The next chapter explores how theatre came to operate as a mechanism for developing debates about the function and structure of colonial and independent, revolutionary and post-revolutionary America.

CHAPTER 3

Performance and Strife in Eighteenth-Century Theatre

The focus I have maintained so far on the key colonisers from Europe shifts in this chapter to emphasise the shaping presence of the English settlements in the regions. At the beginning of the eighteenth century, the southern regions of the continent were an established colony of Spain, and the shape of dramatic output that had been established in the seventeenth century, still developing and diversifying, is a history of theatre in its own right. The northern regions, though, were subject to continual flux in response to a range of wars, between French and English, between French and Native Americans, and between English and Native Americans. French colonial operations, focusing on Nova Scotia and the regions now known as Louisiana, were not densely populated. French Louisiana, particularly, was sparsely settled, and did not ever establish itself as a colonial centre. New France, centred in and around Quebec, fared a little better as we have seen, but again lacked an established base to import and embed French cultural forms. But the thirteen colonies that formed England's territorial conquests were, comparatively, a stable feature throughout the century and cultural operations, such as theatre, did root themselves in the major urban spaces of those regions.

Whilst I am discussing the implications of the importation of theatre as a cultural sign of English imperial power here, though, I am not asserting Englishness as a way of life in the colonies. The population demographic of these zones was diverse, multiracial and multilingual, which informed the development of cultural operations. Politics were volatile and violence a feature of life, through war, uprising and resistance to the imposition of order in slave communities and across Native American tribes, as well as the conflicts that would arise in the later decades of the eighteenth century between loyalists and Patriots. So, whilst I make the point that the English colonies were relatively established, I also note that anti-English sentiment, which grew throughout the eighteenth century, was a product of a distinct lack of solidity of power and control of cultural operations in the colonies.

By the midpoint of the eighteenth century, the thirteen colonies of English settlers in America were operating as satellites of the Crown in trade, economics and social structures, if not in name (five of the thirteen states were not officially registered as Royal Colonies). This is not to suggest that we see a homogeneous cultural development across the colonies (any more than we see stable boundaries to the colonies: land disputes were a feature of these early spaces), but it is worth noting that the antipathy of Sectarians to England's laws, demonstrated in the Puritan and Quaker communities, as we saw in the last chapter, gave way to greater links, mainly because of the economic need to trade. England assumed, then, a position of power, politically, ideologically and economically, as goods passed with increasing rapidity from home to colony. Nevertheless, as Jon Butler points out, 'European goods and ideas fit into a society not like Europe at all' (2001: 5). The colonial settlers in the 'new' world, then, responded to vastly different geographies and populations, in their reconstruction of social and cultural operations. And those operations were different, even transformed, based on the needs and economies of the individual colonies. Whilst all maintained links with the English centre, communication between the colonies themselves was less rigorous, therefore disparate responses emerged to theatre productions.

Despite the distinction between responses to theatricals within the colonies, we can be certain that the audience for colonial theatre would be made up almost entirely of white and wealthy settlers, although there were distinctions: in the northern colonies, the urbane professional patronised the arts; in the south, the plantation aristocracy assumed that role. Nevertheless, audiences were not representative of all echelons of colonial society. Ticket prices varied, but were usually in the region of a 'full day's wages', even for the cheapest (Odai Johnson 2006: 227). Colonials without extensive means, then, would have lacked the wherewithal to attend regularly. The means of those non-coloniser groups who lived in contact with colonial centres, such as Native Americans and slaves and free blacks, are trickier to assess.

Some Native American tribal groups lived in reasonable proximity to the colonial centres, but little evidence links tribes with colonial spaces of performance. One of the very few accounts of Native American attendance is from a season of the Hallam Company in Williamsburg. *The Maryland Gazette* of 14 December 1752 reports:

The Chief of the Cherokee nation and his family were entertained, at the theatre, with the play (the tragedy of Othello) and a pantomime performance, which gave them great surprise, as did the fighting with naked swords on the stage, which occasioned the Empress to order some about her to go and prevent their killing one another. The benefits of their coming have not yet been made public; but it is said to relate to opening and establishing a trade with this colony, which they are very desirous of. They were dismissed with a handsome present of fine Cloaks, arms and ammunition; and experienced great satisfaction in the Governor's kind reception and several others; and left this place this morning.

Worth noting, there was, in 1752, a contestation between two factions within the Cherokee nation for leadership; and we are not privy as to which of the competing parties was in attendance at the theatre. The reporter's claim that the Native American 'Empress' reacted in such terms to the verisimilitude of the fighting seems farfetched; several Native American rituals were predicated on staged violence and any reaction may have been more framed by a consideration of weaponry for the current inter-tribal contest. The attendance of the tribal group is clearly located as part of a series of trade negotiations, with theatre as part of an extended ritual, featuring a variety of public-performance practices. Theatrical acts, as part of a series of political engagements that were familiar to Cherokee leaders in their dealings with the colonials, become ceremonial in structure, and therefore part of a reciprocal exchange between groups. To colonial Americans, the Native American spectators form part of the show, as exotic specimens fulfilling a colonial narrative of difference; at the same time, the tribal leaders are active participants in the performance of ceremonial negotiation between tribes and settlers.

More famously, a group of Cherokee leaders attended the John Street theatre in New York, fifteen years later, on 14 December 1767. The group had arrived from the regions around South Carolina, as part of a peace initiative. The *South Carolina Gazette* of 1 January 1768 records:

Friday last arrived here from South-Carolina [...] the famous Attakullakulla, or the Little-Carpenter, Ouconnostota, or the Great-Warriour, and the Roven of Toogeloo, with six other chiefs and warriours of the *Cherokee* nation, accompanied by two interpreters; and next day they had an audience of his excellency general Gage, the commanders, in chief [...] to mediate a peace between their nation, the *Cherokees*, and the Six nations or Iroquois, they being deputed here on an embassy for that purpose. They met with a gracious reception from the general, and his excellency has been pleased to give orders, they shall be properly entertained, and attended [...] The chiefs having been informed, that there was a theatre in this city, expressed a desire of seeing a play acted; and the general has thought proper to gratify their curiosity, and has given directions that proper places shall be got for them in the house this evening.

The play scheduled was *Richard III*, followed by a Harlequinade. One reporter suggested, with a mantle of imperial superiority, 'it cannot be supposed' that the Cherokee representatives 'were sufficiently acquainted with the language to understand plot and design' (cited in Odai Johnson 2006: 229). Odai Johnson challenges that suggestion: given the trail of broken treaties already experienced by the tribal leaders, the 'story of an English King who lied and murdered his way into power and holdings may not have been all that incomprehensible to the Cherokees' (ibid.). The express purpose of the Cherokee delegation was to negotiate a peace settlement between themselves and the antagonistic northern tribes, a settlement in which colonial leaders had become embroiled for their own ends. The chiefs had, according to the *South Carolina Gazette* of 29 April 1768,

> at their own request, an audience of his excellency general Gage, in order to return him thanks for his powerful interposition and assistance, in accelerating the business they came about [...] on Friday Night last those chiefs entertained the Audience at the Theatre in this city with a War-Dance.

Hot on the heels of the French–Indian and Ponteach's war, between 1764 and 1767, the prospect of, and fears associated with, a staged War Dance led Douglass to announce 'no Part of the Audience will forget proper Decorum so essential to all Public Assemblies, particularly on this Occasion, as the Persons who have condescend to contribute to their Entertainment are of Rank and Consequence in their own Country' (cited in Odai Johnson 2006: 232). Johnson asks:

> [D]id the performance of a war dance mark the moment when the Cherokee tradition capitulated from the active imagining of war to a formalized but impotent ritual? [...] was it, in short, a war dance or

a representation of a war dance? Was it an act of past ceremony, or a promise of a solution to come? (Ibid.: 233)

The structure and interpretative possibilities of the performance are complicated by European understandings of the function of the theatrical venue as a place for entertainment. Perhaps, as far as the Cherokee warriors were concerned, that war dance was a way of marking the end of the exchange with the colonial politicians. The contractual conditions of reciprocity had been met: the Cherokee had been 'given' a performance, and had now returned that compliment, bringing these failed treaty negotiations to completion and freeing the Cherokee from any burden of debt for the part played by colonial politicians.

There is little evidence that, throughout the eighteenth century, free blacks or slaves were in attendance within theatre or worked as actors or behind the scenes. The Douglasses were slave owners, but there are no records of black actors, or even stage hands, in the Douglass Company. William Dunlap notes that, 'from four until six, and after, the front seats of the boxes were occupied by blacks of every age, waiting till their Masters and Mistresses made their appearance' (2005: 34). Black servants and slaves, then, knew theatre from an intimate perspective, more so than the paying audience. They witnessed preparation and perhaps even rehearsal, whilst the white spectators watched the 'finished' performance, lacking that insight into process. Coach drivers and footservants, also, would have been waiting outside for the final curtain. Several colonies in the north, where slave populations tended to be located centrally, had imposed curfews to restrict the movement of the black population in the evenings, considerably curtailing opportunities to participate in theatrical entertainments.

In the southern colonies, slave populations tended to be located away from centres, making for practical difficulties in travel to venues, even if that had been permitted. And of course, the colonial imaginary that promulgated an inherent inferiority in racial types would deem cultural events as unnecessary for the black populations of the colonies. Seilhamer mentions one instance: 'an aged colored man, Robert Venable, who was born in Philadelphia in 1736 and died in 1844, told John F. Watson that he "went to the first play at Plumstead's store"' (2005a: 4). Odai Johnson comments that Venable attended 'to light home Master and Mistress' (2006: 228).[19] The powers of South Carolina, more relaxed about allowing players into town than their northern counterparts, were far less relaxed about race. From the autobiography of Zamba, an

African slave taken from the banks of the Congo, we have the following account:

> In Charleston there has been always a handsome and commodious theatre, and during the winter season this house of vanity is much better filled and frequented than any of the churches ever are. I never had the honour, however, of being within the door of a theatre, so I can give no description of what is inside; for, by law, no negro or coloured person shall be admitted to the theatre in Charleston: there is generally at the foot of the play-bills – "N. B., No coloured persons or dogs can be admitted." Mr. Thomson informed me that he believed Negroes were debarred from entering such places for this reason, that in some of the plays acted black men or women held too conspicuous and too exalted a position. Does not this display something akin to fear on the part of the whites? (1847: 204–5)

Zamba's account of the popularity and racial dynamics of theatre attendance dates from the latter part of the 1790s, but offers intriguing insights into the racial drama of American stages throughout the century. White audiences could watch 'noble' black characters on stage, but were incapable of translating that to the 'characters' they had built on the backs of a racialised imaginary. At the same time, the unwillingness to permit the black population to observe such characters suggests a consciousness of the fallibility of that racial imaginary.

In another development in theatre during the eighteenth century that had particular implications for America's slave economy, African 'dialect' characters began appearing on stage. One of the earliest incarnations was Mungo in Charles Dibdin and Isaac Bickerstaff's comic opera *The Padlock* (1768), which was brought to the colonies by the Douglass Company in 1769. To William Dunlap, Lewis Hallam, Jr 'was unrivalled to his death, giving the Mungo with a truth derived from study of the Negro slave character, which Dibdin the writer could not have conceived' (2005: 35).[20] The legitimacy of Dunlop's claim is inevitably caked in racialised discourses that enforced a 'type' onto the body of the slave. Nevertheless, Dunlap's assessment of Hallam's portrayal lends weight to the suggestion that the Douglass Company owned black slaves, or employed blacks within the touring company, from which Hallam could make his 'study'. Dibdin's Mungo, with his distinctive way of speaking, was already looked upon as an 'authentic type' by audiences in England. J. R. Oldfield argues that he 'was clearly intended to be more realistic, and the vast popular appeal of the character suggests that it was instantly recognizable' (1993: 10). Unpacking the racial attitudes of the eighteenth century clarifies that the popularity of Mungo resided less in the 'accuracy' of his speech style than in the way that style conformed to expectations of inferiority and intellectual weakness within the establishment of a 'negro' stereotype. As Oldfield notes, the name 'Mungo' passes 'into the English language as a typical name for a black slave' (1993: 11). Mungo becomes the template not only for a 'stage negro' but for popular perceptions of the inferior black.

In the context of performance in America, *The Padlock* and the portrayal of Mungo are complicated. Mungo is, after all, an insurgent who rebels against his 'master'. He may speak in tones that are located as 'inferior', but his character is more complex and challenging than that reading suggests. Mungo occupies much of the dramatic space of the play, and his actions, though circumscribed by racist ideologies nonetheless made him the mouthpiece of Abolitionism in the UK. On 24 September 1787, the *Gentleman's Magazine*, under the editorship of 'Sylvanus Urban' (Edward Cave), printed an extract from an epilogue that had been added to the play at its first performance in 1768:

> O sons of freedom! equalise your laws,
> Be all consistent – plead the Negro's cause;
> That all the nations in your code may see
> The British Negro, like the Briton, free. (Cave 1787: 913)

Current records indicate twenty-six known performances of *The Padlock* in the eighteenth century, the majority taking place in Philadelphia and New York, but only two in Charleston. With a black population exceeding white significantly, a play which dramatised the rebellion of a black servant against his white master, even in comic form, might not have been considered viable entertainment, even if the final epilogue were excluded. The play was performed regularly in the West Indies, Errol Hill claims, between 1777 and 1813 (and, argues Hill, it is 'safe to assume' that the play 'did not end with Mungo's epilogue' [1992: 76]), but as agitation for the abolition of slavery grew in England, *The Padlock* was dropped from the repertoire.

Two key developments were a feature of the early to mid-eighteenth-century colonial theatre: the building of theatre spaces in playhouses and halls and the arrival of touring groups from England. Touring companies did travel across the colonies, bringing theatricals to the different centres.

But this was in response to the willingness and financial capacity of local centres to come up with the subscription funds necessary to construct a suitable building, or rent a proper space. And what would be considered appropriate was uneven. South Carolina, Virginia and Maryland proved relaxed in their attitudes to playing, where Massachusetts, Pennsylvania and particularly Rhode Island were fraught with pockets of distinct resistance. New York was an inflammatory space, and theatre struggled, yet managed, to find a shape within an antagonistic political landscape. Other regions, such as New Hampshire, could not at this time support a formalised theatre, with sparse populations and little means. The development of theatre buildings and touring companies, therefore, across the colonies, was a product of local inclinations and means. Those inclinations and means were not static; a reception at one time could be turned to rejection at another, as happened to David Douglass in Newport during two separate visits in 1762. But Douglass also eased through in Williamsburg in 1760, where Lewis Hallam had struggled in 1752. Odai Johnson argues that, as a Mason, Douglass enjoyed certain privileges in cities with Masonic fellowships;[21] whilst that might have worked in Annapolis and Williamsburg, whatever the means or process of facilitation, it was due to the interests and economic willingness of the colonial communities that theatres existed in the eighteenth century.

By 1660, Charles II had reclaimed the throne in England for the Stuarts, endorsing a restored theatrical culture: but the English colonies in the areas around Puritan Massachusetts and Quaker Pennsylvania, America continued to apply sanctions against any performance endeavours. In later decades, religious exiles, voluntary or otherwise, brought with them an antipathy towards what they regarded as the lewd humour that greeted the reopening of theatrical venues during this Restoration.

Virginia was not Puritan doctrinally, but many of its residents were informed by a Quaker suspicion of players as potentially immoral vagabonds. As with New England, our understanding of performance history in Virginia stems from records of attempts at prohibition. Whilst specific laws were not set up in Virginia to restrict theatrical development, nevertheless, as Odai Johnson and William J. Burling point out, this did not mean the same as 'blanket permission' to perform (2003: 70). Our awareness of one early theatrical performance comes from court records, the account of a case pursued against a group of players. And 'case' here is meant in its specifically legislative context. In 1665, the Accomac County Court account notes: 'Cornelius Watkinson, Phillip

Howard, and William Darby were this Day arrested [...] for acting a play by them called the Bare and the Cubb.' The court further ordered that the accused men should 'appear the next court in those habiliments that they then acted in, and gave a draught of such verses or other Speeches and passages which were then acted by them' (cited in Johnson and Burling 2003: 93). Irony was undoubtedly unintended but nevertheless frames the court's order that the three men accused of playing should appear in costume and effectively stage a performance, in court, of the play that had propelled them into legal trouble in the first place. However, after witnessing this replay of the performance, the court decided against the plaintiff Morton, who was ordered to pay court costs. Johnson and Burling point out that, whilst Morton may have drawn on anti-theatre prejudice in his prosecution, his property shared boundaries with those three men he accused, and 'perhaps something more than a distaste of theatre was at stake in the litigation' (ibid.). That the case was dismissed also indicates that anti-theatrical prejudice was not part of official dogma or sanction in Virginia.

In 1682, the colony of Pennsylvania, more stringently dominated by Quaker distaste for leisure activities and distractions than Virginia, declared those who would:

> introduce into this Province, or frequent such rude and riotous sports and practices as prizes, stage-plays, masques, revels, bull-batings, cock-fightings [...] shall be reputed and fined as Breakers of the peace, and suffer at least ten days' imprisonment at hard labour in the house of correction, or forfeit twenty shillings. (Ibid.: 95)

Although the Pennsylvanian ban was repealed in England in 1692, it was re-ratified in the colony in 1699.

In Massachusetts, Puritan culture, which had been unsettled by Thomas Morton's Merrymount maypole, attempts at introducing performance were carefully policed. Increase Mather, minister and activist for the stringent enforcement of the Separatist codes of the founding settlement, wrote *A Testimony Against Several Prophane and Superstitious Customs* in 1686, whilst Rector at Harvard College, in Cambridge, New England. In his *Testimony*, Mather specifically cites Prynne as a consulted source, as 'proof' of the problem with stage plays. To Mather, plays 'had their Original from those Devil-Gods whom the Gentiles Worshiped [...] Hence Ancients call such Theaters, the Devil's Temples, and Stage Plays, the Devil's Lectures, and the Actors in them, the Devil's

chief Factors'. Isani points out that 'Cotton Mather, whose family owned
at least five volumes by Prynne, exhibits his sympathies but not a knowledge unusual for the times when he notes in his copy of the *Histriomastix*', noting that Cotton Mather had written in his copy of Prynne's
text: 'for this work the Author was imprisoned and grievously censured
though licensed by authority' (1972: 183).

That the Mather household were familiar with Prynne's work is clear;
that Increase Mather, father to Cotton, was as hysterically opposed to the
licensing of theatre as Prynne is also clear. Theatres to Mather, as much
as to Prynne, were the 'Devil's temples'. Not just the players but those
in attendance were at 'risk' in these evil dens: again, the link between
theatrical activity and the spread of discord and rebellion is apparent.
Mather's treatise acknowledges, implicitly, that the theatre, in the words
of Antonin Artaud, 'invites the mind to share a delirium which exalts its
energies' (1958: 19), in this instance, through the vital energies of satanic
forces. Mather prefaced his *Testimony* with the commentary: 'there is
much discourse of beginning of Stage-Plays in New-England. The last
Year Promiscuous Dancing was openly practised, and too much counte-
nanced in this Degenerated Town' (1687), suggesting that the urge to
repress theatre was not held in common by all members of Boston's
Puritan communities.

For example, in 1687, according to Louis B. Wright, Boston tavern-
keeper John Wing 'fitted up a room with seats where he proposed to
allow a magician to perform his tricks' (1962: 178). He was visited by the
local judiciary, and was persuaded to acknowledge that his plans to house
the performance were unlawful. Judge Sewall catechised the tavern-
keeper regarding the matter, and recorded that Wing 'saith [...] seeing
'tis offensive he will remedy it [...] the man's practice was unlawful, and
therefore [...] could not lawfully give him accommodation for it' (cited
in Wright 1962: 179). Given that Wing had made the arrangements for
the magician's performance in the first instance, it is reasonably safe to
assume that his 'acknowledgement' of offence was more to do with an
urge to ensure his personal safety against austere authorities than any
epiphanic realisation of fault or lawbreaking.

The development of staging, across medieval Europe, had shifted
performance practices from external spaces – streets, market squares –
to an internal locus, the playhouse. And at the same time, of course, the
focus of drama was increasingly secularised: we witness, therefore, the
coincidence of physical interiority with the inception of a drama of the

human condition on earth, superseding the liturgical drama of human relations within the spiritual sphere. In our considerations of theatre in America, we should bear in mind that the concept of a theatre as we might conceive now was a recent innovation. By the time of the English Civil War, the role of the playhouse, as both a venue for playing and a meeting space for potentially disruptive elements, had been established. Thus the ban on theatre in England from 1642 to 1660 could be enforced in significant measure by the closure of those designated theatre spaces. It is hardly surprising, therefore, that the construction of playhouses was not part of the building mandate of the Sectarians for New England's cultural landscape.

The antipathy against the playhouse, as a venue, is made clear in a letter of complaint to the Boston authorities, from Chief Justice Lord Sewall, in March 1714:

> There is a Rumor, as if some design'd to have a Play acted in the council-chamber [...] Our Town-House was built at great Cost and Charge, for the sake of very serious and important Business [...] let it not be abused with Dances, or other Scenical divertisements. (Cited in Johnson and Burling 2003: 98–9)

Well into the eighteenth century, suspicion and antipathy towards theatre persisted. In March 1750, there was an amateur performance of *The Orphan*, staged in a coffee house on Stet Street. William Warland Clapp suggests that the 'innovation was looked upon with horror', and very soon the general court of Massachusetts passed another act 'to prevent stage plays and other theatrical entertainment' (1968: 2–3). Clapp goes on to suggest that private theatricals 'were clandestinely given', and attempts were made to overturn the law (ibid.: 3). Students at Harvard were, according to Johnson and Burling, presenting plays, also, in the mid-1750s (2003: 190). Nevertheless, no building existed for staging plays – and no building was to be co-opted for that purpose in Massachusetts at that time. Thus the operations of a physical theatre in the manner of English stages were stifled.

Although performances were repressed through the restriction of physical space in Boston and across Massachusetts, we do have some record of dramatic literature in circulation through the auspices of booksellers' correspondence. Thomas Goddard Wright's study of the literary culture of New England makes reference to a letter from John Dunton, a London bookseller, who notes that 'the chief Books' bought by one of his female customers were 'Plays and Romances; which to set off the better, she wou'd ask for Books of Gallantry' (1920: 120). Subsequent lists, noted by Wright, also show that Christopher Marlowe's *The Tragical History of Dr Faustus* was also made available for sale: thirty copies were purchased on one invoice, eighteen on another, within the same month, by far and away the highest quantity of any book ordered (ibid.). Another popular book, John Bunyan's *Pilgrim's Progress*, sold well both through booksellers and hawkers. Louis B. Wright claims that *Pilgrim's Progress* 'was undoubtedly regarded as a moral treatise' (1962: 144). But, albeit a guidebook for the mission of each individualist Christian to achieve the grace of God, the content is also set out in the form of a dramatic text. The *New England Weekly Journal* also published extracts from dramatic texts, as we have seen in the case of *The London Merchant*. Reading matter, then, publicly traded across Boston, despite the prejudice against theatre, featured theatrical texts, which contests received understandings of Boston's puritanical stance against theatre. Perhaps, though, this conflicted narrative suggests that whilst the 'portable theatre' of the book might be tolerated, the physical theatre of the stage, which had operated in London as a site for political gatherings, would not.

Certainly, across English colonies in New England and Pennsylvania, theatre was made subject to state control or banned outright. Such legal restrictions, and cases prosecuted, provide the few records in existence that attempts to stage performances were indeed recurrent events in the history of English colonisation in the Americas. Pennsylvania, displaying a stringently anti-theatrical attitude, repeatedly introduced laws forbidding performance between the 1690s and 1713, as a direct challenge to the government in London. By 1724, there is evidence to suggest some form of theatrical activity had begun to take place in the region: Johnson and Burling make reference to an article published in the *American Weekly Mercury* (30 April–7 May 1724) advertising 'your old friend Pickle Herring', alongside 'several other diverting performances on a stage too large here to mention' (2003: 105). The venue for this performance is not clear, nor is the extent to which the comic tone of 'Pickle Herring' may be exaggerating the size of the stage for satiric purposes; nevertheless, the advertisement suggests that theatrical events were a part of Pennsylvanian cultural life. In 1749, however, Philadelphia's municipal records for 8 January of that year, as noted by William S. Dye, Jr, demonstrate anti-theatrical tendencies continued through the persecution of actors in the city:

[C]ertain persons had lately taken upon them to act plays in this city [...] whereupon the board unanimously requested the magistrates to take the most effectual measures for suppressing this disorder, by sending for the actors, and binding them for their good behaviour. (1931: 353)

In 1750, records Hugh F. Rankin, the Common Council of Philadelphia condemned theatrical performances (1965: 31). This was around the time that the Murray–Kean company had been performing in Philadelphia. Then, on 31 May 1759, the Pennsylvanian Commonwealth, as Johnson and Burling note, banned plays, instituting a system of fines for anyone caught playing. The ban was modified for a few months, from June to December 1759, for the Douglass Company. From the end of 1759, no further public performances took place in Philadelphia till 1766, when again the Douglass Company filed for permission to perform.

In Virginia, where religious dogma was less stringently enforced, as we have seen in the outcome of the *Bare and Cubb* trial, students at the William and Mary College, chartered in 1693, set out to stage a recital.[22] Like Harvard, founded in 1636, William and Mary College was aimed primarily at the production of literate scholars destined for the ministry. Such training of preachers of protestant doctrines, whether Anglican or Puritan, drew on the theatrical arts – specifically the art of oratory – for their sermons. That the Colloquies of William and Mary should be classed as a formative feature in American theatre history would no doubt cause some consternation amongst the religious founders of the College. Nevertheless, the oratory Academy, established as a learning academy for those entering the ministry, demonstrate the rootedness of theatrical performativity in Protestant rhetoric.

A key problem for travelling players and would-be playwrights, though, was the lack of space for performance: in the early decades of the eighteenth century, no theatre had been built for the edification of the colonists. One of the first notable events in the history of theatre building in America took place in Williamsburg, Virginia. Charles and Mary Stagg, who may have been one-time dance instructors in London, entered into a contract with William Levingston of Williamsburg, 'to serve him in the Colony of Virginia on ye Arts, Professions' in 1715 (cited in Johnson and Burling 2003: 99). The contract they signed was an indenture, which bound both the Staggs and any profit from their endeavours to Levingston. Johnson and Burling refer to this contract as evidence of 'colonial America's oldest known company' (ibid.).

In addition to his role in setting up the first Anglo-American theatre company, Levingston is credited with the construction of the first, according to current information, purpose-built colonial theatre in North America in Williamsburg. Information about the setting up of the Williamsburg theatre comes from a contract document, drawn up in July 1716, between the three parties, to set up a theatre and a dance school (cited in Johnson and Burling 2003: 100; Wright 1962: 180). The contract drawn up between Levingston and the Staggs does suggest that although the former had begun to build his playhouse, he still needed to acquire an official permit to perform. Johnson and Burling record that, in 1721, 'Levingston was a familiar face in court [...] bringing complaints against Mary Ansell, Elizabeth Ives, and Mary Peel' (2003: 15), who were all indentured to him; Rankin suggests that their contracted duties were to perform on behalf of the Levingston–Stagg Company (cited in Johnson and Burling 2003: 16). That such complexities should emerge in this set of relations suggests that the concept of 'playing' in America seemed, for the eighteenth-century colonial, twined inextricably with conflict, whether ecumenical, political or economic.

Levingston's venture headed into ruin; by 1723 he had defaulted on the loan he had taken to pay for the build and it would seem that the Staggs had, as a result, moved on, possibly to Philadelphia (Johnson and Burling 2003: 104). Although theatrical performance had been banned within the city limits of Philadelphia, there is evidence of some space for theatrical productions in 1723, set up by players, states Pollock, who 'chose for their Stage a place just without the city verge' (1968: 5). The Staggs would have, we assume, operated similarly in order to avoid the legislature. And, the Staggs seemed financially more secure through the shift in location. On his death in 1736, Charles Stagg was found to have 'left a comfortable estate', according to Wright (1962: 180). Philadelphians themselves, then, were not as antithetic to theatre as their legislature.

By 1736, the operations of the theatre had recommenced through the auspices of amateur performers and students from the William and Mary College. Johnson and Burling make reference to several performances that took place within the old theatre building, specifically *The Recruiting Officer* and *The Busy Body*. The *American Weekly Mercury* of August 1736 clarifies the theatrical operations of the time:

[The] Governors sister and son, in company with one Dr. Potter, Apothecary Gilmore, Abraham Nicholas, A painter, and several others, put plays on the public theatre [...] they performed their parts with so much applause, that they have already got about one hundred and fifty pounds subscriptions, to encourage their entertaining the country with the like diversions. (Cited in Johnson and Burling 2003: 119)

Amateur performers, therefore, appear to have taken over the running of the first Williamsburg theatre, and be intent on maintaining that venue as a viable concern and a site of 'diversion'. Such a view of theatre contrasts significantly with that sense of potential destabilisation that theatre had come to represent in Puritan colonial communities. Theatre, it seems, could be a stabilising force, if a range of community members would join together and contribute: note that the 'cast' list for the amateur company here includes Williamsburg citizens of diverse groups, in terms of social standing and gender, from members of the governor's family to painters and also 'young gentleman and ladies of this Country' (ibid.: 118–19). In Williamsburg, then, we see a very different image of early eighteenth-century attitudes to theatre in the colonies. However, by 1745, the theatre had fallen into disrepair, and was sold off, for conversion into a court house.

Whilst Williamsburg was one of the earliest of the English colonial sites to witness the construction of a purpose-built theatrical venue, New York has witnessed the writing and publication of an early closet drama, by one Robert Hunter, New York's colonial governor. *Androboros* was written in 1714 as a *Biographical Farce in Three Acts*, a satiric attack by Hunter on one of his contemporaries, Francis Nicholson; the two political names, it seems, were somewhat antagonistic towards each other. New York's political landscape was no smoother in the early eighteenth century than at any other time, and Hunter's time in office was particularly marked by his antipathy towards Nicholson, who was a chief governor of many of the English colonies in the region. The rights and wrongs of that discord are debatable; neither figure is particularly sympathetic. The play, though, can be regarded as a satiric commentary by Hunter on specific colonial figures; we know that the writer was, during his time in London, an associate of Jonathan Swift and Alexander Pope. Peter A. Davis argues that the play is constructed in line with 'contemporary theatrical conventions [...] and a wider knowledge of current theatre than most colonials' (1998: 226). The play, though, also demonstrates a recon-ceptualisation of subject matter within its satiric format. The governance of the colonies in America had been unstructured throughout the seventeenth century, with a distinct lack of co-ordinated attention from

England. Attempts to take belated command of the situation, by forming the 'Dominion' in the late seventeenth century, resulted in unrest and direct action. Antagonism towards the colonial homeland, then, was a feature of colonial life at least six decades before the Revolutionary war. Hunter was the British-appointed governor in New York, and *Androboros* was an expression of loyalty to the Crown in the face of some significant dissatisfaction with the current economies of colonial status.

Androboros was written prior to the building of theatres in New York and was never performed in any public space. By the 1730s, though, New York apparently featured two theatres. Although the presence of two venues staging plays simultaneously at this time has yet to be proved conclusively, evidence in support of such a claim is, Johnson and Burling claim, compelling, though lacking distinct physical evidence (2003: 108). Certainly a venue existed on Nassau Street, and there are records of performances there in 1732. But, argues Mary Henderson, there was also a theatre house 'in existence on Broadway, east of the commons' (2004: 14). This may have been a temporary theatre, though, set up within the established tavern of Abraham Corbett (ibid.: 21). Such a divide predicted what would become a bifurcated theatrical landscape of New York in the nineteenth century, predicated on sites of venues for elite and popular performance modes. 'Those who sided with the governor (and the Crown)', Henderson argues, headed to the theatre on Broadway, whilst those 'who were aligned with Van Dam and Zenger (and local rule)', attended the New Theatre at Nassau Street, in the lower east side (ibid.: 15).

The names mentioned by Henderson here are worth exploration. Rip Van Dam was a senior member of New York Provincial Council, and acting governor until the arrival of William Cosby in 1731. Cosby attempted to claim financial remuneration through the courts from Van Dam for his period as acting governor, unsuccessfully. Chief justice William Morris decided against Cosby, and was summarily dismissed from his post by the unhappy governor. Cosby also pursued Peter Zenger, printer of the *New York Weekly Journal*, which had produced an editorial criticising the sacking of William Morris. Intriguingly, the Nassau Street theatre venue was the property of the acting governor, Rip Van Dam. So, at the time, New York was experiencing the pangs of what would become revolutionary fervour against the English monarch and his New World representatives. And we can see that division emerging quite specifically in the theatrical make-up of the city.

One of the most notorious voices in colonial New York against theatre was that of George Whitefield, the 'Grand Itinerant' Evangelist preacher, who is considered the force behind the Great Awakening that swept through the colonies between 1740 and 1760. Mary Henderson argues that 'whenever Whitefield preached at the Presbyterian Church at the head of Wall Street, the result was a "suppressing of the usual public amusement"' (ibid.: 22). However, Whitefield himself managed to draw large audiences, and his biographer, Harry S. Stout, describes the preacher as a 'representative man', in the manner of Benjamin Franklin – and British theatre heavyweight David Garrick. Peter A. Davis argues that whilst it might be 'tenuous to argue that [...] George Whitefield helped to create a theatrical audience in America', there is certainly evidence to suggest 'the connection is not unreasonable, and certainly his popularity coincides with a rise of commercial theatre in the colonies' (1998: 230). Whilst that might be stretching the bounds of 'theatre' in terms of formal operations, and of the growth of American audiences in terms of history, there is a compelling argument that Whitefield was a star performer in the manner that would become the standard for stage professionals in the nineteenth century. Stout's biography of Whitefield is subtitled *The Divine Dramatist* (1991), in recognition of the preacher's youthful theatrical activities, as actor in school performances. Whitefield may have preached against the deviltry of theatre in his later works, but his formative years were spent reading and acting in such performances: theatre taught him how to best promote his religious trade.

Along with Williamsburg and New York, Charleston in South Carolina was proving to be something of a locale for theatrical ventures. One of the earliest players in the colonies was Antony Aston, and he writes of Charleston as the place where he initiates his playing in the New World in 1703.[23] That Charleston was permitting and even encouraging playing in its very early days, at a time when the northern colonies were enacting laws to suppress performance, demonstrates the diversity of attitudes in the colonial representations of England. By the 1730s, Charleston was a thriving economic and cultural hub. Founded in 1670 as Charles-Town, in honour of the restored English monarch, the town was a centre of trade and commerce, based on the demand for rice and indigo, then cotton and altogether founded on slavery – the Spanish had signed over the *Asiento*, the contract to bring in slaves to the British as part of the peace settlement following Queen Anne's war (Treaty of Utrecht, 1713). Peter Coclanis's account of the growth of the colonial

centre points out that 'the town's population had [...] increased by over
500 percent between 1700 and 1740 and its total area had nearly doubled'
(1985: 611). Coclanis is non-specific about the racial demographics of
that population growth. But, according to Kenneth Morgan, 'the slave
trade to South Carolina was significant in scale. Some 93,000 slaves
were imported into that colony in the period 1706–75' (1998: 905), with
35,000 entering prior to 1750. And Peter H. Wood contends that 'during
precisely those two decades after 1695 when rice production took permanent hold in South Carolina, the African portion of the population drew
equal to, and then surpassed, the European portion' (1994: 36). Hennig
Cohen also measures the substantial black presence in the region: the
'twenty-five years preceding the Revolutionary War', he argues, 'saw the
slave population in South Carolina increase to more than one hundred
thousand, outnumbering the white by almost two to one' (1952: 105).
The black population increased, initially through the transatlantic trade,
and then through the enslavement of subsequent generations of those
already held as chattels. Apart from Barbados and the other British-held
islands of the West Indies, South Carolina was 'home' to one of the
largest slave populations in the colonies.

Whilst we can locate records relating to building of theatre spaces in
colonial regions during the eighteenth century, what we lack is information about the development of 'white' theatre in the colonies in relation
to the participation of black Americans and indigenous populations. We
know, for example, that across the colonies trade between white settlers
and tribespeople was regular, at least in the earlier decades, and that much
of the trade would have taken place within the main streets of the town
centre, where the building of the theatre would have been taking place.
But we have little or no information about how tribespeople reacted to
the establishment of performance institutions in the space where they
lived and traded, apart from the brief accounts I discussed earlier in this
chapter. We can conjecture, also, that African slaves formed a significant part of the workforce that built Charleston's first theatre in 1735–6,
but we have no knowledge about whether the builders would become
in any way involved in the activities of the venue once that theatre was
established.

Inevitably, the African slave population would not have been
regarded as capable of contributing to the cultural shape of the colony.
A combination of legislation, custom and the experience of slave owners
who settled in South Carolina from Barbados, produced a set of codes

that were some of the most repressive and brutal of the colonies. Yet, the slave population was important to South Carolina for more than the labour provided; this was a skilled workforce, one that educated the white settlers in the arts required for the cultivation of crops in the region. The urban centre of Charleston also benefitted: Robert Rosen argues that, 'during the colonial era, most of the carpenters, masons, coopers, sawyers and blacksmiths were slaves [...] many of Charleston's building are a monument to their skill' (1992: 69). The rapidity of economic growth coincides with the construction of a purpose-built theatre in 1736. Given that the black population of the region was so significant a part of the workforce, one can assume that the theatre house would have been built on the back of slavery. Free blacks are also listed in the population of Charleston; according to Maurie Dee McInnis, there were 586 free blacks in Charleston by the time of the first official census in 1790 (2005: 20). And Juliet Walker demonstrates that free blacks were involved in the setting up and management of colonial businesses, from brick-making to participation in the arts (2009: 43).

The black population that were subject to the slave system of South Carolina were significant in number and also culturally diverse, from different regions, speaking distinct African languages. A communication system developed, most specifically in the Lowcountry with the evolution of 'Gullah' linguistics, through which Africans began to construct a cultural space. The processes of Gullah were acknowledged by the white slave holders, and the slave workforce operated within a dual naming system, within which the white plantation owners clearly acknowledged the existence of a pre-slavery 'country name'. Hennig Cohen's 1952 essay on slave names lists examples of both 'country' names and imposed slave names (1952: 104–5). For the purposes of this study, it is worth noting that one female slave was named Monimia, the name of one of the main characters from Otway's *The Orphan*. Also worth noting is that the significant slave rebellion, that took place in 1739, was led by a slave who had been given the name Cato: the play, by Joseph Addison (1712), which tells of Cato's sturdy defence of 'commonwealth' and individual liberty in the face of Caesar's advancing imperial army, had been performed both at the court house and at the Queen Street theatre between 1735 and 1737.

Addison's *Cato* became a favourite of revolutionary generals later in the century. By that time, slavery was enforced across the thirteen colonies, and the play would become a complex platform from which to declare the rights of the individual in the New World. None of the political leaders, most of whom were slave owners, seem to have commented on the irony of their decided preference for a play that speaks against shackling humanity, a telling commentary on the racial discourses of colonial Americans.

That we see names from plays in such wide circulation suggests to us that a theatrical imagination was taking hold in the region. And, there is firm evidence of a more formal approach to staging theatrical activity in the city before the building of the theatre house. Eola Willis's study of the theatre in Charleston during the eighteenth century quotes from the *South Carolina Gazette* (18 January 1735): 'On Friday the 24th instant, in the court room will be attempted a tragedy called "The Orphan, Or the Unhappy Marriage"' (1924: 9). Prior to the opening of the official theatre, then, through the auspices of one Henry Holt, the court room was made available for a series of performances that ran throughout 1735. The *South Carolina Gazette* of November 1734 reports the arrival of Holt from England, and notes that the dancing master 'danced a considerable time at both the Play-houses'.[24] Holt began his colonial career advertising teaching at his 'dancing rooms', twice a week; very soon, performances of plays were being advertised.

The official opening of the Charleston theatre was advertised in the *Charleston Gazette* (24 January 1736): 'On Thursday February 12th will be opened the New Theatre in Dock street in which will be perform'd "The Recruiting Officer."' The Holt company continued their performances at the new Theatre when its doors were opened. Holt's 'company' was not necessarily an imported troupe, direct from England, though. Johnson and Burling records that he 'quickly assembled a small company of students' (2003: 112).Where these 'students' came from is not specified: the college of Charleston – the first university in South Carolina – did not open its doors until 1770. But the sons of the wealthier elite of the region were sent to other colleges, such as William and Mary in Williamsburg; as discussed in the previous chapter, these were, in the main, divinity colleges, training the youth of the colonies in the art of spiritual rhetoric.

The Recruiting Officer appears to have been as popular with theatre sponsors in Charleston as it was proving to be in New York; unsurprisingly, as the performances were frequently promoted: 'BY Desire of the Officers of the Troop and Foot-Companies' (*South Carolina Gazette*, 6 March 1736). The play was performed several times during the Queen

Street theatre's three-year existence, alongside *The Orphan*. The theatre also witnessed new material, such as George Lillo's *A London Merchant* (1731) and Charles Coffey's musical *The Devil to Pay* (1731). On 26 May 1737, *The Recruiting Officer* was staged for the final performance at the theatre. In 1739, the *South Carolina Gazette* carried an advert for the sale of: 'the Lott in *Charlestown* whereon the *Theatre* is built' (23 June 1739). The theatre would be used for dances and balls over the next few years, until its destruction, along with many of Charleston's buildings, in 1752.

Throughout its short but important existence, the Queen Street theatre made an impact on the cultural shape of the centre. In part the theatre brought the town into connection with 'Old World' culture, staging plays very much associated with 'home'. Our information regarding theatrical audiences in Charleston is scant. But there are certain assumptions that seem probable. The audience at Charleston theatre would have been white, from the more established colonial and financially well-set families, of the type that would feed the myth of the southern slave-holding aristocrat in the nineteenth-century imaginary. Such an audience, inevitably, would have been influenced by the vagaries colonial living, and their view of English imports on stage shifted in response to those conditions.

From the date of Holt's departure from Charleston in 1737, there are no adverts in the *South Carolina Gazette* for any public performance until 1754, although there is evidence of several performances organised by private subscription. For example, on 27 November 1749, the paper advertises: 'ON Friday Evening next, at the Court-Room at Mrs. Blythe's, several DRAMATICK ENTERTAINMENTS will be performed, by Mr. Stokes, who for several Years acted on the Stages in Dublin, Edinburgh and Goodman's-Fields.' Two years following the destruction of the Queen Street theatre, the Hallam Company arrived in Charleston, and the gazette noted that a performance of 'A COMEDY , called A Bold Stroke for a WIFE' and 'The M-D, [*The Mock Doctor*] or Dmb Lady cur'd' was to take place (10 October 1754). The venue, though, is unspecified, and there had been no reports of the construction of a new theatre in the *Gazette*. But, a theatre clearly had been built on or around the site of the original building on Queen Street very soon after the demise of the first. Eola Willis speaks of the Hallam Company as coming 'to Charles-town to open her theatre' (1924: 38). Johnson and Burling suggest that the Hallam Company had 'apparently built a new theatre' in Charleston (2003: 172). As with other endeavours, no doubt, a subscription was taken up by the local populace to fund the construction of a new theatre. Howsoever the funding was managed, the Hallams were indeed performing in the 'New Theatre', Charleston, in October 1754.

Three theatre companies dominate the records of theatre in the middle decades of the eighteenth century: Murray–Kean, Hallam and Douglass. The companies were responsible for promoting the building of theatres in colonial centres as well as promoting themselves as commercial theatrical enterprises. The Murray–Kean company toured between 1749 and 1752, Lewis Hallam's troupe from 1752 to 1755 and Douglass's company from 1756 to 1774. But as important as these companies have been for theatre historians, America's theatre history encompassed further varieties of performance, embedded within the distinct operation of colonial life.

A hub for theatrical activity, for example, was also a feature of everyday life for eighteenth-century colonists: the British military. The ongoing and ever-changing negotiations between Native American and colonials, as well as conflict with Spain and France in American territory, had led to the establishment of military bases throughout the region. In Halifax, Nova Scotia, Molière's *The Misanthrope* was performed in 1744. In Albany, New York in 1757, *The Beaux' Stratagem*, *The Recruiting Officer* featured at Fort Cumberland. The latter performance owes its archival existence to George Washington, whose diary recorded 'by cash gave the Players at Ft Cumbd' (cited in Johnson and Burling 2003: 186). Far south in Havana, Cuba, *The Fair Penitent* was performed in honour of the 'birth of the Prince of Wales [...] by the officers of the army, in a theatre built for that purpose' (*Pennsylvania Gazette*, 27 November 1762). Controversy broke in Boston, as the *Evening Post* published an exchange between commentators on army activities: on 13 March 1769, an anonymous letter, in response to an advert for a set of military performances, demands, 'I should be much obliged to any one to inform me what right the commanding officers have to give leave to their men to perform any such entertainments here?' (cited in Johnson and Burling 2003: 328). The response, published on 20 March in the same paper, reads: 'I would inform this writer and all other intermedlers, that there is an Act of Parliament licensing theatrical performances throughout the King's dominions, which I take upon me to say [...] intirely supercedes the Act of this province' (ibid.: 330). Theatrical performance, then, was integral to the inflammatory debate between monarchists and Patriots, and specifically in republican zones, such as New York and Boston, was indeed tangibly politicised.

At the time of this conflict between Native and colonial residents, Pennsylvania was the stage of an uprising organised by a group of Presbyterian frontier settlers, dramatised in the anonymous play, *The Paxton Boys* (1764). The actions of the piece expose the political factionalism of Pennsylvania, where the rule of the Penn family had come under scrutiny since the infamous Walking Purchase swallowed lands occupied by Delaware tribal groups. As a result, Pennsylvanian border regions came under attack during the French and Indian Wars. Pennsylvanians began to adopt a creed of self-defence; the Paxton Boys, though, took that concept to a more aggressive stage and formed a militia. They marched against the Conestoga tribe with whom trade and established economic relations had been peaceful and co-operative, and killed twenty of the tribespeople who were fleeing from the militia. Following the massacre, the militia headed towards Philadelphia, to confront the Quaker-dominated assembly. It is this latter part of the Paxton Boys' campaign that the play of 1764 examines. Tellingly, the extermination of the Conestoga is not part of the dramatic remit.

The play, written as a farce, satirises the attitudes of all factions, though seems to sympathise ultimately with the Quaker council. Philadelphians who do not arm themselves for the purposes of defence are critiqued, as are those staunch Presbyterians within the city who support the Paxton boys. The final speech, uttered by a 'Quaker' resident who has been in moral conflict with the concept of taking up arms declares:

> Stir then good People be not still nor quiet,
> Rouze up yourselves take Arms and quell the Riot;
> Such Wild-fire Chaps may, dangerous Mischeifs raise.
> And fer unthinking People in a blaze. (2003: v, 95–8)

The machinery of dramatic construction has been put to use for the purpose of exploring local issues and deeds. Sympathies may have been with official bodies and therefore expressive of loyalty to the Crown: but tensions between groups had become the subject of dramatic projects negotiating political agitation and attempting to secure social order. In its attempt to secure a loyalist perspective, *The Paxton Boys* dramatises the conflict and, ultimately, lack of order within the Pennsylvanian colony.

At the same time, *The Paxton Boys* can be seen as a dramatisation of tensions growing in the colonies in response to French, British and

Native American activities. As Brooke Hindle points out, the activities upon which the play was based 'grew out of the difficulties of the French and Indian War, and they looked forward toward the American Revolution' (1946: 461). The play was published in pamphlet form, as part of a propagandist publishing industry that was rooting itself in colonial culture. In addition to this play, a series of pamphlets based on the Paxton attacks emerged, titled *A Dialogue, Containing some Reflections on the late Declaration and Remonstrance, of the Back-Inhabitants of the Province of Pennsylvania*, *The Quaker Vindicated*, and *The Author of Quaker Unmask'd, Strip'd Stark Naked*. As tensions increased between factions across the colonies, whether religious, moral or political, or indeed mostly all three, so, too, did the market in dramatic dialogues in pamphlet form, also appearing in propagandist newspapers.

Not only in Philadelphia did such pamphleteering that made use of dramatic form take place. In Massachusetts, one of the most prolific of such dramatic writers in the revolutionary period was Mercy Otis Warren, whose brother and husband had been actively involved in political agitation in Boston against British rule. In the years leading up to the war between Britain and America, three plays that were published anonymously have been attributed to Warren: *The Adulateur: A Tragedy As It Is Now Acted In Upper Servia* (1772), *The Defeat* (1773) and *The Group* (1775). The events of the plays are immediate responses to events of the times: the subtitle to *The Adulateur*, as Jared Brown notes, 'refers to the playing out of incidents [...] rather than theatrical performance' (1995: 13). The incidents, in this instance, are those leading to the Boston Massacre. The plays, taken together, are keenly satirical, and clearly form an attack on Massachusetts Governor Thomas Hutchinson and his replacement, in 1774, General Gage.

Drawing on the imagery of Roman patriots, in the manner of Joseph Addison's *Cato*, Warren redefined dramatic character in the shape of the Patriot hero, the man who fights valiantly against the tyranny of British oppression. Jason Shaffer argues that 'the intrinsically theatrical figure of the patriot is ideally suited to provide a defining centre for the public imagination in such moments of crisis' and that, ultimately, it was George Washington, 'inveterate playgoer', that fulfilled the public imaginary (2007: 27). Warren's dramas, however, contributed significantly to an extension of range for heroic characterisation. Precursing Patrick Henry's 1775 'liberty or death' speech, and echoing Cato's declamations on freedom, Warren's Junius declares 'That man dies well who sheds his blood for freedom' (Warren 2003: II, iii) and in the Patriot's theatre of war, all 'men' can perform as American heroes. Her plays rendered symbolic characterisations of John Adams, Samuel Adams, John Hancock and her brother James Otis as a new breed of hero. George Washington, though, is the ultimate Patriot hero, inter- polated as a character into the classic battle against the tyranny of an imperialist centre. This hero can be inclined domestically rather than a cerebral head of state; he can be of the professional classes, not intrinsi- cally 'noble'; and, most significantly, he can be a foot soldier, not neces- sarily a general. Interestingly, Warren does not develop any significant women in her plays; her focus is on the character of the hero, the fighter in the theatre of war. Drawing on a tradition of British eighteenth- century playwriting, Warren also participates in the development of a shifted sense of heroics, one that would inform the status of all American Patriots and inform an ideology of democratic masculinity that would continue to stalk American stages.

Such productions, Walter J. Meserve observes, form 'a prominent part of the "War of the Belles Lettres"' (1994: 14). These closet dramatic productions were part of the conflicted narrative of colonial life. Abjured as performance in major colonial centres, plays had become scripts for political agitations and acts, and also, very significantly, a motivation for the rituals of public protest which were a precursor to revolutionary war.

During the years leading to the outbreak of the Revolutionary war, colonials were participating in a range of political activities that resonate with attributes of festival, carnival and street theatre. The setting up of a maypole at Merrymount may have disturbed early New Englanders, but it was Boston that would become one of the key centres for the enact- ment of dramatic rituals in the 1760s and 1770s. The symbolism of ritual drama particularly translated to the establishment of the Liberty Tree, from which space the Sons of Liberty could manage their tableaux of resistance. The 'Boston Massacre' became, according to James Bowdoin, Joseph Warren (Mercy Otis Warren's husband) and Samuel Pemberton, *A Short Narrative of the Horrid Massacre in Boston* (1770), a 'shocking tragedy' that was 'acted' before an audience of Bostonians keen to make use of the language of performance to instil the full horror of the event (1849: 8). The 'audience' also makes record of the 'dreadful' tragedy, the 'bloody' tragedy, in the 'tragical scene', which unfolded (ibid.: 24, 29, 33). Jeffrey Richards locates the structure of the *Short Narrative* as 'highly charged', with 'the theatrical realm of pitch, stagger and fall'

(1991: 215). By the dawn of the revolution, then, a theatrical imaginary had taken hold of the most stalwart of the anti-theatrical colonies.

One of the most infamous acts of pre-revolutionary fervour is that event famously titled the Boston Tea Party. The story is familiar: Patriots dressed as Mohawks attacked the British ships in port, which were carrying the heavily taxed tea. Bruce McConachie locates the action as a 'scenario of a ritual of misrule, complete with the overturning of a "civilised" custom (tea drinking) by "uncivilised" savages' (1998: 128). The ritual here, though, is in itself a carefully conceived sleight. Page Smith refers to the event as 'guerrilla theater', and makes an important assessment of the participants: 'there were no rioters among the carefully drilled Mohawks who dumped the tea in Boston Harbor' (1976: 384). As a staged event, the Boston Tea Party appeals to ritualised drama, building on the popularity of 'folk' rights such as the Liberty Tree – by now, most if not all colonial centres were in possession of this totem.

The drama, though, as Philip J. Deloria notes, resonates more significantly:

> The tea party had been a street theater and civil disobedience of the most organized kind [...] in the national iconography, the Tea Party is a catalytic moment, the first drumbeat in the long cadence of rebellion through which Americans redefined themselves as something other than British Colonists. (1998: 2)

'Playing Indian', as Deloria notes, was not a replication of native customs: 'White Indians laid claim, not to real Indian practices, of course, but to the idea of native custom – the specifics to be defined not by Indians, but by colonists' (ibid.: 25). In American dramatic productions developed over the eighteenth and nineteenth centuries, the concept of 'playing Indian' is aligned with the framing of the 'vanishing Indian', as native cultures become replaced by white versions of the primitive native, noble or savage. Yet, at the same time, the 'native' is a consistent feature of that output. In 'playing Indian', the Bostonians may have been capturing, owning and reconstructing the concept of 'native' American behaviours; but they had, in the process, declared themselves as 'American' characters in a shifted context – and as Deloria points out, become 'something other than British colonists' (ibid.). Those 'Americans' were thus framed and informed by an exploration of the meaning of 'native', in a complex and shifting landscape of identification that negotiated quests for independence and self-determination through a colonial status that had become consciously and deliberately shaded by an evocation, albeit faked, of tribal operations.

The first Continental Congress was preceded by Associations who passed resolutions to boycott the importation of British goods; Odai Johnson lists 'slaves, wine, beef, spirits, cheese, tallow candles, broadcloth, upholstery, watches, clocks, readymade furniture, and the like'. There was no embargo placed directly on theatre, but a resolution was passed to 'discourage all manner of luxury and extravagance' (cited in Johnson 2006: 90–1). On 20 October 1774, the Continental Congress set out its Articles of Association. Point eight declared that the Association would: 'discountenance and discourage every species of extravagance and dissipation, especially all horse-racing, and all kinds of games, cock fighting, exhibitions of shews, plays, and other expensive diversions and entertainments' (ibid.). Early 1775, in response to Congress's declaration, the American Company decamped to Jamaica, where David Douglass retired, leaving Lewis Hallam, Jr in charge of the troupe.

In Boston, Faneuil Hall was requisitioned by British troops as a theatre in 1775, an insult on a number of levels. In the first instance, this was one of Boston's leading meeting places; then, Boston had passed anti-theatrical legislation in 1750; additionally, it was from Faneuil Hall that Samuel Adams demanded the removal of British troops from Boston following the Massacre. The damage done to relations between soldiers and colonists was further inflamed by the staging of a play written by the British commander, General Burgoyne, a farce titled *The Blockade of Boston*, on 8 January 1776. Burgoyne had dabbled in both politics and playwriting, in addition to his army career. He was elected Member of Parliament for Preston, Lancashire in the late 1760s and had written a play taken up by star actor David Garrick and performed at the Drury Lane theatre in 1774, just prior to his departure for the colonies. Burgoyne was also associated with what we might term parapolitics; he was, according to Richard Hargrove, convicted of aiding and abetting rioters during his parliamentary election in Preston, Lancashire (1983: 53). *The Blockade of Boston* was a satire on American rights, a challenge to the sons of Liberty.

A riposte to *The Blockade of Boston*, titled *The Blockheads; or, the Affrighted Officers*, has been attributed to Mercy Otis Warren, prolific writer for the revolutionary cause. This farce locates the British troops as 'looking like French cooks, in a hot day's entertainment' and the officers as 'terrify'd as old women' (cited in Brown 1995: 72). Another challenge came in the form of *The Fall of British Tyranny* (1776), attributed to

John Leacock and written under the name Dick Rifle. The play features Washington as a character, and another significant name from American history occurs in the play, the Delaware chief Tammany, whose friendship and amenability with William Penn and the Pennsylvanians had become a matter of legend. Tammany became St Tammany and interpreted symbolically as an embodiment of the American continent, with a feast day set onto May Day. Two shepherds of *The Fall of British Tyranny* sing of 'St. Tamm'ny the bold', and 'He, as king of the woods, of the rivers and floods, / Had a right all beasts to controul; / Yet, content with a few, to give nature her due: / So gen'rous was Tammany's soul!' (Leacock 1918: III, vi). Tammany, the Native American chief, is compared favourably to England's St George, aligned with George Washington, and thus elevated, for colonials, to a position of canonised patronage for this new America.

Throughout colonial life, the antipathy to performance did not extend to performativity of the written word. The wording of the 1774 Constitutional ban is here significant: to 'discountenance' exhibitions of 'shews and plays'. The writing of drama does not fall within that remit. As we saw through the early endeavours of actors in the colonies, strollers, like in England, were vagabonds and morally suspect – the act of acting was wrong; but drama expressed in the twists and shifts of metaphoric language as performed on the page, are not only tolerated, but operate actively, as a weapon of the revolutionary war.

On 12 October 1778, the Continental Congress passed another resolution 'for the suppressing [of] theatrical entertainments, horse-racing, gaming, and other such diversions as are productive of idleness, dissipation, and a general depravity of principles and manners' (cited in Brown 1995: 62). Four days later, the Congress passed another, more punitive motion, resolving that 'any person holding an office under the United States who shall act, promote, encourage or attend such plays, shall be deemed unworthy to hold such office, and shall be accordingly dismissed' (ibid.: 63). Opposition was voiced by North Carolina and Georgia; also this time, New York, Maryland and Virginia objected. Throughout the spring of 1778, George Washington, stationed in Valley Forge, had permitted a series of performances by American soldiers, and on 14 May had attended the staging of Addison's drama of besieged bravery, *Cato*. Odai Johnson suggests that Washington's complicity with theatrical endeavours may have been in the minds of the Continental Congress as they passed the anti-theatre resolution (2006: 92). Given that the 16 October Resolution is aimed at those 'holding office', such an argument does seem likely. In response, American troops curtailed their theatrical endeavours for the remainder of the war, whilst British troops continued to perform. Revolutionary dramatists produced a plethora of plays as critiques of the British military theatrical activity. British character was established as dissipated because it was associated with the immoral concept of playing, whilst Americans were good patriots because they were not vagabond strollers. The conflicts of the revolution, then, were expressed specifically through a prolific output of playscripts and performances.

Following the end of the Revolutionary War, Boston finally acquired an establishment for the presentation of theatrical spectacles, although the legislature of Massachusetts still maintained the ban against shows and plays. Various attempts had been made to repeal the ban, but the anti-theatre lobby managed to ensure its continuation. Clapp reports that, as a response to the stringent laws against performance, several local 'friends of the drama' managed to construct a 'theatre in all but name'; they named their building the 'New Exhibition Hall' (1968: 6–7). The 'theatre' opened on 10 August 1792, featuring, according to the handbill, performers who would 'dance a hornpipe on a tightrope, play the violin in various attitudes, and jump over a cane', followed by 'various feats of tumbling', and a 'dancing ballet, called *The Birdcatcher*, with the Minuet de la Coeur and the Gavot' (cited in Clapp 1968: 9). Such acts, formed from a physicality of performance and spectacle in acrobatics or dance, would become known in the nineteenth century as non-legitimate, or even 'illegitimate', theatre.[25] In a prime example of conflict that resides at the core of American theatricals, the very first performances in morally upright Boston were illegitimate both in law and in substance.

In 1792, a pamphlet was published in Boston, titled 'Effects of the Stage on the Manners of the People: and the propriety of Establishing and Encouraging a Virtuous Theatre. By a Bostonian'. The piece was ambitious in its desire to promote theatre as morally improving and indeed suggested that a building that housed a theatre could become a municipal centre, with covered gardens for promenading, and an assembly room for the legislature. The writer, William Haliburton, also proposed an auditorium that would seat 2,000, and free tickets 'as rewards of merit to poor citizens' (Clapp 1968: 18). Larger theatre buildings would become a feature of the nineteenth-century theatre landscape, but, at this stage, seating rarely stretched beyond 500 – in London, playhouses had been constructed to accommodate larger audiences, so perhaps Haliburton's ideas were not quite so 'in advance of the times' as Clapp claims (ibid.). What seems more significant, though, is that that such a piece about the validity and potential expansiveness of theatre both morally and literally was conceived, and published, suggesting that Boston was not so entirely opposed ideologically to theatre as has been argued.

The performance of plays under the guise 'moral lectures' soon followed in Boston and in Newport, Rhode Island, as the legislature loosed its grip over the next five years. The ban on theatre finally passed on, by which time the New Exhibition Hall had burnt down and the Boston Theatre, again supported by local business, had been erected. Susan Porter argues that the theatre following the Revolutionary War 'moved towards the standards, practices and facilities comparable to those found in major English cities outside of London' (1991: 7). Certainly actors were imported from stages across England, Scotland and Ireland (Dublin and Edinburgh also being major centres for performance). Managers imported a series of professionals, and playbills advertised the specific theatrical credentials of their imported stars. Theatre buildings also echoed the stages of England: the Boston theatre, for example, 'displayed a taste and completeness worthy of London', according to John Bernard in 1793 (cited in Porter 1991: 8). For practical reasons, the theatres of the post-revolutionary era may have rifled English stores for their actors, costumes, scenery and even models for theatre buildings. But the performances that took place responded carefully to the contexts and conditions of the new republic. London performance was not lifted wholesale onto American stages.

For example, at the opening night of the first official theatre in Boston, 3 February 1794, the play performed was *The Tragedy of Gustavus Vasa* (Henry Brooke 1739), the story of the Swedish king who stands against injustice and pays with his life. The play was also notorious as the first to be prohibited under the 1737 Licensing Act in England.[26] *The Tragedy of Gustavus Vasa* was subtitled *The Deliverer of His Country*, and was associated during the Revolutionary War with George Washington – also regarded as a deliverer of his country. Jared Brown notes that the play 'was produced on patriotic occasions and always associated with Washington' (1995: 154). According to the playbill, the finale of the evening's entertainment included 'Yankee Doodle' and 'General Washington's March'. Thus the apparent 'Britishness' of American theatre in terms of its constituent parts – imported actors, scenery, playwright – was put together in a distinct format to produce a new drama for and of the new republic.

One of the more famous subscribers to the theatre in Boston was Susanna Haswell Rowson, whose family had been deported to Britain at the outset of the war. She returned to America with her husband, in 1793, as part of the New American Company. She also wrote several plays, one of which, *Slaves in Algiers*, dramatises the kidnapping of American sea travellers by Barbary pirates. The play was premiered at the Chestnut Street theatre, Philadelphia, in December 1794. Unlike the dramas of Mercy Otis Warren, with whom Rowson had been friendly until the deportation of her family, *Slaves in Algiers* offers models of heroism for men and women.

The play is predicated on levels of kidnap, slavery and the desire for freedom. In the early scenes, we are introduced to the key characters: Fetnah is currently enslaved by the Dey; she is the daughter of Ben Hassan, who is a sponsor of Barbary pirates, and had recently taken captive an American woman, Rebecca, whom he has in his turn enslaved. It was from Rebecca that Fetnah has learned that 'woman was never formed to be the abject slave of man. Nature made us equal with them, and gave us the power to render ourselves superior' (Rowson 2003: I, i). The play features another American woman, Olivia, played by Rowson in Philadelphia, who has been captured. The women, then, are captives of men at the outset of the drama. By the end of the play, all are restored to liberty through the auspices of a slave rebellion organised by American heroes Henry and Frederic, who have also been held captive. As part of the live performance, following the conclusion of the main entertainment, Rowson returned to stage, in her role as author, to deliver a telling epilogue:

> Well, Ladies tell me – how d'ye like my play?
> "The creature has some sense," methinks you say;
> "She says that we should have supreme dominion,
> And in good truth, we're all of her opinion.
> Women were born for universal sway,
> Men to adore, be silent, and obey." (ibid.)

At this point, the epilogue draws on a sense of concern amongst women who had been supporters of the Patriot cause in the Revolutionary War. Rowson's epilogue is jocular, in comic tone apparently mocking American women for wishing to be in 'supreme dominion' over men.

Such a tone can be perceived as mocking women's claims for equality; certainly the epilogue also suggests that women's role is 'To raise the fall'n – to pity and forgive, / This is our noblest, best prerogative', consolidating women's social roles as nurturers and care-givers. In the early scenes of the plays, Fetnah describes Rebecca as 'from that land, where virtue in either sex is the only mark of superiority. – She was an American' (ibid.: I, i). Such equality of status is also reiterated in the epilogue, which calls for a humane response to 'slavery's ignominious chain'. Kritzer argues that 'this epilogue speaks on several levels about the potential power of women [...] and the role they might perform in the new nation' (1999: 8). But, I suggest, the epilogue is hesitant about an outright assertion of rights, claiming instead a carer's space that had been allocated already to the American woman. Rather than a radical drama of women's concerns, then, at their absence in the political shaping of the nation, the play stages women's roles as nurturing and domestic. However, those roles are far from passive; throughout the play, plot actions are developed at the behest of its central cast of women, as the domestic becomes located as a space of dynamism and a hub of control. Abigail Adams famously wrote to her husband in a letter dated 31 March 1776, 'remember the ladies and be more generous and favourable to them than your ancestors' and 'Do not put such unlimited power into the hands of the husbands' (1876: 149). John Adams did not heed this warning and as the eighteenth century came to a close, women's rights in America were gradually eroded.

It was in the aftermath of the revolution that one of the most famous of 'American' plays was written and performed: Royall Tyler's *The Contrast*. First staged in New York at the John Street theatre in 1787, the 'polish' and 'deportment' of the Europeanised Dimple threatens to discompose the marital intentions of the unpolished yet worthy American Colonel Manly. Modelled on Sheridan's *The School for Scandal*, *The Contrast* operates as a signal for the drama that would grace privately sponsored theatre houses in the aftermath of the Revolutionary War, locating European posing as degenerate and inappropriate for the rigours of nation-building, whilst acknowledging the role and duty of the privileged (wealthy) elite, who were, in effect, paying the wages of playwright, actor and stage manager. But *The Contrast* is a significant production in the development of American staging, looking to and incorporating post-independence, or more specifically non-colonial, theatrical material. In these early Republic productions, the drama of identity was keenly anti-colonial; the role of the 'good' American nation-builder was that of Colonel Manly, by name as well as in his actions. A stereotype of Calvinist disapproval of pleasure, the Colonel constitutes the figure of the 'honest American' (Tyler 1970: V, ii).

However, *The Contrast* also dramatises what was to become a staple on the stages of the United States in the figure of Jonathan. The embodiment of the 'true born Yankee American son of liberty', Jonathan was conceived as a vehicle to demonstrate, Peter Davis argues, 'the basic goodness inherent in American culture through the common sense and rural humanity' of the American servant (1998: 244). Jonathan's speech patterns are clear markers of his national status: 'why such a tarnal cross tyke you never saw!' (Tyler 1970: V, i). The comic elements of the play derive from the attempts of the Anglophile Jessamy to gull the innocent Jonathan in pseudo arts of decorum with regards to proper notions of laughter. With his 'tarnations' and 'dangs', Jonathan becomes as much as target for ridicule as Jessamy's insouciant Europeanism and thus, argues Bret E. Carroll, 'expresses anxieties of a new nation before resolving them with patriotic reassurances' (2003: 109). Jonathan's status as an American citizen, indicated by his repeated cries of 'tarnation', were, albeit unconsciously, counterpoised against the noble spirit of Colonel Manly as a signal of the vitality and urgency for the theatre's participation in articulating a post-independence body, language and voice – or more accurately voices.

So *The Contrast* dramatises competing concepts of American masculinity. Colonel Manly and Jonathan share certain traits: neither has left the American homeland, both display a dislike of pleasure trips, including the theatre, and both are threatened by the Anglophile team Dimple. The key difference between the two American voices is founded in class: Colonel Manly is a hero, Jonathan a figure of comedy; *The Contrast* thus stages a society formed on social understandings of class.

The end of the eighteenth century is also notable for the burgeoning career of William Dunlap, whose *History of American Theatre from its Origins to 1832* (1832) has done much to persuade theatre historians of the shape of the American stage. During the Revolutionary War, his family, who were loyalists, moved to New York, a British stronghold in the early years of the conflict. His first exposure to theatre was therefore at the hands of the British military performances that took place in the St John Street theatre throughout 1777. Later, Dunlap spent time in England, prior to establishing himself as the writer/adapter of over sixty plays. Dunlap's career is important, in part because of his prolific output, but also because of his critical assessments of American productions. As one of the earliest theatre critics, Dunlap's readings have contributed to interpretations of early theatre as poor, in comparison with European counterparts. He described *The Contrast* as 'extremely deficient in plot, dialogue or incident', but also deplores the 'predilection' of audiences for 'foreign articles', a preference he considers 'discouraging' (2005: 75). Here Dunlap is somewhat hypocritical, given that he was himself responsible for the translation of German and French plays for the American stage. Dunlap is troubling as a source, in that his attitudes towards theatre are informed, inevitably, by his urge to define 'improper or immoral purposes' in theatrical output. But his declaration that, in 1832, 'the drama in its moral character is now purer than in any former time since the glories of Grecian republicanism and literature' (ibid.: 3) is worth noting. At a time when theatre bans were ousted, if not entirely lifted, Dunlap stakes a claim for the moral standing of American drama.

Throughout the eighteenth century, colonial America had been a repository of British acting companies, British scenery and costuming; but, at the same time, the colonial atmosphere had made significant differences to that stock and structure, with performance shifting in line with local expectations, influenced by prevailing conditions of cultural life and tensions between the diverse population groups. Dramatic texts and dramatised events examined colonial existence, as tensions of Englishness and American identity became more and more pronounced. At the end of the century, playwrights born on the North American subcontinent were establishing credentials, at the same time as new playhouses were being constructed for the performance of their plays. Whilst not exactly encouraged by the legislature or religious leaders, theatrical entertainments were less fraught with ban and blockade. Nevertheless, the tensions that had been manifest in the dramas of eighteenth-century theatre continued to feed the stages on the nineteenth, as slave economies became more deeply embedded and attitudes towards Native Americans as 'Americans' came under scrutiny. Such concerns were recontextualised in the next century by an increasingly conflicted federal structure and further colonial wars. Political, economic and cultural conflicts also fed performance production, as can be seen in the policies enacted towards black and Native Americans. Dramatic productions, performances and theatrical shows continued to home in on political and cultural anxieties, as we see in the production of and reaction to the troubling group of

'Indian Plays', the persecution of the African Grove Theatre company in 1820s New York, and the emergence of popular performance such as melodrama, pantomime and the *corps de ballet* of the infamous 'leg shows', which placed women's bodies on stages, in explicitly sexualised terms.

CHAPTER 4

Politics and Plays in the Nineteenth Century

American theatre in the nineteenth century has become synonymous with commerce and with the staging of spectacular entertainments designed to appeal to a mass audience to fill the new theatres that were being built to cater for larger audiences. Bruce McConachie cites the example of Philadelphia's Chestnut Street theatre, reconstructed in 1794 to seat 2,000. At the same time, the demographic of that audience had shifted; of those 2,000 seats only 900 were allocated to the boxes for the higher echelons (1998: 131). The patrician auditorium of the eighteenth century was giving way to a wider, more diverse audience. In the early decades of the nineteenth century, patriotic plays, similar to those of the period post-revolution, continued to be offered, but by the 1820s, theatre managers were looking to attract audiences to fill their bigger theatres, to stay in business.

The economic climate of the nineteenth century was at best uncertain, but very quickly, a form of drama was translated from French and English stages that became a significant presence in American theatres. David Grimsted refers to a 'new dramatic age', in which 'the type of play that would be popular for the rest of the nineteenth century had been acclimatised to the American stage [...] it paid little heed to poetry or characterisation but rather emphasised stage effect and scenic display' (1968: 20). This 'new drama' was the melodrama. With its emphasis on scenic display, on the fullest and most urgent expression of raw emotion, with its battle between hero and villain, and sanctifying of female rectitude and virtue, the melodrama became embedded in the American theatrical repertoire of the nineteenth century. One of the problems with assessments of melodrama is a tendency to locate the form as reactionary and stilted, as sentimental and sterile. Whilst melodrama is indeed a stylised form of drama, one that tends to assert a return to moral order in its closure, its manifestations on American stages invite alternative readings, and I will, in this chapter, discuss the implications of some of the key melodramas of the period.

Immigration played a major role in developing theatre in the nineteenth century, and negotiating dynamics between groups continued to provide subject matter for productions, particularly between racial groups in the antagonistic climate of Manifest Destiny and slave economies. The theatrical endeavours of America's black communities, notably the African Grove Theatre of William Brown, and the production of racial 'types', in 'Indian Plays' and in 'blackface', form a significant part of my discussion. Theatre in its conflicted roles as 'moral' enterprise, or space of immoral activity, was a dialogue maintained throughout the century and one that became entangled with social discourses on proper gendered behaviours. The 'third tier' of theatre auditoria were widely recognised as spaces for the commerce of prostitution and the figure of the actress also came to be regarded as an ambiguous, potentially illicit threat to social propriety. This chapter will examine, therefore, the shifting landscape of theatrical and social roles in response to the burgeoning fleshly spectator sport of burlesque, assessing the social implications of the display of women's bodies on stage.

In the early decades of the nineteenth century, Philadelphia and Williamsburg maintained their colonial position as America's busiest theatre cities, with New York supporting only one major establishment. British forces had occupied New York for much of the Revolutionary War and had made regular use of theatre for their leisure hours, which may have informed antipathy to theatricals in the immediate aftermath of the conflict. By the 1830s, though, that position had changed significantly, and New York had become a centre for theatrical activity in America, as indeed it had become a commercial hub, with the completion of the Erie Canal in 1825. Navigable waterways made New York the most cost-effective entry point for touring companies visiting the New World. For many of the imported stars – Charles Mathews, Edmund Kean, William Charles Macready and Fanny Kemble, to name but a few – the city provided a gateway for touring.

Theatre houses had begun to proliferate across the nation; overall, Leman Thomas Rede counts just fewer than ninety theatres spanning the northern continent by 1827 (1868: 13–18). In the south, New Orleans was a major centre: American star Charlotte Cushman's performance career was initiated there, and Edwin Forrest found an early theatrical home in the city. Following the Mexican War, San Francisco began to establish itself as a theatrical centre as well as a gold-rush town. Londré and Watermeier count over 1,000 productions in theatres of the city between 1850 and 1859 (2000: 133). Edwin Forrest's ex-wife, actress Catherine Sinclair, chose to tour the western shores of America after their scandalous divorce in 1851; in 1853, she was managing the newly built Metropolitan theatre there. And one of America's most famous theatre stars of nineteenth-century theatre, Adah Isaacs Menken, began her stellar career on the stages of San Francisco.

In New Orleans, performances catered for the dominantly French-speaking population, which had been supplemented by Acadians who had headed south following the wars between England and France in the New French colonies and by refugees from the French colony on Haiti. From New Orleans came playwright Victor Séjour, whose father had escaped the Haitian Revolution and whose mother was, according to M. Lynn Weiss, a 'free woman of colour' (2001: xvi). Séjour's plays were performed across Parisian theatres, including the famous *Comédie-Française*. One of the earliest works to be performed in New Orleans was the *Moniteur* by French writer Paul-Louis LeBlanc de Villeneufve, which was based on the life of Native American Chief Poucha-Houmma, who sacrificed himself for his son; like many a play constructed at this time, *Moniteur* celebrates the 'Indian', whilst dramatising the tribespeoples' inevitable demise. Whilst such dramas were popular, the theatres of New Orleans more frequently witnessed operatic performances.

In Philadelphia, an influx of German immigrants in the 1830s led to the establishment of a German Amateur Theatrical Society (Rothfuss 1951: 96; Carvajal 1983: 176). Amateur groups performed in other major cities, including Cincinnati, Milwaukee and New York. Christa Carvajal argues that the 'German Americans were the first to construct adequate theatre halls and public buildings with stages and theatrical facilities, which they usually shared, or made available for English-language theatre production' (1983: 186). Albert Bernhardt Faust argues that, by the turn of the century, it was the standard of production in the German-language theatres that had informed the production ideology of the New Theatre in New York, which shifted focus from melodramatic extravaganzas to 'high dramatic art independent of commercial success' (1909: 693). The establishment of German-language theatres, therefore, offers us a different take on that narrative of American drama, which had fixed on the emergence of Susan Glaspell, Eugene O'Neill and the Provincetown Players as the point when 'good' American drama was initiated.

The influence of Irish immigration in the nineteenth century is the most pronounced. Maureen Murphy argues that 'the Irish who came to America [...] came without a highly developed native drama' (1983: 221). Thus what emerges in 'Irish' drama in America is a form of racialised stereotyping akin to the construction of the 'Indian' and the 'Negro' stock characters. The most famous incarnation of this stage Irish character was Mose, who first featured in Benjamin A. Baker's *A Glance at New York* (1848). Mose is the archetypal Bowery B'hoy, determined, egalitarian, casually violent, but ultimately a hero, as denoted by his status as a volunteer firefighter in an incendiary New York. Dion Boucicault, a famous Irish playwright of the nineteenth century, also engaged in the production of racial types: but the process of characterisation is more nuanced in his melodramatic plays, *The Octoroon* (1859), *The Colleen Bawn* (1860), *Arrah-na-Pogue* (1864) and *The Shaugraun* (1874). Although known on English stages for his social comedy *London Assurance* (1841), in America it was his melodramas of political and racial antagonisms that achieved success. *The Colleen Bawn*, for example, dramatised with the history of the English colonisation of Ireland and was based on the murder of a young Irish girl in 1819. Thus Boucicault shows himself to be a politically minded dramatist: he would, in later years, call for the release of Fenian prisoners from British gaols (Harrington 2009: 74).

One of Boucicault's most famous melodramas, *The Octoroon*, premiered in New York just a few months following John Brown's raid on Harper Ferry. Maureen Murphy argues that Boucicault achieves a balance between 'recognising the injustice of slavery and sympathising with the end of a way of life its loss threatened', and thus 'he offended neither North nor South' (1983: 225). But the play offers a more complex dialogue between attitudes towards race. The heroine, Zoe, is a free 'woman of colour', daughter of the plantation owner and a black slave, whose appearance, in terms of racial codings, is ambiguous; she has received the education of a 'lady' and is admired widely for her beauty.[27] She exists in that liminal zone of the American south, not enslaved, but not enfranchised. Zoe is a spectral figure, an intelligent, educated 'Negro', whose very existence has challenged the South's slave economy and the North's embedded racism. Boucicault, the Irish writer, whose own nation had been colonised and whose population had suffered a form of indentured slavery at the hands of absentee colonial landlords from England, brought into being a character whose multiracial identity challenged the very core of the American nation.

Italian influences on American theatre in the nineteenth century take
several forms: acrobatic tumbling, such as was performed by Donegani's
Tumblers, magicians' shows, as demonstrated by Falconi, and opera,
through the singers that toured widely across the states (Aleandri and
Seller 1983: 239). A form of performance, though, that also had a most
telling impact in the nineteenth century was the gestural language that
came from mime and pantomime. The term pantomime is derived apparently from the single masked dancer known as *Pantomimus* that featured
in Ancient Roman performances, which fed into the Renaissance
commedia dell'arte that circulated from Italy across Europe and England.
In English pantomime, Giuseppe Grimaldi emphasised the role of the
clown – the buffoon of the *commedia dell'arte* – and became very popular
among English and French audiences of the nineteenth century. American
pantomime borrowed variously from Italian and other European forms,
cherry-picking Grimaldi's clowning and slapstick alongside the French
urge towards acrobats and tumblers. America's most famous *commedia*
white-faced clown was George Washington Lafayette Fox, whose incarnations in *Humpty Dumpty* travelled the length and breadth of America.
Humpty Dumpty, premiering in 1867, was performed over 1,000 times
during Fox's lifetime.

American theatres, in the early years of the nineteenth century, were
involved in a process of segmentation that Peter Buckley refers to as
the 'stratification of performance' closely associated with the development of class (1998: 456). In the immediate aftermath of the revolution, much of what was performed, exemplified by Royall Tyler's *The
Contrast*, demonstrated the dominance of the patrician class, consolidating the power base of the revolutionary leaders as the fathers of the
new nation and as controllers of 'culture'. By the turn of the century,
though, the emergence of social strata was reflected in the structure and
format of theatrical endeavours. 'Culture' and 'civilisation' were staged
in legitimate theatres, whilst non-legitimate venues presented entertainments considered purely vulgar and non-edifying, specifically 'commercial' spectacles of cheap thrills and extravaganzas. That class division is
also marked by cultural boundaries. *The Spirit of the Times* explains: 'the
"Corinthian" patronizes the opera, the literary, the legitimate, and the
million go for national, the horrible, and the funny' (cited in Dudden
1994: 107).

The ways in which the works of Shakespeare were staged illustrate
such a divide. American stars Charlotte Cushman, Edwin Forrest and

Edwin Booth made names for themselves performing in Shakespeare. All three starred at various times as the titular Prince of Denmark in *Hamlet*. Pantomime star George Lafayette Fox also starred in an immensely popular burlesque version of the play at the Olympic in 1870 in the regions of the Bowery, as Booth was playing the role at his own Booth's Theatre in the heart of the legitimate theatre district. As was typical of the burlesque format, Fox appeared as a parody of Edwin Booth playing the melancholy Dane. A class boundary, then, can be drawn between these performances of the Bard, one a serious interpretation of tragedy, for which its star was noted, the other a comic spoof for the entertainment of the b'hoys and g'hals of the Bowery. The working class appreciated the bawdy, whilst the wealthy patronised the 'arts'.

Throughout the nineteenth century a whole range of divisions between 'types' emerged in theatres; in addition to class, concepts of race, gender and political ideologies as boundary markers were taking to the stage. What emerged, therefore, across American centres as well as within those individual centres, was an ideological division in the body politic between cultural forms, social structures and economic groups. Theatre became a key space, therefore, through which a range of anxieties were explored and exposed publicly: about Manifest Destiny, about slavery and slave insurrections, about the working classes, about gender and social behaviours, and about the condition of the nation.

William Dunlap was one of the foremost in examining the social contribution of the 'histrionic arts' in the early years of national autonomy, arguing for legislative oversight of theatre. At root, in his assessment, responsibility lay with the 'governmental patronage', to secure theatrical integrity from the 'uneducated, the idle and the profligate, mercenary managers', who would 'please their visitors by such ribaldry or folly, or worse, as is attractive to such patrons, and productive of profit to themselves' (2005: 71). Dunlap argues that by 'taking the mighty engine into the hands of the people as represented by their delegates and magistrates, "nothing could be represented that was not comfortable to patriotism, morality, and religion"' (ibid.: 72). His plan is detailed, including a payment scheme for actors and a section process 'for their morals as well as their talents; they would be instruments of good at all times; and sheltered from the temptations which now beset the profession' (ibid.). At that time, then, Dunlap seems to suggest that theatre does cater to ribald tastes – indeed, that ribald tastes were the order of the day. Dunlap's plea for legislative control implies that commerce did hold sway at that time, and intellectual proprieties were not observed in playhouses. In his plea for government patronage, he asks for nothing short of government intervention.

Dunlap's cogitations on the control of theatre output were formed at a time when the concept of a national legislation was a matter of urgent debate between Federalist and Anti-Federalist factions. The revolutionary Articles of Confederation had stated: 'each State retains its sovereignty, freedom and independence' (cited in Kramnick 1987: 18). But the Constitution, argued Richard Henry Lee, represented a 'transfer of power from the many to the few' (ibid.: 43). Dunlap's concerns about theatre, therefore, reflect a wider concern about the relationship between the nation, the state and the individual American. Dunlap speaks in the tones of the Federalist, in favour of national, centred control of theatre. His concerns were associated not just with the drama as it was staged, but with the attitude of the audience. McConachie points out that 'by 1800 most Americans viewed the playhouse as a legitimate arena for the clash of political factions' (1998: 132). Political debate, in the aftermath of the revolution, continued to spill into the format of theatre, a showcase for the expression of what it meant to be American.

Bruce McConachie argues that the oratory style of revolutionary politics, associated with thinkers such as Patrick Henry and Thomas Paine, which had developed 'straightforward locutions and accessible vocabulary', became a feature of such performances, producing what Kenneth Cmiel has titled 'a middling style' (cited in McConachie 1998: 113), to replace the 'decorous discourse of neoclassicism spoken among the gentry at public events before 1776' (McConachie 1998: 113–14). In theatres, such patriotic rhetoric was also a popular feature. McConachie argues, for example, that Addison's tragedy *Cato*, popular with colonials in the lead-up to the Revolutionary War, 'was rarely performed after 1790', its 'neoclassical cadences' out of step with the new emphasis on 'appeals to the heart' (ibid.: 124). New 'native' plays began to appear on stages, funded by private subscribers keen to promote and assert national certainty through dramatic forms. Theatre, banned by the Continental Congress, now became an integer in the post-revolutionary political drama.

One of the exemplars of the 'middling style' was American 'star' Edwin Forrest. Forrest's career stuttered into life in Philadelphia, in 1820; in 1821, he was in Cincinnati, then a city of around 30,000. The theatre company was struggling financially, and toured considerable distances, including a successful interlude in New Orleans, before ending up at the Park Theatre in 1826. By the mid-1820s, his profile was secured, and Forrest had become the American 'star'. Forrest garnered a reputation for physicality and volume as much as he did for his acting. Indeed his physical presence seems as important to his stage art as the roles he performed. A 'loud mouthed ranting style', was Walt Whitman's assessment (Moses and Brown 1934: 69). In his obituary, William Winter, theatre critic of the New York *Albion*, described Forrest as a 'vast animal, bewildered by a grain of genius'. Winter also commented that Forrest, 'at his best, was remarkable for iron repose, perfect precision of method, immense physical force, capacity for leonine banter, fiery ferocity, and occasional felicity of elocution' (cited in Bordman 1992: 269). Forrest's background – impoverished, lacking a formal education, pushed into work at an early age – is in itself an American myth of rags to riches. Such a story would inevitably feed into his popularity on American stages, and he was championed by the working-class audiences that attended those venues.

Forrest traversed the boundaries between Bowery and Broadway theatrical spaces, and much of his success was also garnered by his repeated touring – he may have been a star in New York, but he was also a mainstay of theatres across the nation.[28] And he was a transatlantic star – appearing on stage in England in 1836 and again in 1845, though less successfully on the latter occasion. Londré and Watermeier (2000) suggest that the lukewarm reception of his second visit was due to activities behind the scenes of William Charles Macready, famous English tragedian, who was concerned that his own reputation had been suffering in the face of Forrest's successes. During this second visit, Forrest famously hissed at Macready on stage in Edinburgh; the event was reported widely in America as a revenge attack on Macready's machinations and the enmity between the two was consolidated in the press.

In 1849, Macready was touring America and in May, was scheduled to appear at the Astor Place opera house, in competition with Forrest who was starring at the Broadway Theatre. Macready was booed and pelted with eggs, and was so outraged that he decided to return to England immediately. The New York literati, including Walt Whitman and N. P. Willis, signed a petition to ask him to remain, and he did. But on 10 May, three nights later, he was attacked by organised forces who had spent the intervening time agitating for unrest. Posters stated: 'Working men, shall

Americans or English rule in this city?' (cited in Grimsted 1968: 72).
The riot duly took place and Macready had to be smuggled off stage; the
army were called out and twenty-two bystanders killed. The theatre had
become, therefore, a literal battle ground for the 'rule' of identity.

The 1849 Astor Place Riot was predicated on the rivalry between
Forrest and Macready, but was less to do with acting than it was with
the construction of national identities and class. The *Boston Liberator*
recorded, on 18 May 1849:

> Ever since the arrival of the distinguished English tragedian Macready
> in this country, he has been dogged from city to city by Edwin Forrest,
> a rival American actor, and by him publicly denounced in low and
> inflammatory language, on the false charge of having disparaged the
> latter when playing in England.

Macready was the English gent – in comparison, Forrest was a native
oaf. To be 'American', as Forrest portrayed that role, was not always
critically welcomed. Such sentiments were echoed by New York Mayor
Philip Hone, who, in his diary, wrote of Forrest's rivalry with the
English actor that it had 'no cause that I could discover, except that one
is a gentleman and the other is a vulgar, arrogant loafer, with a pack of
kindred rowdies at his heels' (1910: 359–60). It should be recognised,
however, that the incident took place during a major strike in New York,
at a time of volatile relations between workers and bosses, and the actions
of the Astor Place Riot, therefore, had more to do with class antagonisms
than theatre. But theatre had operated as a space in which such antagonisms could find direct and indirect expression.

For audiences associated with working-class venues in the Bowery,
Forrest was the exemplar of an expressive heroic style that suited their
ideals of a democratic American nation, and he became the dramatic
embodiment of their quest for representation. Forrest is also associated
with one of the most famous of the distorted racial dramas of 'Indian
Plays' that proliferated in the early part of the nineteenth century.
Another notable play, *Tammany: or, The Indian Chief*, was written in the
latter part of the eighteenth century; the text is no longer extant, although
the songs survive to provide an outline of plot. The play fictionalises
an account of the 'sainted' friend of Pennsylvania, who suffers at the
hands of colonial violence, displaced from eighteenth-century English
to sixteenth-century Spanish forces (Hipsher 1927: 124–5). James Nelson
Barker's *The Indian Princess; or, La Belle Sauvage*, produced in 1808,

produces a bucolic image of 'the Indian as child of nature and helpmate to the white man', argues McConachie, a fantasy that coincided with the 'famine, disease, and frontier violence' that 'continued to decimate the eastern tribes' (1998: 136). Following the 1812–14 war with England, in which Chief Tecumseh supported British forces against the American army, a plethora of dramatic texts emerged, making him, according to Hoxie, an 'American folk hero' (1996: 461). Tecumseh shares with Chief Pontiac, fictionalised in the drama of Robert Rogers, the capability of orchestrating pan-tribal resistance against the newly established American legislative and its land claims. Tecumseh, eventually betrayed by the British forces he had supported in the 1812–14 war, was killed by American forces as his Native American forces stood alone against the American army, the British having fled the scene. Little attention seems to be paid in the dramas to the activities after the battle, when 'Kentucky Militiamen skinned and mutilated' Tecumseh's body (ibid.).

John Augustus Stone's *Metamora: Or the Last of the Wampanoags* (1829), a play written on behalf of Edwin Forrest, stands as one of the most famous of plays dramatising the American pursuit of deracination. Whilst Manifest Destiny physically and dramatically eradicated tribes across swathes of this new nation, romanticised, sentimentalised or lampooned stage versions proliferated in the theatres. The concept of such theatrical characterisation had been visited in early endeavours such as Rogers's *Ponteach* of 1766 and Barker's *The Indian Princess* of 1808. Stone had written *Metamora* as a response to a competition launched by Forrest, with an award of $500, for 'the best tragedy, in five acts, of which the hero, or principal character, shall be an aboriginal of this land' (ibid.). There seems something rather sinister in Forrest's urge to look for tragedy in the dramatisation of the 'aboriginal', as if attempting to suggest some hubris that would inevitably lead to a fall for such a hero, or leading character. *Metamora*, first performed in December 1829, just prior to the 1830 Indian Removal Act, offered a way for audiences to find reassurance in the demise of the tribespeople, whilst still regarding the figure of the 'Indian' within the romanticised parameters of the 'noble savage'.

The role also established Forrest as a pivotal player in the drama of American theatre and contributed to the white American tradition of playing ethnicity. Homi Bhabha points out that such stereotyping 'gives access to an "identity" which is predicated [...] on mastery and pleasure' (1994: 74). The play contributed to circumscribing of such ethnicity as theatrical spectacle; and in asserting control over Metamora's character in dramatic form, the audience could control the body of the Native American outside theatres.

Forrest's portrayal was, according to William Alger, an authentic account of the figure: 'when Forrest came to impersonate [...] Metamora it was the genuine Indian who was brought on stage, merely idealized a little in some of his moral features' (1977: 240). The question of 'authenticity' was indeed a major factor of critical debate. The *American Quarterly Review* hoped that the applause bestowed upon Metamora by audiences was aimed at 'Mr Forrest, rather than the ferocious savage he impersonates' (Grimsted 1968: 218). Based on historical events, the story seems to have appealed to audiences, in part as a nostalgic recollection for ancient Arcadian living that must give way to modern cultural forms, and as confirmation that it was right for those ancient ways to be removed. This play, popularly regarded, or at least urged to be regarded, as the 'history' of the war of King Philip, and an authentic image of the unreconstructed chieftain, therefore, draws on and concretises stereotypes in and for the public imagination. That figure of the doomed, anachronistic tribesman became a history for – as well as a theatre of – the American psyche. Here we see the enactment, most clearly, of the collocation of ideologies, of the manipulation of a mass audience, of the theatre and of politics.

Conditions for Native American tribespeople were deteriorating in the early decades of the nineteenth century. A soldier's toast, made as part of the Fourth of July celebrations in 1779 – 'civilization or death to all American Savages' (cited in Pearce 1964: 51) – sums up that ideology; throughout the late eighteenth century, treaty after treaty was broken by the violent actions of state forces or indeed by pockets of land-seeking white Americans, who refused to recognise national legislation. Andrew Jackson championed the policy of Indian Removal in the early part of the nineteenth century. He also introduced government schemes for the control of what tribal populations survived the various incursions and wars. Michael Paul Rogin argues that, to Andrew Jackson, Native Americans would have to 'become merged into the mass of our population', eradicating all traces of indigenous cultural forms, in other words, cultural extinction: 'in a white scheme civilization meant', as Rogin argues, 'no less than death, the disappearance of the Indians' (1975: 210). The American 'toast' had thus made the brief journey from 'civilization or death' to civilisation as death. Stone's *Metamora* deplores this outcome, but locates it as inevitable.

However, audience reaction, although carefully monitored and indeed directed to encounter the noble Metamora as the 'last' of a type, was not always so firmly controlled. When Forrest performed as Metamora in Augusta, Georgia, he 'was openly charged with insulting the people of Augusta by appearing in a character which condemned the course of the state in dealing with [...] land-claims' (Murdock 1880: 299). At the time, the case of *The Cherokee Nation* v. *The State of Georgia* was being tested, and the context of the broken treaty and renegotiations of land rights informed the reception of the play. Forrest was held personally responsible for the perceived insult to the state legislature. Judge James Shannon declared:

> Any actor who could utter such scathing language, and with such vehemence, must have the whole matter at heart. Why [...] his eyes shot fire and his breath was hot with the hissing of his ferocious declamation. I insist upon it, Forrest believes in that d—d Indian speech, and it is an insult to the whole community. (Cited in Levine 1900: 26–7)

That such a radically alternative account of the play should circulate suggests that audiences were not so monolithically controlled by the concept of having seen the 'last' of Metamora at the close of the play. The violence of the reaction to the play can be seen as in proportion to the depth of the fear experienced in Augusta – fear of being recognised as fallible and flawed, fear of the exposure of the discourses that attempted to legitimate Manifest Destiny in action, and fear that ultimately the concept of the 'vanishing Indian' was never any more than a rigorously pursued and somewhat hysterically enacted theory.

Native American delegates in the various American cities also attended performances of the play. William Alger states, 'many a time, delegations of Indian tribes chanced to be visiting the cities where [Forrest] performed this character [...] and their pleasure and approval were unqualified' (1977: 240). Alger makes specific reference to the reaction at one show, where the delegation 'were so excited by the performance that in the closing scene they rose and chanted a dirge in honour of the death of the great chief' (ibid.). Alger's musings, albeit constrained by the ideology of the 'picturesque' Native, do expose some key points: in the consistent negotiations with the various state legislatures, Native Americans had become participants in the theatrical landscape, as spectacle for a white audience, but also as audience to a dramatic performance. Frequently, as part of the negotiations, tribal spokespersons were invited to attend theatrical entertainments. Although the 'Metamora' played by Forrest would bear little resemblance to the historical figure, the concept of memorialising the death of chiefs was a key part of the performative practices of Native American culture. *Metamora* is not a direct referent to an authentic chief; but the context of memorialising a heroic chieftain bore performative similarities to tribal tributes to the dead. The response of the Native American audience to *Metamora*, therefore, offers us another way of assessing Stone's drama. The play was of course predicated on the ideology of the 'vanishing Indian'; but to the Native American observers, the tribal chief was part of the ongoing cycle of existence – he had not 'vanished' in death: *Metamora* was reconceptualised as an affirmation of the spiritual resonance of the Native American chief.

In Boston, as Edwin Forrest played *Metamora*, William Apess of the Pequot tribe, who had been indentured to a series of white families from childhood, had rented the Odeon Theatre for a performance on 8 January 1836, of a 'Eulogy on King Philip'. Apess had converted to Methodism and become a preacher – his 'Eulogy', when published, was in the name of the Rev. William Apess. Apess declared his intention, in the name of 'justice and humanity for the remaining few', to 'vindicate the character of him who yet lives in their hearts', aiming to redress the 'white' history of this 'character' from the colonial drama, and frame him with the standard of immortality awarded to George Washington (1836: 5–6). The 'remaining few' are, somewhat troublingly, deemed as 'degraded'; but Apess makes it clear that the degradation has been inflicted from external forces; it is not intrinsic to the tribespeople. The 'remaining few' are 'monuments to the cruelty' of colonisers – referred to somewhat ironically as 'those who came to improve our race and correct our errors' (ibid.: 5). Vogel argues that Apess, as an 'Indian' representing the 'Indian' King Philip, just a few blocks away from Stone's fiction of the Indian Chief, 'challenges beliefs that extinct Indians could never responsibly participate in the community' (2004: 50). Apess's Pequot ancestors had allied themselves with the British against the Wampanoag tribe in King Philip's war; yet in the face of a distorted 'white' history of colonisation, a new tribal alignment emerges, between representatives from different tribes and different generations, to perform an American history from the perspective of Native American peoples.

For colonial Americans, American Native American women were also stereotyped, as either the noble child of nature, the 'Princess', or her brutalised, licentious 'other', the 'squaw'. Rayna Green has referred to this condition as the 'Pocahontas Perplex', a set of categories for Native American women that are still prevalent in the white imagination (1975: 714). The nineteenth-century white-American imaginary was caught up with the dramatisation of the 'vanishing Indian', but has also enacted, rigorously, discourses of gender and social propriety on the bodies of Native American women. To all intents and purposes, the dramatisation of the princess and the squaw had rendered the Native American woman invisible: she had, in the white imaginary, already been subsumed to the category of gender.

The history of racial politics in the early nineteenth century is complex, and the theatrical landscape through the century an active participant in that complexity. Theatres in Charleston refused entry to black Americans altogether, whilst others set up segregated spaces, usually in the gallery. In some theatres, in the northern states, the gallery was shared by black and white working classes. At the Camp Theatre, in New Orleans, mixed-race audiences were permitted to attend the theatre on one night in the week, in the main section of the auditorium; Grimsted points out that '"escorted coloured women"' were 'given access to all parts of the house' and 'by tacit agreement, white women did not attend the theatre on those evenings' (1968: 53). Such an arrangement speaks volumes of tacitly acknowledged interracial relationships within the slave states. Although persecution and discrimination were standard, and racism effectively institutionalised by varying degrees of segregation, some states had actively worked towards the abolition of slavery in the late decades of the eighteenth and the early decades of the nineteenth century. The Vermont Constitution of 1777 declared slavery unlawful. In the 1780s, Massachusetts and Rhode Island had passed legislation to enable emancipation of older slaves. New York legislated in 1799 for the freedom of slaves over the age of twenty-eight; and in 1817, formally decreed that by 4 July 1827, all remaining slaves would be freed.

It was in New York, within that time of transition following the 1817 emancipation decree but prior to the formal decree of 1827, that William Brown launched the African Theatre. In the first instance, Brown's venture was known as the African Grove and operated within a pleasure garden, a form of venue popular amongst New Yorkers in the summer, but one that was generally segregated. The *National Advocate*, in August 1821, reported the opening of a garden 'somewhere back of the hospital called African Grove; not spicy as those of Arabia [...] but somewhere at which the ebony lads and lasses could obtain ice cream, ice punch, and hear music from the big drum and the clarionet' (cited in McAllister 2003: 1). Brown's pleasure garden, argues McAllister, operated as a form of 'whiteface minstrelsy', in which black Americans could '"other" Euro-New Yorkers', in an 'extratheatrical performance of whiteness that allowed New World Africans to construct a distinctly black urban style and to rehearse their most coveted social aspirations' (ibid.: 12). Hill points out that the pleasure garden 'did not last long', as complaints from the residents of the area led to an official demand for closure (2003: 25).

Almost as soon as he was forced to close the pleasure garden, Brown developed a theatre space in his rooms, and launched the African Theatre, with a performance of Richard III on 17 September 1821. Over the years of its existence, the theatre moved; mainly due to protest against its operations, or violence. But one location is of particular significance: in January 1822, Brown moved his theatre to Hampton's Hotel, which was on Park Row, Manhattan, and located next door to the Park Theatre, which was at that time just restored, following a devastating fire in 1820.

The announcement of the opening of Brown's 'pleasure garden' had been written by Mordecai Manuel Noah, a playwright and novelist, as well as editor of the *New York Advocate*. Noah continued to write up reports on the African Theatre, which staged one of his own plays, the perennially popular *She Would be a Soldier, or the Plains of Chippewa; An Historical Drama, in Three Acts* (1819). Although named after a battle between white and Native Americans, that historical action is somewhat marginal to the main plot, the union of deceived lovers. Worthy of note, however, is that Noah's chief does not die and the play concludes with the gift-giving of a wampum belt from the American General in return for a declaration of peace by the Chief. Demonstrating the fascination with the 'noble savage', the survival of Noah's Chief, and the forming of a reciprocal understanding between warring factions, does, nevertheless, offer a more nuanced attitude towards the shaping of racial consciousness.

Noah's attitude towards the black American theatre group, though, was consciously and overtly racist. Mordecai Noah was an important figure in New York, both culturally and politically. He was, according to Lee Levinger a 'member of Tammany Hall [...] an active Mason, a major in the New York State Militia, an officer of the Jewish congregation and president of Jewish charities' (1930: 162). As a member of an ethnic group historically marginalised in countries founded on racist ideologies, a playwright and a Democrat, therefore vested in ideologies of racial hierarchies, Noah's engagement with Brown's early endeavours is significant. McAllister argues that Noah constructed his accounts of Brown's activities in the language of 'racial terms most consistent with prevailing attitudes and stereotypes' (2003: 26). Hill and Hatch suggest that Noah's reviews were 'often condescending' and 'probably had the unintended effect of attracting Whites to the shows' (2003: 27). Noah stands as a concatenation of New York's demographic flux and the anxieties embedded within that fluid social, cultural and racial landscape. In an expanding, shifting and mutable space, with a complex atmosphere of racial plurality and sensitivity, the establishment of a black American leisure space proved tricky to negotiate. The default response, though, was invoked soon enough, as acts of violence forced Brown's venture to move.

The African theatre was subject to several violations by the white audiences that attended, and at the hands of the authorities, but it was the move to Park Row that brought about one of the most telling attacks on the theatre troupe. McAllister records that on 7 January 1822, the theatre company were arrested and confined in jail, until they 'promised never to act Shakespeare again' (2003: 49). William Dunlap's divided dramatic landscape can be seen enacted here; the racial ideologies of America could not accept that black Americans could perform 'high', Shakespearean, drama. Brown had scheduled *Richard III* for that night's performance, which had been playing at the Park, starring imported British actor Edmund Kean. Brown's decision, then, looked to be a direct challenge to the Park's position as the privileged stage for legitimate drama. Noah, according to McAllister, accused Brown of 'invading Park Row to increase his profits and rival the "great Park Theatre"' (ibid.: 49). That Brown had factored economics into his move to Park Row is undeniable; a political motivation is as clear: staging the same play as the Park was a direct challenge to 'white' ownership of the Bard. Brown's decision to set up his African theatre absolutely next door to Price's venue proved to be anathema. As a result of the attack on the Park Row site, the Hampton Hotel venue was shut and Brown forced to move once again. To inform his audiences of the move, Brown posted a bill stating that 'in consequence of the breaking up of his theatrical establishment, there will be no performance this week' (cited in McAllister 2003: 48), further advising that the 'break-up' was due to 'the influence of his brother managers of the Park Theatre' (Hill and Hatch 2003: 30).

The phrasing is careful, but specific: Price literally broke up the African theatre company.

Following a tour (of which there are no records) in Albany, the group returned to one of their previous sites, on Mercer Street. The material chosen for the performances at Mercer Street does support the contention that Brown's theatrical endeavours were politically charged. One of plays staged was *Obi; or Three-Finger'd Jack*, by John Fawcett (1800), based on the story of a runaway slave who remained free for two years. Brown's own play, *The Drama of King Shotoway*, was also performed. We have no existing script, but the playbill claims that the dramatic action was 'founded on facts taken from the Insurrection of the Caravs in the island of St Vincent' (cited in Hill and Hatch 2003: 34). The plays performed by the African theatre company, then, were predicated on an examination, whether based in fact or founded on fiction, whether comic or serious or melodramatic, of the formation and enactment of racial identities, from the perspective of considering blackness and whiteness from the black American point of view.

Two actors emerged from the African Theatre Troupe following Brown's eventual cessation of operations in 1823: James Hewlett and Ira Aldridge. Hewlett, who had been popular amongst audiences for his impersonation of English 'star' Edmund Kean as Richard III, toured as a one-man show, eventually appearing in Trinidad in 1839, before disappearing from view. Hewlett's acting seems to have been an inspiration for a series of stereotypes in American and English theatres. Following a trip to America, the English comic actor Charles Mathews produced a one-man show, titled *A Trip to America*, which included the figure of a 'Black Tragedian', apparently based on Hewlett – though whether Mathews ever witnessed the African Company's performances is unproven (see McAllister 2003: 159–60). More likely, Mathews's caricature was based on Mordecai Noah's accounts of Hewlett's acting and therefore constitutes a caricature of a stereotype drawn by the pen of a representative of America's dominantly racist ideology. Ira Aldridge had been briefly a member of the African Company, and had direct experience of the violent response of white America; he was, according to Hill and Hatch, assaulted in the street outside the theatre house by one of the ringleaders of the attack at Park Row (2003: 30). Aldridge left America for England, and throughout the nineteenth century toured across Europe, developing a reputation as the 'African Roscius'. His performances were, generally, of black characters, such as Mungo from *The*

Padlock and *Othello*. A free American black and skilled actor, Aldridge performed in works by comic bawd and serious Bard, and thus demonstrated the blatant lie of white America's racial typing.

In America, Mathews's burlesque inspired other actors: notably, in the 1820s, Edwin Forrest, who paid for and got the role of 'Native American' Metamora, also performed as 'The darkey Tragedian, and Ethiopian sketch in One Scene', in which, according to McAllister, 'an ambitious "Negro" actor implores a theatre manager named "Mr Brown" to allow him to perform *Hamlet* or *Richard III*' (2003: 161). Whilst the impact of Brown's theatrical endeavours seems to have been in the inspiration of mocking burlesque, that actors such as Forrest should have made conscious reference to the African Theatre suggests that the entertainment for 'people of colour' had a more profound and nuanced effect on the theatrical landscape. Shortly following the demise of the theatre troupe, minstrelsy took to American stages and acted to consolidate racial stereotypes on behalf of a white audience. But the first noted minstrel performer staged a more carefully framed response to the living conditions of black Americans.

Thomas Dartmouth Rice, in 1828, developed a 'blackface' character, Jim Crow, who found favour on American and English stages in the nineteenth century; 'Daddy' Rice's performance of race, then, became one of the most successful exports from the New World to the Old. English stages had already been enjoying Charles Mathews's 'blackface' one-man show, *A Trip to America*, since 1822, but it was Rice's portrait of what W. T. Lhamon, Jr refers to as 'perceived blackness' that would appeal most profoundly (2003: 2). In the early stages of the shows, Jim Crow occupied an ambiguous space in the drama of identity of the post-revolutionary era, Lhamon argues: 'Rice knitted together publics who were normally separated or opposed outside of theatre's fantasy space. Every night he blacked up, he embodied a character who stitched filiation across class, region, even nationality, and race' (ibid.).

However, by the mid-nineteenth century, minstrelsy's stereotyped race-lines had taken hold and Rice's Jim Crow capitulated to the demands of racist stereotypes. According to Lhamon, the 'inertia of social misreading overcame the meaning of Jim Crow' (ibid.: 31). Perhaps, though, it was the accuracy of social reading that led to the 'capture' of Jim Crow: a character who transgressed established racial parameters so blatantly was a direct threat to hierarchical conventions and needed to be controlled. The *Boston Liberator* of 6 June 1835, for example, makes appalled reference to 'an army of *Jim Crows* and their white associates' who were threatening to 'desecrate Faneuil Hall' by holding a series of abolition talks. No doubt the reporter intended a racial slur against black abolitionists by naming them 'Jim Crow'; nevertheless, it is the fear of the subversive black rebel that communicates itself most profoundly. The report makes specific use of the term 'Jim Crow' to symbolise the politically radical act of staging a meeting against racism and slavery, thus demonstrating the anxiety the character inspired for white America.

'Jim Crow', that symbol of potential challenge to white racism, was appropriated as a racist stereotype, and the laws of racial segregation in the aftermath of the Civil War would be known as the Jim Crow laws. Thus Rice's character, who confronted racism at its core, was silenced, or at least made to conform, to speak in the voice of the comically 'low' subordinated slave or servant, exemplified by servant Zeke in Anna Cora Mowatt's popular *Fashion; or, Life in New York* (1845). With the advent of minstrelsy in the mid-nineteenth century, non-white characters were frequently written in accordance with stereotype; nevertheless the staging of racial dramas was by no means at an end, and theatre, both consciously and unconsciously, continued to perform and explore the racial shape of the American nation.

One of the most famous 'race' dramas on American stages in the nineteenth century was adapted from Harriet Beecher Stowe's novel *Uncle Tom's Cabin*, which had been serialised between 1851 and 1852. Initial dramatic adaptations did not succeed, but in 1852, George L. Aiken launched a version at the Troy Museum in New York, which enjoyed an unbroken run of over 100 performances. In 1853, at Barnum's Museum Theatre in New York, H. J. Conway's version also attracted large crowds. According to John Frick, Stowe's anti-slavery morality was diluted in both plays: 'evil was ultimately shifted away from the institution of slavery and embedded in the individual villains of the narrative' (2007: 48). Conway's script has not survived, but Bruce McConachie argues that, whilst Conway's version was 'pro-South', Aiken's was 'altogether a more faithful rendering of Mrs. Stowe's intentions' (1982: 149). A review in the *New-York Daily Tribune*, 15 November 1853, concluded:

> The effort of the dramatist has evidently been to destroy the point and moral of the story of Uncle Tom, and to make a play to which no apologist for Slavery could object. He has succeeded; and in doing so, has made a drama which has nothing to recommend it but its name.

A review of Aiken's dramatisation, however, in the *New York Herald* of 3 September 1852, comments:

> Here we have nightly represented, at a popular theatre, the most exaggerated enormities of Southern slavery, playing directly into the hands of the abolitionists and abolition kidnappers of slaves, and doing their work for them. What will our Southern friends think of all our professions of respect for their delicate social institution of slavery, when they find that even our amusements are overdrawn caricatures exhibiting our hatred against it and against them?

The two plays, then, need unhitching, in order to assess fully the implications of their melodramatic interpretation of race.

Frick's combining of the two plays stems from his reading of melodramatic structure. He cites Sarah Meer's assessment of melodrama's tendency to 'individualize issues and hence reduce them to matters of private choice, and where suffering or a social problem could be blamed on the villainy of a single character, there was little room to denounce an oppressive class or institution' (in Frick 2007: 47–8). The melodramatic structure, though, was as mutable as the shape of America's cultural landscape. Originally a drama accompanied by music, in the late eighteenth century, melodrama had become in post-revolutionary France a drama of specific class divisions, where the upper classes, traditionally the aristocracy, were representatives of evil, as Peter Brooks notes, 'a social order to be purged' (1979: 17). David Grimsted argues:

> Though there were no titled aristocrats in America, the melodrama reflected the realization that money made gradations of social level less lasting perhaps than aristocratic rank, but no less important. The differences between rich and poor played much the same role in plays set in America as those between peasants and nobles in Europe; they caused false social distinctions rather than judgement on the basis of merit. (1968: 209)

The melodramatic mode could and did function to expose 'false social distinctions', fixing an enemy in a group, not just in terms of individual villainy.

In Aiken's play, Legree's 'individualised' evil is nuanced by another trope of melodrama: his love for his dead mother. In itself such an appeal is typical of the melodramatic form, but it does complicate readings of Legree as a plain-dealing villain. We are informed that Legree was 'born of a hard-tempered sire', whose brutalising influence has resulted in his debasement – the 'sins' of the father visited on the son (1858: VI, iii). Significantly, Legree's sentimentalised mother is described, in terms of the standard melodramatic heroine, as 'a fair-haired woman' who, 'at the sound of Sabbath bells', led her infant son 'to worship and to pray' (ibid.) She dies alone, a victim of the cruelty of husband and son. In one of the most significant sequences of the play, Legree tells us that he has been subjected to night visitations from the ghost of his mother and, as he speaks of his terror at her ghostly presence, declares: 'I thought I saw something white rising and glimmering in the gloom before me, and it seemed to bear my mother's face! I know one thing; I'll let that fellow Tom alone, after this' (ibid). With the vision of 'something white' glittering before him, Legree faces his own racialised ideologies and, momentarily at least, understands the evil face of slavery that he represents. As the play concludes, though, the brutal 'parent', the American south, wins, and the violence essential to the perpetuation of slavery is enacted on the body of Uncle Tom. The play was produced just prior to the outbreak of the Civil War and continued to play throughout that period – and, indeed, beyond into the nineteenth and twentieth centuries. Although the play becomes tangled with the era of blackface minstrelsy in a series of performances known as 'Tom shows', as Hill and Hatch argue, *Uncle Tom's Cabin* was significant in providing 'opportunities for black performers to participate in productions, initially as jubilee choruses or extras in crowd scenes, and eventually as characters in the play, including the title role' (2003: 55). The play thus required a cast of black and white actors to mingle in rehearsal as well as performance. Aiken's dramatic and sympathetic version of *Uncle Tom's Cabin* became a powerful embodiment of changes in racial dynamics as much as its titular lead was a symbol of the need for that change.

The work done by Aiken's dramatisation of *Uncle Tom's Cabin* for the Abolitionist movement was significant. Also worthy of note was *The Escape; Or a Leap for Freedom* (1858) by black American writer William Wells Brown. In his preface to the play, Brown locates the play as a closet drama, 'written for my own amusement, and with not the remotest thought that it would ever be seen by the public eye' although it 'had been given in various parts of the country' (1996: 37). Black American drama critics have been ambivalent about the value of the play: Sterling Brown considers it to be a 'hodge-podge with some humour and satire and much melodrama' of a piece, therefore, with the standard production form of the mid-nineteenth century (cited in Hatch and Shine 1996: 36). Loften Mitchell locates the play as unfortunately 'close to blackface minstrelsy' (1996: 37), but also points out that the play is worthy of consideration in its staging of potential rebellion. The play incorporates a marginal comic figure, in the 'negro' Cato, who makes a bid for freedom, 'an action', as Mitchell points out, that 'no white playwright of that period would ever have considered for a low comedy character' (ibid.). The name of character is worth noting: Cato was a recurring slave name – and also the titular hero of the Joseph Addison play that had been so popular with General George Washington at the end of the previous century.

The contribution of women to the shape of the new nation was also explored on stage, whose roles were consistently dramatised, as actors, as bastions of morality within the auditorium – or as threats to that morality through their exploits in the gallery, and as Americans.[29] Anna Cora Mowatt, playwright and actress, was an active participant in the debate about women's roles in theatres. In her autobiography, she quoted Mary Hewitt's call for the 'benign influence of womanly spirit' in theatre to improve and even transform what was regarded as a sadly neglected and immoral format (1859: 215). Theatre in the early nineteenth century was attended largely by a male audience who regarded their nights out as an opportunity to escape the confines of 'good society', to mingle with men, and also, perhaps, encounter the pleasures of the 'loose' ladies of the third tier. The association of theatre houses and actresses with prostitution has been critically assessed at length. Rosemary K. Bank, for example, produces a statistical analysis of the proximity of houses of prostitution to theatres in New York. Between 1830 and 1839, 34 per cent were in two and a half blocks of the vicinity of theatres; a percentage that increased over the decades until over 50 per cent had appeared within that same distance by the 1860s (1993: 55). Claudia D. Johnson writes of the 'guilty third tier', that hosted prostitutes within theatres, a 'fact of theatrical life which probably shaped the American stage' (1975: 575). William Dunlap notes, in 1832, that 'in most theatres', we 'see a display of the votaries and victims of vice in one part of the house, and the allurements to inebriation in the other' (2005: 407). The prevalence of prostitution in, and indeed around, theatres meant that women in the audience could find themselves ravelled in tricky discourses of social propriety.

The impact of prostitution in theatres was also felt by female performers themselves. Faye Dudden argues that:

For nineteenth-century minds, actresses lived on the edge between art and immorality. Theatre surrounded them with an ambiguous aura. To become an actress a woman would leave the home – her proper, natural place for women to live and improve – and plunge into the public sphere. (1994: 131)

At the same time, the female performer, as Miriam López-Rodríguez argues, becomes a 'symbolic option for women who stood at the crossroads of marriage and prostitution' (2004: 154). The role of actress teetered close to the precipice of potentially illicit proclivities, and at the same time, offered a pathway from both marriage and its dark double, prostitution. The actress, then, even without the complication of breeches roles, already stood at the gateway to ambiguous territories, and many famous 'names' on the American stage were less renowned for their skills in performance and drama, than for their uncertain origins and lives, played out in the scandalising reportage that foamed in their wake.

Yet, one of the earliest female performer on American stages and a major American star, Charlotte Cushman, transgressed all concepts of such roles, on stage, playing Romeo, Hamlet and Wolsey, and off stage, as the major financial provider and decision-maker for her family (Merrill 2000: 22–3). A review of Cushman as Romeo, dated 16 November 1860, argued that 'generally mankind does not love to see a woman acting the part and wearing the grab of men', but, in this instance:

> There is a delicacy in Romeo's character which requires a woman to represent it, and unfits almost every man for its impersonation. The luscious language which draws its rich, lascivious colour from the fiery blood of Young Italy sounds ridiculous alongside of the rather blasé sensible style of love-making of Young New York and here seems strange of a man. (Cited in Merrill 2000: 126)

As Merrill notes, Cushman could represent the young romantic Italian hero, as 'he' was already feminised by 'his' comparison to the muscular masculinity of the young American. Cushman's 'Romeo', Merrill argues, 'inhabited that contested borderland between "acceptable" exceptions that proved the general rules about appropriate male and female behaviour and those that threatened to topple the norms altogether' (ibid.: 127). Operating at and as a threshold that passed between licit and illicit behaviours for theatrical cross-dressing, critical debate centred on discussion of how 'realistically' Cushman performed the role of Romeo. Emphasising Cushman's mimicry of effete Italianate masculinity as a realist strategy, theatre writers could circumvent the potential radicality of ambivalent performativity.

By the 1850s, the critical tide had firmly turned against female actors in trousers, and the *New York Herald*'s protest against 'mannish' women, who 'wear the breeches', was widespread, playing its part in the suppression of 'serious' cross-dressing roles for women on stage.

By the 1870s, 'leg shows', disguised in a range of costumery from ballet to burlesque, proliferated across all stages. One of the earliest importers of the 'leg show' spectacular was Broadway manager Laura Keene, who worked initially as an actress, starring in the popular comedies staged at Wallack's Broadway venue. One of Laura Keene's early financial successes was *Camille*, a play that would continue, in revised versions, to appeal to audiences in New York's 'high' theatres, despite its disturbingly sexualised courtesan heroine, who trades on her looks and 'buys' respectability – a challenge to an audience, as Dudden notes, familiar with the 'prostitute's powers and dilemmas', in the auditorium (1994: 134). Keene's other successes, though, were spectaculars, burlesque shows that incorporated spoof performances of popular plays, posed tableaux, dance and song – and great scenery. *Our American Cousin*, a farce, was instrumental in changing the shape of theatre economies across America. Up to this point, the 'star system' had been supported by stock companies established at theatre venues. Now, combination companies would be put together to take the show around the country, disposing with the need for theatre to employ local actors to support the stars. The divide between owner-managers and theatre-workers became, at this time, significantly pronounced and would be, in the twentieth century, a source of contention and antagonism.

Another of Keene's major productions was *The Seven Sisters*, which ran for 200 plus performances between 1860 and 1861. Whilst those in the auditorium seemed more than happy with the supply of entertainment, critics were less certain. *The New York Times* regarded the production as 'a wealth of fancy and artistic finish' (cited in Creahan 1897: 86), whilst the *New York Herald* swiped: 'many a dull play has been saved by a judicious and liberal display of nether limbs' (cited in Dudden 1994: 143). Such a consideration of legs as 'nether limbs' is striking, hinting at Shakespearean bawdy but also, more sinisterly, of a prejudicial animus that dehumanised the staged female form; 'nether limbs' are, after all, the back legs of a quadruped. Such critical analogies damaged attitudes towards the performance skill sets of the women on stage. A review of

The Seven Sons, a follow-up to *The Seven Sisters*, in *The New York Times* of 24 September 1861, comments that the 'charming ladies' who form the *corps de ballet* – or leg ensemble – 'were not remarkable for their intellectuality'. The display of female flesh does seem to have provoked an outcry in the news – great publicity for the managers – but also a clear attempt by theatre critics to 'intellectualise' their distaste for the shows, a distaste directed specifically at actresses, who were, for their time on stage at least, freed from the bounds of corsets and crinolines. Such women who engaged in an overt display of their bodies, critics argued, were inevitably and unquestionably stupid.

One of America's most famous nineteenth-century performers, Adah Isaacs Menken was regularly subjected to such critical derogation. Infamous for her appearance in the equine extravaganza *Mazeppa* as the 'male' lead, who in one scene is 'stripped' naked, Menken scandalised and delighted American audiences. The role required Menken to be visibly 'stripped' to apparent nudity, and bound by ropes onto the back of a horse, which was sent careering across the stage. Menken's stage performances in flesh suits melded with salacious reporting in the press, as her body was paraded for a male audience, in an exposed and titillating sexuality. *The Clipper* of 1862 reports that Menken wore her hair 'in that tantalising style', suggesting an alluring provocation (cited in Mullenix 2000: 257). Mullenix contends that 'by reducing Menken to a sum of fetishised parts, male critics could control the danger implied by her societal transgressions as an outspoken forceful woman' (ibid.: 251). Not for Menken, then, within this analysis, do we see the potentially transgressive ambiguity that was a feature of breeches roles in the 1840s; such radical ambivalence had now been displaced by overt sexploitation. Mullenix argues that:

> Because of Menken's influence, the image of breeches actress shifted from innocuous boy, a feminine hero, or even a directly transgressive masculine woman to a silent sexualised object [...] no more talented than a horse and no more professionally empowered than a 'pretty waiter girl'. (Ibid.: 264)

However, Menken's participation in theatre seems to me to be more radical than such a reading suggests. Before Menken, performers had generally gracefully bowed out from that final scene, and a stuffed body of straw performed the role of the naked young prince lashed to the horse. Menken, though, had insisted on taking that wild horse ride. So, as Mazeppa, Menken was, within the same performance, cross-dressed as an exoticised Tartar chieftain, and then as the stripped body of a woman. Menken's gendered instability can also be linked to her very public racial indeterminacy. As Dane Barca points out, 'Menken identified herself variously as Black, as Jewish, as Spanish, and as Caucasian, among others' (2004: 294). Rather than regarding Menken as merely capitulating to the sexualising discourses of the critics, her performance can be regarded as exploiting those very discourses.

Menken's wild-horse ride earned a reputation for bravery at a time when Civil War battles and bloodshed meant that Americans were seeking out acts of individual heroism – bar a handful of southern venues, theatres had not shut their doors during the conflict. *Mazeppa*, touring across America throughout the war, was as popular in Confederate states as in the Union. As a story, *Mazeppa* emphasises overcoming the odds, and its cross-dressing lead, like all good melodramatic heroes, triumphs over aristocracy and restores democratic order. And Menken as Mazeppa brought notorious nudity into middle-class theatres. The body of the remarkable Menken, therefore, as a 'naked' display, appeared prominently in legitimate venues, and thus transgressed middle-class, gendered and racialised performance proprieties.

The Civil War forms a radical fracture in American history; but its impact on theatre history was comparatively minor. Perhaps the most significant theatrical event of the Civil War era was the assassination of President Lincoln. The murder was committed by John Wilkes Booth, brother of famous 'star' actor Edwin Booth, on 14 April 1865, at Ford's Theatre, Washington DC.

The types of performances popular before the war continued to be performed following its conclusion and, apart from venues in the worst affected areas of the southern states, theatres remained open throughout. Some of the theatres in southern cities inevitably sustained serious damage, and emphasis on the re-establishment of those venues in the aftermath of the war was not necessarily a priority. And some theatres had been destroyed by 'enemies' within; the Baltimore Plug-Uglies (an equivalent to New York's Bowery B'hoys) were suspected of an arson attack on the Marshall Theatre in Richmond, whilst a fire in Charleston, that destroyed a major part of the city including the playhouse, was allegedly deliberate.[30] Richmond had continued to maintain a theatre, and even premiered a new production, the propagandist play *The Guerrillas: A New Domestic Drama* (1862). Written by James Dabney

McCabe, Jr, the play was predicated on 'Dixie' heroine Rose Maylie, and was widely performed in Confederate theatres. Few dramas seem to have been written at the time, and theatres tended to stage favourite shows – *Uncle Tom's Cabin* and *Mazeppa*, for example, remained popular across all stages.

Racist ideologies that supported the minstrel show before the war were maintained and indeed consolidated post-emancipation. The economic poverty of the southern states, the enactment of Jim Crow laws, the establishment of the Ku Klux Klan in 1865 and the threat of the lynch mob also led to a mass migration into northern cities, and by the end of the nineteenth century, black Americans became significant enclaves – and indeed ghettos – of city spaces. Mainstream 'legitimate' theatres were still segregated, although black performers were more and more entering into engagements with mainstream theatre managers. Many black Americans, though, supported a series of theatres for the staging of productions specific to a non-white American experience (Cullen et al. 2006: 11). For Native Americans, the War had led to an intensification of the federal assimilation programme, and treaties were made and broken, as reservations became increasingly institutionalised. As discussed in Chapter 1 of this book, performance rituals were banned, feared as expressions of potential violence against the United States government. At the same time, Buffalo Bill Cody launched his 'Wild West, Rocky Mountain and Prairie Exhibition', that featured Native Americans as 'Indians' attacking stagecoaches.[31] L. G. Moses argues that 'Indian attacks became set pieces in all Wild West Shows. Without them the shows would have remained raucous, but hardly wild' (1999: 1). The popularity of such shows internationally, and their subsequent impact on Hollywood 'Indians', has led to a pervading construction of a 'wild west' Native identity that is difficult to circumvent. In the early decades of the nineteenth century, 'serious' dramatist John Augustus Stone wrote Metamora out of history and onto stage, to perform the 'end' of Native American existence; in the latter decades of the century, the urge to construct and therefore control the 'role' of the 'Indian' continued in Buffalo Bill Cody's popular spectacular. That the Wild West Show also coincided with the development of the Ghost Dance (discussed in Chapter 1) is significant: the 'Indian' had not 'vanished', and even though a stereotyped version had become staged as an extra in white American cultural productions as well as in white history, Native American tribes-people had carved out an alternative platform on which to perform the struggles for existence and the renewal of spiritual energies.

In American theatres at the end of the nineteenth century, Garff B. Wilson declares: 'realism begins to upstage melodrama' (1973: 223). James Herne is considered an exemplar of this shift, with his 1890 production, *Margaret Fleming*, a play which draws on the sentimental styling of melodrama but also makes use of realist stage settings. This is what Thomas Postlewait refers to as the 'suspect history of American drama' (1999a: 39). Such a 'history' Postlewait argues, 'slights or sets aside' the range of other performance types that were in circulation across the nineteenth and twentieth centuries. But, as I have been arguing, nineteenth-century stages were diverse, dynamic, vibrant and complex – melodrama was important but did not speak for or to all America, nor did it send out one clear moral message.

The dramatic productions of the nineteenth century under discussion in this chapter have been consigned to a naïve and somewhat embarrassing 'past' of American theatre. The melodrama, the 'leg show', and the equine extravaganza, *Mazeppa*, have been critically damned; but as I have been discussing, these formats were flexible feasts. Melodrama, for example, as we have seen in Daly's *Under the Gaslight*, investigated the social roles of men and women. In analysing *Metamora*, *The Octoroon* and *Uncle Tom's Cabin*, we have seen that melodramatic productions engage with concepts of race and racial identities in the American nation. To look to melodrama for consciously and subtly worked subversion is a fraught task – the mode is intrinsically two dimensional and many plays, at least textually, reproduced racial, national and gendered stereotypes. Yet such plays could be bold and dynamic articulations of social issues. Thomas Dartmouth Rice's comic 'blackface' also vexes interpretations of racial codings in America, albeit that the format of the show would be overwritten by minstrelsy. I am not claiming that such portrayals were innocent of racial slurs – indeed they were not. However, the continuous and shifting incorporation of a range of racial types in such productions speaks volumes about the shape and cultural structure of the nation – America was not and never could be the assimilating parent. Theatre in nineteenth-century America was not structured or fixed: a range of performance types, characterisations and critical attitudes were developed. The variety of nineteenth-century American theatrical productions functioned as an investigation of the range of national concerns and anxieties that could not be collocated into one particular American dramatic 'type'.

Nineteenth-century theatre operations cannot be summed up in one form any more than the term 'realism' can contribute much to our understanding of the theatre of the twentieth century. In the next chapter, I explore the range of dramatic material that develops in response to emerging technologies such as film and television, but also, more significantly, to the radical shift in the shape of American history, as propagandist plays dramatised the tensions and violence experienced by marginalised groups across the American nation.

CHAPTER 5

'Modern' American Theatre and the Twentieth Century

American theatre in the early decades of the twentieth century saw significant shifts in structure and output. The demise of the 'star system', innovations in stage setting, combined with developing technologies of moving images on screen, contributed to a series of reconsiderations of theatre's social role. At the outset of the twentieth century, legitimate theatre maintained its love of sensational drama and complex realistic setting in vast theatres seating upwards of 3,000 per show. Broadway stages had also been lured into the 'leg show' business of the non-legitimate stage. Such theatre had become located as feminised therefore passive, performed for an audience that consisted of more women than men – a complete shift from the early nineteenth century. Critical attitudes, shaped by twentieth-century concepts of 'business' and 'the professional', poured scorn on nineteenth-century output, and looked to the professional playwrights of 'new drama' of emerging repertory theatre as an antidote to what Susan Harris Smith neatly terms 'America's Bastard Art' (1989). This chapter looks to unpack that narrative of progression in theatre. As part of that discussion, I will explore the works of Clyde Fitch, one of America's most prolific, successful and overlooked playwrights. Fitch was responsible, according to theatre critic William Winter, for the production of 'female' dramas and therefore for the 'death' of the stage. Conversely, Fitch is also regarded as a 'transitional' figure in the 'realism to melodrama' narrative history of theatre and the conflict in critical opinion that surrounds his work is worthy of exploration.

In the early twentieth century we do indeed see a conscious reconsideration of dramatic writing, but not one that supports wholesale critical notions of progression from melodrama to realism. Eugene O'Neill and the Provincetown Players have become most closely associated with that shift. This analysis assesses how the 'new' drama of playwrights like O'Neill and Paul Green, however experimental in form, continued to engage in structures of racial identities in America. Black American artists were also contributing to the development of debates about race and racial identities, notably the work of W. E. B. Du Bois, Alan Locke and the black artists of vaudeville. In the 1920s, the Barsum Bill had been passed, another attempt to secure land from Native American tribes; at the same time, scholars concerned with explorations of 'authentic' folk culture and 'primitive' life began to look askance at government land claims; their endeavours, though, were founded, as Wilmeth argues, on a desire 'to see the Indian as a frozen artefact' (2000: 145). I will examine, therefore, the impact of attitudes towards Native American culture, through an assessment of plays 'about' and plays by Native Americans.

This chapter will also examine the development of immigrant theatre across this apparently 'American' century, which initially became consolidated, in a variety of forms and languages, in the early decades of the twentieth century. In many instances, though, immigrant theatres were thwarted by two world wars and the ideologies of the McCarthy era. But in the latter decades of the century, and in response to the aggressive policies of policing national identity, a range of ethnic theatres resurged, inspired by immigrant groups as well as second- and third-generation writers and artists, who explore the problems of America's plurality from the perspective of multiculturality. What we find in the twentieth century, as we have seen throughout this book, is a theatre that dramatises gender, class, race, ethnicity and sexuality; the context of debate was, inevitably, subject to slippage, in response to world wars, the renegotiation of social roles for men and women in 'business' America, racial tensions and antagonisms, immigration, restrictions on movement and political affiliations, and intolerance. This chapter demonstrates that twentieth-century drama maintained its fascination with socially constructed difference and division, examining the fault lines of ideologies, and thus participates in the formation of social debate.

In the aftermath of the Civil War the economic power of America became increasingly shaped by entrepreneurial business practices. The impact on theatre of such practices was the development of booking syndicates, who controlled the activities of the now commonplace combination touring companies. The most commercially viable of the syndicates was operated by Marc Klaw and Abraham Erlanger. The system worked through partnerships with businessmen who controlled the leases of regional theatres across the nation. Klaw and Erlanger also partnered with Charles Frohman, the theatre producer who had staged Bronson Howard's successful play *Shenandoah* in Chicago in 1889. Together they created the Theatrical Syndicate, which negotiated exclusive rights over clients. At the beginning of the twentieth century, then, much of what was seen around regional theatres was controlled by booking agents based in New York.

Almost as soon as its dominance was secured, however, the Syndicate came under challenge from a group of even more efficient business entrepreneurs. Sam, Lee and Jacob Schubert, who owned several major theatres in the north-east, had been signed up to the Theatrical Syndicate, but had been buying theatre houses for their own agency. *The New York Times* in July 1906 announced that 'the theatre being built at Broadway and fifty-sixth street has been acquired by the Schuberts', the acquisition making 'the number of so-called anti-trust houses equal to the number controlled by the Theatrical Syndicate and affiliated interests' (27 July 1906). The Syndicate continued until 1916, when competition from the Schuberts became too intense, and their operations ceased. Another famous booking monopoly emerged in Boston, with the partnership of entrepreneurs B. F. Keith and Edward F. Albee, who formed the United Booking Office in 1906 for vaudeville productions.

By the early years of the twentieth century, financial pressure from increasingly exorbitant transport costs meant that syndicates were struggling to support tours to regional theatres, whose managers looked to alternative forms of entertainment. As John Frick notes, the combination touring company that had become the staple of syndicate operations was displaced by stock companies in local theatres, who could negotiate directly with Broadway playwrights and producers for best-selling shows (1999: 218). Regional theatre, therefore, came into direct competition with the syndicates. The ever-popular vaudeville had become monopolised by the United Booking Office, whose cheaper entertainments could be more readily accommodated in regional theatres.

The cost-effective nickelodeon, developed by Thomas Edison and made infamous by Edwin S. Porter's *The Great Train Robbery* in 1903, also competed with the larger-scale, expensive productions. The history of twentieth-century nickelodeons was relatively short, though; by 1915, the movie industry has taken over many of the buildings that had been accommodating nickelodeon shows. But in the time that the nickelodeons flourished, between 1903 and 1915, the exclusive power of the theatre syndicates was dislodged. And following 1915, the film industry itself competed with the large-scale, expensive touring shows. Robert

McLaughlin records that, in 1910, there were an estimated 236 touring companies across America per week; by 1920, that number had fallen to thirty-four (1974: 2). Adopting and adapting the syndicates' business practices ensured that, as Hollywood developed, a steady stream of actors relocated west, and playwrights and producers found themselves in negotiation for film rights before a play had even been staged (ibid.: 8).

The monopoly of booking agents over their 'stars' contributed to a growing labour movement amongst American actors. In 1898, a small group of actors, including comedian Francis Wilson, who would become the first president of the Actors' Equity Association in 1913, attempted to stand against the syndicates. Their attempt was unsuccessful, but had at least been noted in the theatre press, and the syndicates came under pressure in the theatre press. The critics, although concerned with unfair labour practices, were mainly concerned that the syndicates were, as Frick argues, 'debasing the art of theatre' (1999: 215). Syndicates were accused of debilitating acting, of ignoring American playwrights and of choosing scripts based on commerce rather than craft. As Frick notes, though, not only is there no evidence to indicate that the overall quality of acting did, in fact, decline during the Syndicate's reign, but that Klaw and Erlanger promoted works by American playwrights James Herne and Clyde Fitch as well as staging productions of Ibsen, Barrie, Goldsmith and Shakespeare (ibid.: 215–16). Rather than collapsing under pressure from theatre critics' repeated claims of dramatic paucity, the syndicate system, then, came under financial pressure, as economic circumstances and alternative booking operations participated in the shifting landscape of America's theatrical history.

The criticism of the syndicates as harbingers of mediocrity, commerce and poor theatre, therefore, requires reconsideration. Vaudeville producers Keith and Albee made a point of advertising their morally suitable productions, in order to appeal to a dominantly female audience. Such claims to the legitimacy of drama residing in propriety and morality, lend themselves to a particular narrative of improvement in American theatre history, that the 'leg show' of the nineteenth century had been reconstituted as proper entertainment for women. By the end of the nineteenth century, Don B. Wilmeth argues, 'American theatre confined itself to innocuous material that supported middle-class virtues (e.g. monogamy, frugality, temperance, modesty)' and 'rarely challenged rigidly defined social conventions that depicted women as asexual beings who possessed little or no political or economic power' (2007: 148).[32] In

1872, the Comstock Law, officially the Federal Anti-Obscenity Act, had been passed, to control 'vice' in public material; one of the main outcomes of the act was the suppression of material regarding birth control. But the legislation was also manifest in theatres, where productions had to be tamed to accommodate the standards expected for feminine propriety.

Thus a female audience has been equated with domestic dramas and mawkish sentimentality; as a form, the drama of the 'home' is seen as unchallenging, and/or as a capitulation to a rigid status quo. Such an argument, though, is difficult to sustain. The National American Woman Suffrage Movement was agitating for enfranchisement, and an article written in 1908, titled 'The Suffragettes of America', declared: 'The suffragette, it should be carefully noted, is something more than a women suffragist. She is a militant woman suffragist. She does not merely want the ballot, she is determined to have it' (cited in Moore 1997: 90–1). This 'New Woman' was stereotyped mockingly as a masculine figure, who 'smoked, rode bicycles, demanded political power, and insisted in going to popular entertainments' (Frick 1999: 198). Nevertheless, the assertive, political and public presence of this stereotype conflicted with the concept of passive feminised consumption. Further, as David Sehat argues, 'the middle class was never as unified in its tastes, or as prudish in its desires, as proponents of the legitimate theatre maintained' (2008: 331). The social structure of the United States in the early twentieth century was no more rigid than it had been in the nineteenth century. That women in the auditorium, for example, were considered to be desirous *de facto* of a certain type of mass-market sentimentality is a fallacy: what we see inscribed onto the female body is a prescriptively feminised passivity to secure the identity of the American bourgeois woman, as the myth of feminine propriety within dominant masculine cultural operations.

One of the most famous and popular playwrights and stage producers of the early twentieth century, William Clyde Fitch, has been relegated to critical obscurity, his plays regarded as part of that mass market of entertainment for women. Yet, one of the earliest moments of dramatic tension of the twentieth century was the staging of Clyde Fitch's adaptation of Alphonse Daudet's novel *Sapho*. The play features the seduction of a young man by an unmarried mother, Fanny Legrand, whose status as 'fallen' renders her, symbolically if not literally, a prostitute. On 5 February 1900, it opened at Wallack's Theatre in New York, a centre of that bourgeois commercial capital, and one of those theatres that had been, allegedly, 'feminised' by its predominantly female audience.

The play, though, became a symbol of the controversy over women's social and theatrical roles. On 6 March 1900, *The New York Times* recorded the headline: '"Sapho" stopped by police'. That afternoon, Olga Nethersole, the actress who took the leading role of Fanny Legrand and had collaborated with Fitch over the script for *Sapho*, had been detained by the magistrate's office. The chief of police was reported as stating that the play had been stopped under a violation of section 385 of the Penal Code, as 'an offence against public decency' (*The New York Times*, 6 March 1900). Famous theatre critic William Winter was not complimentary about Olga Nethersole as a performer. She had, he said, 'devoted herself largely to a parade of theatrical transgressors' (1913: 309–10). Indeed, Nethersole had carved a name for herself playing women of ambiguous reputation. Nethersole herself, an extremely able manager of the media, ensured a degree of display, wearing a loose-fitting gown, which would billow around (and up – and down) as she moved. The performance, the press and the court case, then, focused on the body of the woman, as a public icon of potential impropriety.

Nethersole and *Sapho* were acquitted of indecency, and the publicity surrounding the case led, inevitably, to the play's popularity across American stages. *Sapho* was only one of the sixty-two plays that Clyde Fitch wrote, adapted or contributed to, in the course of his career. During 1900–1, Don B. Wilmeth notes, ten of his plays 'were seen simultaneously in New York and on the road' (1998: 9). His productions travelled across Europe, earning him the distinction, according to Wilmeth, of being 'the first American playwright to attain a truly international reputation' (ibid.). Critically, though, Fitch had been repeatedly dismissed. According to his obituary in *The Independent*, Fitch's plays concerned themselves almost exclusively with 'the delineation of feminine characteristics' ('*Death of Clyde Fitch*', 9 September 1909: 614). Fitch thus becomes an exemplar of a critical practice that locates successful productions of the early twentieth century as written to appeal to a female audience.

To William Winter, *Sapho* was 'dull and stupid [...] there can be no doubt as to its dirty character, or its pernicious tendency [...] a rigmarole of lust, sap-headed sentimentality, and putrid nonsense' about 'a harlot and a fool, showing how, in a carnal way, they fascinated each other' (1913: 313). Winter critiques *Sapho* as the type of drama that excuses its 'portrayal of licentiousness and turpitude', by claiming that there is a 'moral lesson' to be learned (ibid.: 315). Winter's attack on *Sapho* was also aimed at its writer: such 'tainted plays', he declares, 'emanate largely from weak sisters of the male sex, or of no sex at all, emasculated puppies, suckling collegians and the like' (ibid.). Fitch's sexuality was repeatedly subject to indirect interrogation and he had, during his time at Amherst College, performed in several cross-dressed roles. The playwright was also rumoured to have been one of Oscar Wilde's 'liaisons'.[33] Montrose J. Moses, who published a collected edition of Fitch's letters, spoke of the playwright in his youth as 'something of a dandy' (1924: 48). Such publicly indeterminate sexuality rendered Fitch feminised in the eyes of masculine America. *Sapho* dramatised sexual liaisons between unmarried men and women, substantially challenging theatre propriety; in Winter's somewhat hysterical critical assessment, though, the 'taint' of the plays relate directly to Fitch's sexual ambiguity, conflating gender and sexuality in the image of the 'weak sister of the male flesh'.

Yet, as early as 1927, theatre critic Arthur Quinn Hobson had reclaimed Fitch from critical obscurity:

> His contribution to our drama lies primarily in his portraiture of American men and women, prevented by their social inhibitions from frank expressions of their complete natures, but presenting in the consequent struggle a drama quiet yet intense, so restrained in power that his own generation mistook its fineness for weakness. There has rarely been so complete a reversal of critical judgement for he is now placed securely among the foremost writers of high comedy. (II: 296)

Despite Hobson's critical praise, Fitch has remained in relative obscurity for most of the twentieth century. More recently, he has come under critical review, assessed as a 'transitional' figure in the history of American drama, from nineteenth century to twentieth century. Mark Evans Bryan argues that Fitch's 'melodramas of contemporary society bridge the gap between the tradition of American romantic melodrama and social realism' (2007: 6). As such, Fitch becomes part of a canon of twentieth-century American playwrights who shifted theatre from the control of 'the professional theatre artist' to 'the literate, professional writers' (ibid.: 5). Realism on stage was associated, courtesy of William Dean Howells, with a professionalisation of playwriting; the sentimental melodramas of the popular stage were a product of the profession of theatre, rather than the profession of writing. In short, melodrama was commercial, therefore tainted, whilst realism was literary, therefore acclaimed. Whilst Fitch now forms a part of discussions of American theatre history, his status as 'transitional' between melodrama and realism, between the stage professional and the writing professional, reasserts the 'suspect history' of American theatre, which claims that there was, in the early twentieth century, a progression from melodrama to a more 'literate' form of realist playwriting.

Not only Fitch, but early twentieth-century playwrights David Belasco, Rachel Crothers, Langdon Mitchell and Percy MacKaye are regarded, in Arthur Hobson Quinn's words as 'the advance guard of the new drama' (1927, II: 4). One of the key figures in the development of the 'melodrama to realism' narrative in American theatre history, though, is Eugene O'Neill, whose status as America's 'first' playwright has been reiterated repeatedly. In an article on O'Neill commissioned by the National Theatre in London for its production of *Mourning Becomes Electra*, Tony Kushner claims: 'it is not excessive to write that O'Neill created serious American drama. He was the scion of what had come before: the sensational, historical, narratively novelistic melodrama, a flashpot-and-sheetmetal theater of noise and exclamation' (2004: 249). Kushner refers to the 'blood and thunder' melodramatic expressions of the nineteenth century, of the type performed by O'Neill's actor father. Eugene O'Neill was indeed dismissive of the type of melodramatic plays that had made his father, James O'Neill, a star – O'Neill senior was famous for his appearances, 6,000 in total, in *The Count of Monte Cristo*. Eugene O'Neill famously commented: 'I saw so much of the old, ranting, artificial romantic stuff that I always had a sort of contempt for the theatre' (ibid.: 251). According to Thomas Postlewait, the apotheosis of O'Neill's dramatic trajectory, and the 'history' of theatre's shift from melodrama to realism, is found in *A Long Day's Journey into the Night* which was written between 1939 and 1941 and published posthumously in 1956. The 'realist and aesthetic agenda' of the play stands as a 'defiant rejection of the melodramatic heritage of American theatre' (Postlewait 1999: 42). By the 1940s, then, melodrama is located critically as dead, or dying, and realism has won the genre war.

But, the abiding antagonisms between melodrama and realism, as Thomas Postlewait argues, do not stand up. Rather, throughout the nineteenth and twentieth centuries, we are 'confronted with numerous joinings of melodramatic and realistic forms and functions [...] most of the time we can find melodramatic elements in realistic forms and realistic elements in melodramatic plays' (ibid.: 54–5). The narrative of progression from sentimental melodrama to social realism relies on an assertion of hierarchy: realism is constructed, critically, as a 'better' form than melodrama, a construction tied in with the complex of theatre, art and money. For critics, a female-centred audience's need to consume domestic, sentimental melodrama led to a paucity of style and literary value: realism regenerated art and brought back substance. David Sehat assesses the role played by W. D. Howells in setting out the terms of this shift: 'Howell's advocacy of realism [...] sought to move the literary profession from the feminised realm of letters into the manly business of the world' (2008: 332–3). Realism was the masculine response to the feminisation of American theatre. The production of realist plays was an assertion of playwriting itself as a manly pursuit.

Although the concept of melodrama's passing in the face of realism's emergence in playwriting has been debunked, there was, undeniably, a shift in dramatic focus on stages, from epic-scale spectacles to understated and concise performances, with scenic displays of verisimilitude replaced by suggestive setting. One of the delights of stage melodrama was to render setting as authentically a reflection of the 'world' as could be got with the technologies at the disposal of the set designers; but in the early twentieth century, scene designers were looking to incorporate more experimental, more abstracted dressings. The innovations of the little theatre across Europe also informed the building of smaller theatres for more intense and intimate dramas, and playwriting likewise took a shift to the intimate. Attention became focused on conditions of living, specifically in the post-Darwinian determinism of the technological world: Sophie Treadwell's *Machinal* (1928), examines such a world from the perspective of women, locked into domestic spaces by an over-determined, damaging masculine world. The play is based on the story of Ruth Snyder, who was executed for murdering her husband, and the title's overt reference to automation and mechanisation reflects the 'machinery' that imprisons women in the home.

The Provincetown Players were one of a group of repertoire theatre companies that explored the possibilities of what has become known as the 'New Stagecraft', linking European expressionism with American stages, and particularly with Eugene O'Neill.[34] The organisers offered slots for one-act plays from new writers, in their early years at least. After 1922, as a result of internal fractures, the company reshaped itself as The Experimental Theatre, Inc., and was producing longer productions, frequently by Eugene O'Neill; but they also staged *In Abraham's Bosom* by Paul Green, which won a Pulitzer Prize in 1926. Green, from

Chapel Hill, North Carolina, had been a member of Frederick Koch's
Carolina Playmakers. Koch published an account of the players, titled
Carolina Folk Plays, in which he lists a series of aims for the players,
the second of which was to 'serve as an experimental theatre for the
development of plays representing the traditions and various phases of
present-day life of the people' (1922: ii). The concept of 'experimental'
theatre in America, then, was not confined to the urban centre of New
York; burgeoning interest in cultural anthropology and investigations
into 'authentic' American via folklore had become popular in theatre
scholarship. The concept of 'experimentation', for Koch, though, did
not extend to an inclusive theatre: 'negro' theatre was still segregated in
format. But Green's *In Abraham's Bosom*, set in North Carolina's rural
regions, faces directly the problem of 'the colour line' in rural America.
The setting is 'somewhere in the southeastern part of the United States',
and the time 'the latter part of the nineteenth century and the first part of
the twentieth' (Green 1998: 17). The play, then, dates to the era when the
promise of Reconstruction gave way to segregation and Jim Crow laws.

In Abraham's Bosom is subtitled *The Tragedy of a Southern Negro* and
tells of Abraham McCranie (Abe), a black fieldworker, who aspires to
set up a school for the education of young black children. In the opening
scene, the black fieldworkers discuss Abe's current plight – he had cut
down a lynching victim and given him a burial – and only the interfer-
ence of Colonel McAllister, ex-slave owner and current employers of the
field hands, had saved him from being lynched himself. Abe is beaten in
the early scenes by Colonel McAllister – his father – and is also struck by
his half-brother, McAllister's 'white' son Lonnie. The stark materials of
southern 'traditions', then, are obliquely dramatised.

Yet, the play is not without problems: Colonel McAllister is a 'patron'
to Abe, granting him land and offering him a teaching post at the school
that he is setting up for black children. *In Abraham's Bosom* does take
white America to task for its sordid slave 'history', and for its betrayal of
black Americans in the institutionalisation of Jim Crow laws. The play
also challenges concepts of a racialised hierarchy: of the two brothers,
'black' Abe and 'white' Lonnie, it is Abe who demonstrates ambition,
skill and determination. But ultimately the play resorts to the 'colour
line' for its melodramatic conclusion, as Abe kills his brother and all
but murders one of his charges in the school. The 'tragedy', finally for
Abe, resides in the flaw of race: he is the product of miscegenation. As
Brenda Murphy points out, the play is a version of the '"tragic mulatto"

theme in which the greatest tragedy of miscegenation was the battle of two conflicting "race" impulses within one nature' (1999: 309). Sitting alongside O'Neill's *Emperor Jones* (1921) and *All God's Chillun Got Wings* (1924), *In Abraham's Bosom* is one of a series of 'representations of blacks on the New York stage' that were 'overwhelmingly by whites' (Murphy 1999: 308). In all three plays, resolution cannot be found to the social issue of racial boundaries. O'Neill and Green did challenge Broadway's segregationist policy by casting African American actors Charles Gilpin and Paul Robeson in lead roles for their plays. But the plays themselves were ambiguous vehicles for assessments of social constructions of race. For example, *Emperor Jones*, as Annemarie Bean notes, was criticised for its liberal use of the term 'nigger', a term which was a prominent marker of racial abuse by the early twentieth century, and for dialect 'embarrassingly similar to blackface minstrelsy and its misrepresentations' (2007: 97). The experimental theatre of the early decades of the twentieth century capitulated, therefore, to the intrinsically uneven racial structures of segregated America, even as it attempted to alert audiences to the problems of those structures.

The 'tragedy' of miscegenation had been explored, also, by Edward Sheldon's 1909 production, *The Nigger*. Sheldon's play had been, arguably, more provoking, premised on the concept of passing: 'white' southern landowner and leading politician, Philip Morrow, is exposed as 'black'. In the first act, stalwart southern aristocrat Morrow declares: 'if we want t' keep our blood clean, we've got to know that *white's white* an' *black's black* – an' mixing 'em's damnation!' (1910: 33). Nevertheless, he tries to hide a black labourer, Joe White, who has been accused of rape; despite his best efforts, the man is taken by a mob and lynched. The play, then, asserts the equivalence of blackness with sexual violence – the southern white woman is still threatened by the lascivious black sexual predator. In the final scenes, the 'black' Philip Morrow vows to commit himself to the cause of his 'race', although he still asserts 'black' and 'white' as two distinct and racialised identities, explaining the rules of segregation to his ex-fiancée. In all the political intrigues that have accompanied his rise to power and the unfolding of his past, Morrow maintains a sense of dignity and heroic presence.

There are several ways of interpreting the play: on the one hand Morrow disturbs any intrinsic concepts of racial difference – he is, within the play, both 'white' and 'black'. But, at the same time, his nobility of character resides in his ability to match the stereotype of the 'white' Southern aristocrat. In such a reading, Morrow's ability to 'be' white renders him 'better' than the likes of sexual predator Joe White; miscegenation, then, 'saves' him from the violence of blackness. Such a reading, though, raises problems for attempts, in the era of segregation, for African Americans to assert any presence in the United States. Only by mimicking whiteness, argues the white playwright, could the black American be American.

In the same year that Sheldon's play premiered, the National Association for the Advancement of Colored People was formed, setting out to challenge racism in America. One of their earliest targets was D. W. Griffith's film, *The Birth of a Nation*. Thomas Dixon, Jr had published the novels *The Leopard's Spots* in 1902 and *The Clansman* in 1904; he adapted them for stage and in 1905, the play, *The Clansman*, was premiered in Norfolk, Virginia, at the Academy of Music. The script, published in New York through the American News Company, was billed as 'The Play That is Stirring the Nation'. The introduction describes the play as 'a sequel to "Uncle Tom's Cabin"', claiming 'the historical accuracy of this picture is absolutely unassailable'. The play is significant, not only for its attempts to assert racial hierarchies for a 'new' post Civil War nation, but because it was made into one of the first full-length films by D. W. Griffith, as *The Birth of a Nation* in 1915, which was appropriated as propaganda for the resurgent Ku Klux Klan. Dixon's books and the film echoed the judgment of *Plessy* v. *Ferguson*, that black Americans were essentially, biologically, inferior. In an article on Booker T. Washington, Dixon stated: 'No amount of education of any kind, industrial, classical or religious, can make a Negro a white man or bridge the chasm of centuries which separate him from the white man in the evolution of human nature' (1905: 1). The subject matter, which situates the Ku Klux Klan as protector of virtuous southern womanhood threatened by the 'free' and inherently lascivious black man, is familiar territory well-trod by white writers, and forms part of an ongoing production of racial stereotypes. The patient pathos of Uncle Tom and comic stereotypes that had fed minstrelsy in the nineteenth century had become displaced by a racialised villainy in the aftermath of Reconstruction and the enforcement of Jim Crow laws. Thomas Dixon, Jr's imposed sexual villainy on the figure of the black American man, aided and abetted by D. W. Griffith's starkly plotted movie, propagates a racial melodrama that would resonate throughout the twentieth century.

'Serious' drama of the early twentieth century invoked troubling racialised images, 'dehumanising' as Bean argues, black Americans, 'in their quest for "authenticity,"' (2007: 93). At the same time, African American dramatists were engaging with the creative possibilities of theatre as a vehicle for the exploration of folklore, culture and heritage. Studies of cultural anthropology were not confined to accounts of racial tensions from the perspective of white American scholars. African Americans were also engaged in theatrical production that investigated the conditions of cultural operations for black communities, examining the very specific conditions of living within a nation founded on a racialised exploitation. Howard University had been established in 1867 for the education of African American ministers, but had developed courses in liberal arts and sciences, and introduced a theatre programme in 1921, becoming a hub for African American scholarship in performance, drama and anthropological studies.

In 1913, W. E. B. Du Bois's pageant *Star of Ethiopia* premiered at the National Emancipation Exposition in New York, between 22 and 31 October. Freda Scott Giles (1996) notes that over 14,000 people attended the pageant, which was repeated in Washington in October 1915 for three nights at the American League Baseball Park, in Philadelphia in May 1916, and in Los Angeles for two nights in June 1925. The performance is predicated, in line with the pageant structure, with the giving of symbolic gifts: the 'Gifts of Black Men to the World' (Du Bois 1996: 89), which, in sum, demonstrate the centrality of Africa and its people to the world, from the discovery of iron, the basis of industrialisation, to the production of 'freedom' and 'hope' that accompanied the end of slavery. Although Du Bois's attempts to inspire a genre of African American pageantry did not materialise, nevertheless, his development of the pageant over a thirteen-year performance period, involving local communities, stood, Giles argues 'as a source of social cohesiveness and artistic pride' (1996: 88).

Although his pageants have been relatively obscured in studies of Du Bois, his impact on theatre, and more generally on artists of the Harlem Renaissance, has been well documented. In 1925, Du Bois contributed to the programme for the Krigwa Players Little Negro Theater and in *The Crisis* magazine of September 1924, reproduced Du Bois's four criteria for theatre from the inaugural Krigwa Players' programme:

> The plays of a real Negro theatre must be: 1. 'about us.' That is, they must have plays which reveal Negro life as it is. 2. 'By us.' That is, they must be written by Negro authors who understand from birth and continued association just what it means to be a Negro today.

3. 'For us.' That is, the theatre must cater primarily to Negro audiences and be supported and sustained by their entertainment and approval.
4. 'Near us.' The theatre must be in a Negro neighbourhood near the mass of ordinary Negro peoples. (Cited in Walker 1988: 348)

Alain Locke also assessed the function of theatre for the 'new' generation of black Americans, but, unlike Du Bois, advises playwrights to look beyond America for its material. The 'contemporary stage', argues Locke in an article for *Theatre Arts Monthly*, has 'choked' the 'emotional elements of negro art'; looking to Africa, for Locke, offers 'a wonderfully new field and province for dramatic treatment [...] a world of elemental beauty with all the decorative elements that a poetic and emotional temperament could wish' (cited in Charles 2005: 48). The key problem, as Charles argues, with Locke's call for dramatic engagement with Africa, is that it resonates with the ideologies of exoticising wish-fulfilment that fed imperialist discourses about Africa. Locke imagines Africa as an empty land, lacking indigenous populations, 'elemental' in its primitive, bucolic state. Charles points out that 'even though Locke rejected essentialist, ahistorical ideas about race in the most sophisticated terms, he nonetheless reinforces popular ideas of the connection between African heritage and the primitive' (ibid.: 50).

One of the problems for Harlem Renaissance writers was the need to match the expectations of their wealthy, generally white, patrons. Playwright Langston Hughes, for example, found difficulty with his sponsor, Charlotte Osgood Mason, who liked to be referred to as 'Godmother'. Hughes said of the break between the two: 'She wanted me to be more African than Harlem – primitive in the simple, intuitive and noble sense of the word. I couldn't be, having grown up in Kansas City, Chicago and Cleveland' (1956: 5). Hughes's work, investigating class and racial politics in the context of the Great Depression, lacked appeal for the white patron. Locke's urge, however, to imagine a 'free' African space of creative potential, offered the primitivist Mason the type of material she wished to purchase and following her break from Hughes, Mason did sponsor the work of Locke. This is not to suggest that Locke deliberately set out a primitivist agenda to ensure funding; but rather to acknowledge the racialised structures that were entangled with the exploration of aesthetic potential for black Americans.

Whilst black American artists were exploring the possibilities for a legitimate theatre movement and the production of non-stereotypical black characters, vaudeville maintained a sturdy support for traditional, racialised comic characters. By the turn of the century, though, vaudeville was becoming shaped by black Americans performing blackness as well as by the white American 'mimics'. At the end of the nineteenth century, the Hyers Sisters Combination performed in a variety of musical entertainments; one of the most successful was *Out of the Wilderness* (also billed as *Out of Bondage*) in 1876, written by Joseph Bradford. Bert Williams and George Walker were also popular comic actors in the late nineteenth and early twentieth century. One of their most famous productions was *In Dahomey: A Negro Musical Comedy*, a collaboration between Jesse A. Shipp, Paul Lawrence Dunbar and Will Marion Cook. According to John Graziano, this was 'the first African American show that synthesised successfully the various genres of American musical theatre at the beginning of the twentieth century – minstrelsy, vaudeville, comic opera, and musical comedy' (1996: 65). In other words, the show is an important marker in American theatre history, standing as an amalgam of forms made popular by American performers from a range of cultural backgrounds.

In Dahomey is also significant for the development of African American theatre, for a variety of reasons. The writers and cast were made up of black Americans; the play, having premiered in Connecticut, was performed on Broadway, at the New York Theatre on 18 February 1903, making it, according to Gerald Bordman, 'the first full-length musical written and played by blacks to be performed at a major Broadway house' (1978: 190). The performance draws on specifically African American experiences, with Dr Straight selling products to straighten hair and whiten skin; as Graziano points out, 'to African Americans in the audience, this scene was a satire of the many advertisements that appeared in Black newspapers of the day' (1996: 64). The play also satirises various tenets of 'back-to-Africa' campaigns: Dahomey, now part of Benin, had been a wealthy and, according to Thomas Riis, 'aggressive military power', a potential symbol of 'darkest part of the Dark continent', in mainstream newspaper coverage (1996: xix). References to Africa as a creative source for black American arts tended to focus on Ethiopia, as a symbol of cultural superiority and aesthetic beauty, as in Du Bois's *Star of Ethiopia*, in which Africa is the centre of civilisation. The writers of *In Dahomey*, instead, opted for a symbol of the most challenging concept of Africa for a white audience: a wealthy, aggressive and potentially cannibalistic nation, one that was newsworthy as a sign of 'savagery'. The very name Dahomey, then, performed as a symbol of the potentially violent 'primitive' that was at the root of white fears of blackness. Structured as a vaudeville production, to be played to multiracial audiences (allowing for rules of segregated spaces), *In Dahomey* plays on fears embedded in the construction of racialised identities. Sitting on the cusp of non-legitimate theatre, *In Dahomey*, as a racialised satire that mocks attitudes and behaviours across racial lines, operates as a comic critique of constructions of racial identities.

Considerations of racialised identities in America, then, formed a core of American theatricality. Blackness, in the early twentieth century, had become a major theme, as the entangled histories of slavery, Civil War, reconstruction and segregation were embedded in the national psyche. But the 'problem' of the Native American population was also still subject to scrutiny. William C. De Mille wrote *Strongheart: An American Comedy Drama* in 1909, featuring Native American Soangataha, also known as Strongheart, who attends college and plays on the football team. The comedy of the earlier scenes is predicated on his identity as Native American: three of his friends kneel in his presence, referring to him as the 'big chief' (1909: 26); he makes tea, whilst one of his friends intones 'behold the future chief of a war-like people making tea for pale-faced squaws' (ibid.: 29); one of his friend's sisters asks him, 'how do you like America' – his grave, unconsciously ironic, response: 'my people have always been very fond of the place' (ibid.: 30). In an atmosphere of detribalising and assimilation for Native Americans, Soangataha himself sees the condition of 'white' America as the future for himself and his tribe. Soangataha declares to Dorothy, the sister of one of his white college friends:

> You have told me of the advantages civilisation would bring to my people. That when we learned your ways and obeyed your laws, you would call us brothers. From that day, my one thought, my one ambition, has been that your words might come true. Your people and mine dwelling together in peace. (Ibid.: 32–3)

Throughout, however, Soangataha is consistently reminded of 'difference'. When the football team find there is a traitor in their midst, the first name called out is 'Strongheart'. When he proposes to Dorothy, he is told by her brother he cannot marry her because he 'is not one of us' (ibid.: 82). In the final act, Soangataha and his friend Dick, rivals for Dorothy, find that 'prejudice has cut the ties of friendship' (ibid.: 94). In the final scene, news is brought by messenger Black Eagle that

Soangataha's father has died and he must assume responsibility for the tribe. Black Eagle tells Soangataha he cannot bring Dorothy with him to the tribes, a 'white' woman being unable to cope with the privations of tribal life in the cold winter. Although Soangataha and Dorothy have declared that they love each other, the 'law of the races' separates them, as each returns to the family that will not accept their relationship. Don B. Wilmeth argues that the play stands as a 'prime example of the shifting attitudes towards Indians' in the early decades of the twentieth century, in its critique of 'racial prejudice amongst the so-called educated, liberal, white men of the play' (2000: 142). Whilst such a critique of white racism is apparent in the play, the plot structure is still predicated on the racialised body of the performing 'Indian', as demonstrated by Soangataha's capitulation to the ideologies of the 'civilised' white world. His 'white' education 'improves' his individual condition and expectations in the world; but the brutalising conditions of his racial identity are perpetuated, as he returns to reservation life. If Soangataha lives a 'tribal' life, he can never hope to be 'civilised'.

Native Americans as dramatic characters continued to be a feature of stage but more increasingly of screen, as the Hollywood industry opened operations by adapting large-scale spectacles of Buffalo Bill-style horsecraft and warfare; courtesy of Hollywood, the wigwam-dwelling, horseback riding, hunting 'Indian' formed the popular racial imaginary. At the same time, *Green Grow the Lilacs*, written by Rollie 'Lynn' Riggs, was produced in 1930 and formed the basis of one of the major Hollywood successes, *Oklahoma!*. Riggs, a descendent of the matrilineal Cherokee nation, had written several dramatic pieces, but *Green Grow the Lilacs* was his most successful production. Opening on Broadway in 1931, the play was performed by the Theatre Guild and nominated that year for a Pulitzer Prize. Riggs's historical drama is set in the troubled, western landscape of the Indian Territory of the early 1900s, and is predicated on the ramifications of a transition from territory to state. The political background to that debate is one that divided Oklahoma's white pioneering settlers from the Native American residents of the Indian Territory; both sides had sought statehood independent of each other. Both were thwarted and the state of Oklahoma came into being in 1906. The political situation is subtly unfolded within the framework of a lover's tale, as Curly and Jeeter fight over Laurey. Over the first five scenes, we see Curly and Laurey's courtship and eventual union; but Curly's rival, Jeeter, takes revenge on the couple by waylaying and threatening to burn them to death. In a scuffle with Curly, Jeeter is stabbed through the heart and the former is taken up for murder. Thus far, the play is focused on the lives of individuals; but in the concluding scene, the conflict between local and national identities is played out. Curly escapes from his cell and hides in the house Laurey shares with Aunt Eller. In scene six, the final scene of the play, the deputies arrive to return Curly to jail and Aunt Eller protests against their right to do so:

> Why, the way yau're sidi'n' with the Federal Marshal, You'd think us people out here lived in the United States! Why, we're territory folks – we ort to hang together. [...] Whut's the United States? It's jist a furrin country to me. And you supportin it! Jist dirty ole furriners, ever last one of you! (2003: 103)

One of the temporary deputies responds: 'Now, Aunt Eller, we hain't furriners. My pappy and mammy was both borned in Indian Territory. Why, I'm jist plum full of Indian blood myself!' (ibid.). One might read this statement as wry, an ironic commentary of the 'white' American's urge to be 'native', to 'play Indian'. At the same time, the statement is clear: to be local, in the Indian Territory, is to be 'plum full of Indian blood'. To be of the United States, is to be foreign – to be 'other'. Centre and margin have been disrupted, as the United States are moved to the margins of 'Indian' life. Up until that point in the play, little reference is made to forms of racial identity. Characterisation, then, does not rely on racial codings; yet racial dynamics are prevalent in the cultural backdrop to the play. The drama, then, in its climax gives voice to the interplay of multiple identities. Notably, *Oklahoma!*, the Rogers and Hammerstein musical version of Riggs's play, was stripped of its implicit racial complexities.

One of Riggs's later dramas, *The Cherokee Night* (1932), was concerned more overtly with the condition of living for tribespeople in early twentieth-century America. The play was not as successful as *Green Grow the Lilacs*, but has been noted by contemporary Native American scholars and playwrights as an important development in the history of American theatre: a play about Native Americans written by a Native American playwright. The tensions that abound in the play are, Craig Womack argues, a product of Riggs's own psychological tensions: caught within identity markers of Cherokee in the United States, homosexual in a heterosexual sphere, and as a lyrical poet, 'contrarily drawn to gritty realism' (1999: 282). *The Cherokee Night* is an atmospheric drama; the opening scene takes place on Claremore Mound, where Cherokee and Osage tribes fought each other in the early nineteenth century, a battle that was informed by the antagonisms of treaty negotiations for the cessation of land rights carried out by Andrew Jackson. The play stages continued unrest between Osage and Cherokee, symbolically drawing on the history of tension between tribal cultures. Internal strife and violence are also key markers of the drama, as members of the Cherokee tribe turn on each other in antagonisms related to 'blood' – 'half-breed' Gar is mocked as 'Big Chief' and 'Chief Squat-in-the-grass' (Riggs 1999: 14–15). However, the source of tension resides ultimately in the racial antagonisms of the United States: 'this is God's country out here', says Tinsley, 'and God's a white man' (ibid.: 101). In a sense, the ultimate and pervading decay and death of *The Cherokee Night* follows the pathway of the 'vanishing Indian' constructed by writers such as John Augustus Stone. The play's dramatic tensions are, inevitably, framed by the history of white racial antagonisms, but Riggs's play does more. *The Cherokee Night* is an investigation of the complexities of tribal histories from a tribal perspective, a dramatic rendering of the history of tribal existence. The play also explores tensions through a range of individuals and personalities that explode the mythical status of both noble and barbaric savage that were, by the 1930s, a staple of Hollywood film production.

Green Grow the Lilacs was performed on behalf of the Federal Theatre Project, and the 1937 version of the play script is stored in the organisation's archive in the George Mason Library, Virginia. According to Rena Fraden, the 'leftist cultural politics' of the productions sponsored by the Project had caused its 'banishment from the archival centre of Washington' (1994: xii). The Federal Theatre Project was part of the Works Progress Administration's New Deal organisations, set up with the aim of reducing the relief rolls. The Project, whose director, Hallie Flanagan, was questioned by the House Un-American Activities Committee, was closed in 1939, as the anti-New Deal administration had succeeded in capitalising on the conservatism of the media. During its lifetime, the Federal Theatre Project had been associated with many left-wing plays, not least of which is Clifford Odets's propagandist *Waiting for Lefty* (1935), a call to unionisation for New York taxi drivers. The contribution of the Federal Theatre Project is undoubted, yet perhaps not entirely radical. Barry Witham argues that whilst the Federal Theatre Project 'would be remembered most for some of its "leftist" productions, they actually made up only a small sampling of the total repertoire' (2003: 1). Attitudes towards black actors were troubling, as Fraden points out, citing the example of a director in Seattle who said that, in order to be able to represent black characters that matched expectations of the predominantly white audience, some black actors needed to be taught 'negro dialect' (1994: 177–8). In Los Angeles, also, black actors were 'kept as segregated as the Yiddish unit' (ibid.), suggesting that the uneven politics of race and ethnicity were as endemic to the Project as to other aspects of American social and cultural life.

Hallie Flanagan declared that the project should, as Fraden points out, support 'regional plays and historical pageants and instituted ethnic and language-based units' that were to 'represent and reflect America in all its diversity' (1994: 3). Such a 'diversity' programme had not been undertaken previously on a national scale in America's theatre history; but regionally, such distinct theatres had already existed, albeit that the economic crisis of the 1930s had closed the doors of many a theatre across the nation.

Arthur Hobson Quinn declared that 'there is no medium so powerful and so competent to carry the meaning of America to our assimilated and our unassimilated population as the drama' (1923: xii). Quinn's statement presupposes that there is a single 'meaning' to be conveyed, and that Americans fall into two categories: those who 'are' American, and those who are not. The state of in-between being and becoming American is bridged by American drama. As Joyce Flynn points out, though, 'on the whole the melting pot image, though not the concept of mixture, was a white literary favourite' (1986: 429). Quinn's statement is also troubling as it overrides any distinction other than American and non-American. But groups settling within the States did not share cultural backgrounds, and antagonisms travelled to America. Nor, as Maxine Schwartz Seller points out, were immigrant communities necessarily welcomed in established communities. Seller cites the example of the burning of a German theatre in New Ulm, Minnesota, by Native Americans in 1862, a response to fears of yet further incursions into the ever-decreasing lands granted by treaty (1983: 4). Some immigrant communities were also harassed, states Seller, for holding theatres on Sunday (ibid.). Indirectly, the antipathy between Islam and Judaism (Jewishness being associated with mainstream 'white' entertainment, particularly Broadway) contributed to the political and artistic endeavours of the Black Arts Movement. But ethnic theatres operated as a site for the negotiation of the multiple meanings of America, and of ethnic conditions of living in America.

In reality, there were, and are, many different types of ethnic theatre in America. Maxine Schwartz Seller's collection of essays on ethnic theatre examines a plethora of productions that came into their sharpest focus in the early years of the twentieth century. Indeed, theatre became an important way for ethnic communities to maintain a sense of cultural identity within America. Seller cites journalist Mark Villchur's survey, which demonstrated that 'immigrants who had never attended a theatre in their native villages in Russia became regular theatregoers in the United States, and Matthew J. Strumski's article, which argues that 'Polish immigrants to the United States took theatre far more seriously than their counterparts in Poland' (Seller 1983: 16). Irish, German and Italian theatre companies, who had established themselves in the nineteenth century, continued to thrive into the twentieth century. Chinese theatre had become established in San Francisco, if consistently harassed, especially following the 1882 Exclusion Laws. Yiddish theatre has been one of the most enduring, argues Julia Listengarten, and its influence is seen throughout American mainstream theatre, particularly in the comic works of Neil Simon, Herb Gardner and Wendy Wasserstein (2007: 456).

The productions of ethnic theatres were varied: in addition to plays from countries of origin, Shakespeare, as Seller points out, was a staple on many stages (1983: 6). Ethnic performances, also, were not confined to one space, and troupes were accustomed to touring for the benefit of non-ethnic audiences. Ethnic theatres, then, whilst providing entertainment for ethnic audiences, were not exclusive spaces, and interaction between audiences from a range of backgrounds was not uncommon – although racial segregation was an issue for all theatres. Indeed, the German theatre of Irving Place, New York, was regarded by Norman Hapgood as 'our only high class theatre' in 1901 (cited in Smith 1997: 73).

The condition of being American and of being in America became the subject matter of plays written by immigrant writers. For example, *The Submission of Rose Moy* by Ling-ai Lee, first performed in Hawaii in 1924, features a female protagonist whose father wishes her to marry in accordance with his wishes, whilst she wishes to join the movement for women's suffrage. It is too uncritical to suggest that Rose Moy's leanings towards suffrage, therefore liberty, are unequivocal symbols of the promise of American citizenship, whilst her father's restrictive traditionalism equates to an unreconstructed Chinese culture. But, the dramatisation of antagonisms that accompany the negotiation of multiple cultural positions is a key feature of Asian American and, as Guiyou Huang argues, 'other ethnic theatre' (2006: 17).

There was a backlash against certain ethnic theatres in response to national and international events. German theatre suffered, following World Wars I and II. As Waldemar Zacharasiewicz notes, the prejudice constructed in cultural works 'undermined the self-confidence of the German ethnic component in the United States and dramatically accelerated its assimilation' (2007: 12). In 1924, the Quota Laws regulated immigration numbers, and concomitantly reduced audiences for ethnic theatres. The Depression had its most significant impact on lower-paid groups; in America that included groups of immigrant labourers as well as segregated black and Native Americans. The Federal Theatre Project kept some language-based theatre afloat, but many closed in the Depression era. And ethnic communities suffered considerably from the exclusionism of the Cold War era in the aftermath of World War II, not only from the practice of violent enactments of racism, and in the case of Japanese Americans actual internment, but also from the practice of racist stereotyping in American performances.

The negotiation of racial tensions so much a feature of American theatre was influenced significantly by the events of World War II. In the era post 1945, arguably the most notorious of racial dramas was the collaboration between Broadway's Joshua Logan, producer Leland Hayward, Robert Rogers and Oscar Hammerstein II. *South Pacific* premiered on Broadway on 7 April 1949 at The Majestic Theatre. The racial tensions of the musical are most apparent in the attitudes of American nurse Nellie Forbush and naval Lieutenant Joseph Cable. Forbush is in love with French émigré Emile de Becque; but turns down his proposal of marriage because he has two Polynesian children from his first marriage. Cable falls for Liat, but cannot bring himself to propose to her, as his family would object to his marriage to a non-white woman. It is Cable that sings one of the more probing pieces of the musical, 'You've Got to be Carefully Taught', an indictment of the forces of family and institution that come together to enforce racism. Cable dies, 'punished' for his racism, and Nellie Forbush learns to overcome her prejudice against de Becque's children. *South Pacific* is not without its problems; not least, Liat and her mother are caught in Rayna Green's 'Pocahontas Perplex': Liat as the 'Indian Princess' and her 'crafty' parent as the unpromising 'squaw'. Overall, though, the musical constructs a dramatic framework that does not affirm a 'colour line', even if it does not quite break through the ideologies of that racialised barrier.

The construction of racial, national and local identities continued to provoke drama throughout the latter half of the twentieth century, and a diverse body of plays contributed to the cultural, social and political movements that advocate radical change to the American nation. America's entry into World War II had been predicated on an attack on American soil – in World War I, events had been distant. An attitude of pervasive mistrust circulated, particularly as fear of Soviet nuclear power grew and was fanned in the popular press. At the same time, groups who had been marginalised prior to the war had become part of the nation's endeavour for victory: women had found themselves called upon to work in 'male' jobs – a radical shift in the practices of gendered operations. Between 1941 and 1945, William H. Chafe notes, over six million women, many married, were employed in a range of jobs, 'from manoeuvring giant cranes in steel mills to toppling huge redwoods in the Oregon forest' (1992: 330). Following the war, this workforce was expected to return to domestic duty. The rhetoric enforces the inherent domesticity of women – *Modern Woman: The Lost Sex* (1947) declared that 'the independent woman [...] is a contradiction in terms' (cited in Chafe 1992: 331). Betty Friedan's *The Feminine Mystique* explored the concept of the 1950s 'happy housewife'. Arthur Miller had portrayed the role in somewhat stereotypical, if nightmarish, terms with loyal and supporting wife Linda Loman of *Death of a Salesman* (1949). Yet, as Chafe points out, women's employment rates increased four times faster than men's in the 1950s, suggesting that the ideology of gendered domesticity was, as it had been at the beginning of the twentieth century, tricky to support (ibid.).

The conflict between gendered ideologies and living conditions informed the structure of social satire in theatre, most famously Edward Albee's *Who's Afraid of Virginia Woolf?* (1964). Attitudes towards sexuality also provoked dramatic material, as demonstrated by Tennessee Williams's *Cat on a Hot Tin Roof* (1955), which explores the difficult negotiations of desire between injured footballer Brick, his wife Maggie and his friend Skipper. In his editorial preface to the 1956 publication of the play, E. Martin Browne records:

> I saw this play on Broadway. It contains some passages on sexual matters which are extremely outspoken and some of the audience of which I was a member indulged in Bacchanalian laughter; appropriately these

Maenads were female. This was the only source of embarrassment in the evening.[35] (Cited in Williams 1976: 16)

The sexual references of the play are seen as part of the aesthetic of dramatising 'life in the raw' (ibid.). Women in the audience, though, to Browne, do not possess the intellectual capacity to experience such pleasure. The complexities of dramatising non-normative sexuality are caught up here with the rigidity of gendered expectations in the auditorium.

The construction of sexuality was also a feature of an earlier play that receives far less attention than Williams's tale of unspeakable desires. Lillian Hellman's *The Children's Hour* (1934), predicated on the malice of gossip, dramatises the collapse of a friendship between two teachers at a school, a broken engagement for one of the teachers and suicide for the other. The works of Hellman are coming more into critical focus, as are those of her contemporaries in the 1930s and 1940s; but, overall, critical accounts of women playwrights in the years between 1945 and 1960 tend to be few and thin. In his essay on American drama of the 1940s and 1950s, Thomas P. Adler (2007) mentions only Kitti Frings, who adapted Thomas Wolfe's novel *Look Homeward, Angel* in 1957 and Hellman's *The Autumn Garden* (1951). In the *Cambridge Companion to American Women Playwrights*, discussions of women from the 1940s and 1950s are scant compared with those of the 1930s and of the 1960s. Judith E. Barlow suggest that the demise of the little theatre movements, which had been more accommodating of women dramatists, led to a dearth of women playwrights at this time, and cites George Jean Nathan's 1941 article 'Playwrights in Petticoats', which states 'even the best of our women playwrights (Hellman) falls immeasurably short of the mark of our best masculine' (2001: vii–viii). The comparative lack of women playwrights in the early decades of the twentieth century is crucial: at a time when critics were locating American drama as coming into being, 'due' to the 'skill' of playwrights such as Arthur Miller, Edward Albee, Tennessee Williams and William Inge, women writers have been absented from the field.

Indeed, the marginalisation of women playwrights has been a consistent feature of American drama throughout the twentieth century. In 1973, *The New York Times* published an article titled 'Where Are the Women Playwrights?' by Mark Fearnow. The article cites Helen Epstein's biography of Joseph Papp, founder of the Public Theatre, which claimed that this 'hotbed of creativity' was 'a hard-drinking, cigar-smoking circle of aggressive young male playwrights' (Fearnow 2007: 430). Such an environment of exclusivity demonstrates the marginalisation, rather than the paucity, of female playwrights. One might contextualise Papp's 'male' circle as specific to a particular time and cultural atmosphere: this was the 1970s, the decade of hypermasculinity and macho posturing. But even in the twenty-first century, the debate continues. On 21 December 2003, Jason Zinoman, in *The New York Times*, wrote an article on 'The Season of the Female Playwright', which relates the following anecdote:

> About 10 years ago, the playwright Theresa Rebeck was having drinks with a well-known male director when he made the kind of blunt comment you hardly ever hear in polite society. As Ms. Rebeck remembers it: '"Women don't write good plays,"' he said, adding, '"Look at history: they write good novels, but as for plays, they just don't have the knack for it."' Ms. Rebeck calls this prejudice 'the dirty secret of the American theater,' and while it's unclear how commonly it is held, there is no question that most of our celebrated playwrights are male and that female writers are responsible for only a small minority of the plays produced in this country.

Although Zinoman comments, 'historical trends are starting to change', in 2008, another article in *The New York Times*, by Patricia Cohen, points out that, for women playwrights, the greatest obstacle is the 'difficulty in getting their work produced'. Any canonical 'gap', then, in the numbers of male and female playwrights in America, is a matter of gender bias in the production of theatre, rather than abstention by female writers.

Throughout the 1940s and 1950s, the US government was beginning to rescind legislation that had enforced segregation on America. In 1948, discrimination in the armed services on the grounds of race, colour, religion or national identity became illegal. In 1954, the Supreme Court ruling in the *Brown* v. *Board of Education of Topeka, Kansas* effectively prohibited segregation in schools. In 1955, Martin Luther King was voted inaugural president of the Southern Christian Leadership Conference. In 1964, President Lyndon B. Johnson signed the Civil Rights Act, which prohibited discrimination based on race, colour, religion or national origin, and granted to the federal government powers to enforce deseg-regation. But racism continued to be part of material life for all America. Most starkly, in 1955, Emmett Till was murdered by two white men. The men were acquitted in court, but then famously boasted about the murder in an interview for *Look* magazine. Three Civil Rights workers were murdered by the Ku Klux Klan, having been kidnapped by the local police force in Neshoba County, Mississippi.

Politically, the atmosphere of American in the 1960s was charged with racial violence, the murders of Malcolm X and Martin Luther King being the most notorious. In 1966, the Black Panther Party was formed, with actor Bobby Seale as a founder member. Mike Sell points out that performance was central to the movement, which 'attempted to exploit and seduce the media (and wealthy liberals) by way of outrageous, blatant displays of hypermasculine "Blackness"' (2001: 56). At the same time, the Black Arts Movement emerged, partly in response to the international Asian-African Conference of April 1955, which initiated the Bandung humanist movement, and also in response to the specific racial atmosphere of America. One of the most significant participants was playwright LeRoi Jones, who had already produced several notable plays, including *Dutchman* and *The Slave*, which both premiered in 1964. Jones converted to Islam in 1968 and changed his name to Amiri Baraka. He was one of the founder members of the Black Arts Repertory Theatre/School, formed in April 1965, which looked to incorporate the avant-garde theatre of Artaud that had influenced Edward Albee's work with cultural traditions of Africa and African American experiences. The institution was short-lived, though – the organisation had its funding withdrawn. But, argues Sell, perhaps more damaging to the Movement was the attempt to yoke in a performance strategy – avant-gardism – that was interpolated with 'racist tendencies' (ibid.: 61). Ed Bullins of the San Francisco Drama Circle had produced absurdist drama *How Do You Do* in 1965, but then subsequently dismissed the form for its overriding aim to 'perpetuate and adapt the white man's theatre, to extend western reality and finally to *rescue* his culture and have it benefit his needs' (cited in Hill and Hatch 2003: 389). Henry Louis Gates, in an article for *Time*, wrote that:

> [The] Black Arts writers imagined themselves as the artistic wing of the Black Power movement. Amiri Baraka, Larry Neal and Sonia Sanchez viewed black art as a matter less of aesthetics than of protest; its function was to serve the political liberation of black people from white racism. Erected on a shifting foundation of revolutionary politics, this 'renaissance' was the most short-lived of all. By 1975, with the Black Arts Movement dead, black culture seemed to be undergoing a profound identity crisis. (1994)

In 1976, however, Ntozake Shange's choreopoem, *For Colored Girls Who Have Considered Suicide/When the Rainbow is Enuf* (1974), part of the New Federal Theatre's productions, opened on Broadway. The New Federal Theatre, founded in 1970, is still in operation, sponsoring new playwrights, and running training courses at its arts centre.[36] Whilst the Black Arts Movement's political edginess may have unsettled many black scholars, and indeed many white audiences, without its work, Hatch suggests, there may not have been an opportunity for the black-oriented productions that came onto Broadway in the 1970s, a decade of some creative innovations in black arts. Yet, with the upsurge of neo-conservatism in the 1980s and the concurrent tactics of institutional racism (Ronald Reagan, for example, tried to veto the Civil Rights Restoration Act of 1988, which was established to prevent segregation in private institutions that benefitted from public funds – a sign of how endemic racist practices were still a feature of America), the possibilities for black American theatre came under challenge.

All theatre suffered under Reagan, who presided over severe cuts in public arts funding, which meant that minority theatre would struggle to afford venues for performance.[37] Smaller venues, though, in American cities could be more cost effective; appealing to smaller audiences, for a 'niche' performance, then, was a cost-effective way of circumventing arts cuts. Smaller theatre venues had been staples for off-Broadway productions early in the twentieth century, with the little theatre movement. Regional theatre groups had continued to operate smaller venues throughout the twentieth century, and as Mark Fearnow points out, 'the energy that built up a new and positive theatre came largely from formerly silenced groups – feminist, gay and lesbian, African American, Latina/o, and Asian American playwrights' whose works constitute the most radical response to 'the conservative environment of 1980–92' (2007: 423). In the post-Stonewall era, from 1969, plays engaging with sexualities had become more prominent, although it would be the late 1970s and early 1980s before consciously worked analyses of homosexual relationships would be performed on Broadway. Jill Dolan argues that 'white gay male playwrights adopted more conventional forms to describe their experiences and their liberatory practices after Stonewall' (2007: 489). But feminist and lesbian groups tended to form collectives that experimented with staging and dramatic form. The Women's Experimental Theatre, which was formed in 1977, assessed the role of women from the perspective of women, examining a matrilineal space of mother–daughter relationships in *The Daughter's Cycle Trilogy*, a collaboration between the three founders, Roberta Sklar, Clare Coss and Sondra Segal, that addressed contemporary debates about shifting definitions of gender and sexuality. One of the most enduring of theatre groups that emerged at this time is Spiderwoman Theatre. Originally the group included Peggy Shaw, Lois Weaver and Deb Margolin, who left to form the feminist-lesbian company Split Britches in 1980, as well as sisters Muriel Miguel, Gloria Miguel and Lisa Mayo (Kuna/Rappahannock). Spiderwoman Theatre, as Ann Haugo argues, 'drew on the techniques of collective theatres', a feature of many feminist groups of the 1970s, but also 'maintained a firm connection with their native identity and cultures' (2000: 238). Spiderwoman Theatre is informed by the context of a feminist theatre dynamic and also by the work of the American Indian (now Native American) Theatre Ensemble, founded by Native American playwright Hanay Geiogamah in 1971, which fuses ritual performance strategies with theatre staging.

Theatre, then, continued to thrive throughout the difficult financial climate of the 1980s, and an innovative body of work emerged that addressed a range of perspectives and contexts. By the 1990s, though, it was legitimate theatre that had begun to suffer from financial insecurity. One way of ensuring the success of a theatre, June Schlueter argues, was for 'artistic choices' to yield to 'financial imperatives, with investors placing their money on the big-cast, full-orchestra, star-powered spectacular that would fill a five-hundred-plus-seat house nightly' (2007: 505). In 1994–5, Schlueter points out, there were 'no new musicals or plays on Broadway' (ibid.). Revivals were prominent throughout the 1990s, with Eugene O'Neill and Tennessee Williams a significant presence. Some new plays did appear, scripted by 'heavyweights' Arthur Miller, Sam Shepard and Edward Albee, not always to accolades, although Albee's *Three Tall Women* won a Pulitzer Prize. However, in 1990, August Wilson's *The Piano Lesson* had premiered on Broadway. Wilson had garnered a reputation with mainstream audiences, and his first play, *Fences*, had run for over 500 performances on Broadway between 1987 and 1988. And in 1993, Tony Kushner's *Angels in America: A Gay Fantasia on National Themes* (1991) proved to be popular with audiences and critics. According to David Savran, '*Angels in America* has almost singlehandedly resuscitated a category of play that has become almost extinct: the serious Broadway drama that is neither a British import nor a revival' (1997: 13). The debate is familiar and one which is to be found in the words of all American critics engaging with theatre: the body of 'serious drama' is threatened with the disease of popular, mass commerce.

'Serious' drama, though, was appearing across American throughout the 1990s – although it would be more accurate to consider such dramas as innovations, or experiments in theatre, than the troublingly elitist 'serious'. Ehren Fordyce discusses the plays of Cherrie Moraga, Naomi Wallace, Erik Ehn and David Greenspan as 'moderately known writers' (2007: 548). Perhaps the most famous contemporary writer of experimental theatre, though, is Susan Lori-Parks, whose play *Topdog/ Underdog* (2001) won a Pulitzer Prize in 2002. Alongside Tony Kushner, Susan Lori-Parks had become, Fordyce argues, 'the most important American playwright of the 1990s' (2007: 546): Susan Lori-Parks's contemporary works continue to innovate theatre.

One of Parks's earlier productions, *The American Play* (1993), opened at the Public Theatre and revisits the history of America, phrased as the 'Great Hole of History', in the opening of play, punning on hole/whole: the 'history' of America is either encompassing, and whole, or voided, in the 'hole' of narrative construction. Such a homonym stands as a symbol for the 'history' of American theatre discussed in this book. There are many published versions, accounts, narratives that set out to explore, pattern, graph and map America's theatre history. But what I hope to have shown is that such a map is, ultimately, an impossibility; grasping a whole 'history' of American theatre is forever thwarted. American theatres are as divided in their productivity, ethos and ideologies as they ever were.

In an interview for *The Salon Magazine* in 1997, David Mamet declared:

> The job of mass entertainment is exactly the opposite of the job of art. The job of the artist gets more difficult [...] I like mass entertainment. I've written mass entertainment. But it's the opposite of art because the job of mass entertainment is to cajole, seduce and flatter consumers to let them know that what they thought was right is right, and that their tastes and their immediate gratification are of the utmost concern of the purveyor. The job of the artist, on the other hand, is to say, wait a second, to the contrary, everything that we have thought is wrong. Let's reexamine it. (Covington 1997)

Mamet's words echo the debates that were taking place in the early years of America's 'national' theatrical activity. William Dunlap, for example, also argued that commercial theatre meant bad theatre. Performances in America have been repeatedly subject to such binarisms – moral/immoral, legitimate/non-legitimate, commercial/artistic.

But social debates are a feature of American theatre and performance: rebellion, both literal and symbolic; racialisation of character and plot; pageantry, ritual and street theatre; structures of stages and auditoria, stand as facets of performance that have contributed and continue to key into the development of theatre in America by accident, design, fluke and coincidence. This book has attempted to illustrate the continuously shifting atmosphere of America's theatre history. There is not one 'American' theatrical space, dramatic type or gestural language. There are, as always there have been, many ways of producing and consuming theatricality in, across, for and about America.

Notes

1 'Theatre' comes from the Greek *theatron*, which, in translation, means a seeing place – not necessarily a permanent structure, but an arena in which spectators can gather for the purpose of watching a spectacle. 'Drama' derives from *dram*, meaning to 'do' or 'act', literally the 'act' of scripting a play for performance. Thus, drama, as a critical term, has become associated with the privileging of the text, an issue of concern in contemporary theatre criticism, which prefers to research and evaluate a range of performance strategies.

2 'Nova Britannia: Offering most excellente fruites by planting in Virginia. Exciting all such as be well affected to further the same', available at http://www.wwnorton.com/college/history/eamerica/site_images.htm, accessed 29 April 2009.

3 Roy Harvey Pearce's slogan, 'civilization or death to all American Savages' (quoted in Herbert 1980: 27), a product of the Jacksonian push west, still, it seems, flavours the ideological underpinnings of the Reservation.

4 See Deloria 1997; Lovgren 2007.

5 I should point out that anthropologists have investigated the striking similarities between the 'Mound City' that surrounds the Serpent Mound of the Adena- Hopewell period and the Japanese earthworks of Kiysu temple mound. See Joseph 2010.

6 The various attempts to establish the size of the Cahokia population are summarised usefully by Pauketat and Lopinot 1997.

7 Paula Gunn Allen cites the example of the 'sacred hoop' from John G. Neihardt's *Black Elk Speaks: Being the Life Story of a Holy Man of the Oglala Sioux*: 'and I saw the sacred hoop of my people was one of many hoops that made one circle' (2000: 33). Neihardt's reading of the Sacred Hoop is an interpretation of an extract from *The Sixth Grandfather: Black Elk's Teachings Given to John G. Neihardt*: 'The sacred hoop means the continents of the world and the people shall stand as one. Everything reproduces here inside the hoop' (DeMallie 1984: 129).

8 Schechner has attempted to demonstrate that reclamation through his figure-of-eight diagram, effectively 'looping' social drama (overt performance) with stage drama (manifest performance). The 'loop' structure both draws

169

on and reshapes the 'scared hoop' of Native American rituals (2002: 68).

9 'Sioux' as a denomination, is troubling: Guy Gibbon's *The Sioux: The Dakota and Lakota Nations* tells us that the name allocated to these plains tribes came into being in the seventeenth century, and was a translation from an Ojibwa term, *na-towe-ssiwa* (people of an alien tribe/snakes), into the French *Naudoweissioux* and then shortened by English settlers to *Sioux*. The name was, in the first instance, not that which the Lakota and Dakota (and Nakota — whose language, however, is somewhat distinct from that spoken by the Lakota and Dakota) tribal groups gave to themselves (within the tribes, the collective name translates as 'the allies'), but one used by Ojibwa, and at this time, was a term to denote an enemy force (2002: 2–4).

10 Letter from Thomas Galbraith to Clark W. Thompson 27 January 1863, held in *Annual Report of the Commissioner of Indian Affairs* serial 1182: 398.

11 *New York Times*, 24 September 1867.

12 James Mooney speaks of the participation of Chief Sitting Bull. Sitting Bull was, Mooney records, responsible for the introduction of hypnotic visions to the dance, having induced a trance in dancers at arguably the biggest and most extensive of the ceremonies, in September 1890, attended by over 3,000 from many tribes. The visions induced were of 'departed friends' and joining in with 'old time amusements' (1973: 92). In other words, the visions were a representation of an alternative way of living than that being imposed through Removal and reservation laws. Mooney argues that from the time of the September 1890 event, managed by Sitting Bull, 'the Ghost Dance was naturalized in the south and developed rapidly along new lines. Each succeeding dance resulted in other visions and [...] other hypnotists arose, until almost every camp had its own' (ibid.: 899). However, Sitting Bull appears to have been involved inasmuch as he was a chief and a revered religious figure. Russell David Edmunds cites the record of teacher John Carignan, who notes that, as participants entered a trance state, they would be 'carried into a tepee where Sitting Bull waited for him to recover sufficiently to tell of his "dream" and what he saw in his "vision." [...] Sitting Bull would interpret the vision' (1980: 168). As Stanley Vestal points out, Mooney acknowledged that the Lakota tribes would not speak to him about the Ghost Dance, and his information about the Dance and Sitting Bull came from the Agency Offices (1934: 311). And Sitting Bull himself apparently declared 'I did not start this Ghost Dance [...] I told my people to go slow, but they were swept into this thing' (cited in Vestal 1934: 310). Sitting Bull's participation, therefore, is far more ambivalent than Mooney suggests, and was very likely used as an excuse by the Indian Bureau to eradicate a powerful opponent to the programme of detribalisation.

13 A 1993 excavation of Nanny Town, one of the major sites of Maroon society in the early to mid-eighteenth century, has revealed that Arawak tribes-

people, escapees from the previous Spanish conquests, were also part of the community.

14 See Clark 1950 for a detailed account of the symbolic register of the Dance across Europe.

15 http://www.optative.net/neptune/deconstruction.html.

16 A pamphlet, 'A Discover of the Bermudas, otherwise called the Isle of the Divels; by Sir Thomas Gates, Sir George Somers, and captain Newport, with Divers others', written by one of the travellers aboard Gates' ship, Sil. Jourdan, in 1610, delivered an account of the shipwreck, and of the bounties of the island, described as a 'never inhabited by any Christian or heathen people, but ever esteemed a most prodigious and enchanted place' (quoted in Furness 1892: 313). Such an account, argues Furness, informed the development of the dramatic landscape and shipwreck for Shakespeare. Although evidence is not rock solid, certainly, the drama of the Bermudan adventure was in general circulation in the UK at the time the play was being written.

17 As can be seen in John Smith's *The Generall Historie of Virginia* (1624) also William Bradford's *Of Plymouth Plantation (1606–1646)* and Thomas Morton's *New English Canaan* (1637), amongst others – although all written from very different perspectives, these texts share a desire to record 'observations' of native performances.

18 In *The Theatre and its Double*, Antonin Artaud argues that 'The Theatre is a disease because it is the supreme equilibrium which cannot be achieved without destruction. It invites the mind to share a delirium which exalts its energies [...] impelling men to see themselves as they are, it causes the mask to fall, reveals the lie, the slackness, baseness, and hypocrisy of our world' (1958: 31).

19 W. E. B. Du Bois, also referencing Watson's *Annals of Philadelphia*, notes that Robert Venable was a free black in Philadelphia in the mid-eighteenth century, and may, therefore, have been in attendance in his own right (1899: 18).

20 Oldfield notes, however, that Charles Dibdin had been advised by John Moody, who had recently returned from Jamaica, on the subject of speech patterns and also points out that 'Moody was to have played the part of Mungo in the original production of *The Padlock* but later declined it in favour of Dibdin' (1993: 14).

21 Johnson argues: 'What better place for Douglass to find support for building than a society of Masons? And once supported, what better place for Douglass to find a builder than a Masonic lodge?' Thus Douglass 'facilitated his introduction' to Williamsburg in 1760 (2006: 108).

22 The homepage of the William and Mary website informs us that Royal Governor Francis Nicholson, in a letter to the Archbishop of Canterbury on 22 July 1702, reported that "a Pastoral Colloquy in English verse,

spoken by some younger Scholars in the College hall" was presented. This performance is also noted in several examinations of America's colonial cultural history, the earliest of these accounts being Lyon Gardiner Tyler's *Williamsburg, the Old Colonial Capital* (1907).

23 Anthony Aston kept a journal of his travels, and he recorded his straitened experiences of the New World: 'We arrived in Charles-town, full of Lice, Shame, Poverty, Nakedness and Hunger. I turned Player and Poet and wrote one Play on the Subject of the Country' (cited in Hill 1992: ix.). No play survives, however to support this claim. But a 'Sketch' of his life, which was published as preface to his *The Fool's Opera* (1731, written under Aston's pen-name, Mat Medley), claims performances in 'New York, East and West Jersey, Maryland [and] Virginia (on both sides of the Chesapeek)' (cited in Johnson and Burling 2003: 97). Aston's attempt at producing drama in the colonies seems to have been mainly unsuccessful, and he made his way back to London and the relative reliability of theatrical endeavours in England.

24 'Both' theatres here referenced most likely would be the Drury and Lincoln's Inn Fields Theatres; however, in 1720, the little Haymarket had opened its doors, and was established as a theatrical venue with some rapidity – but may have been overlooked in this analysis.

25 According to the *Oxford English Dictionary*, the terms 'legitimate' and 'illegitimate' did not come into circulation until the1800s; certain performances types, such as pantomime and other forms of physical theatre, did tend to be dismissed critically.

26 The play was, however, performed in Dublin on 3 December 1744 as *The Patriot*, according to 'Miscellaneous Notes', *The Modern Language Review*, Vol. 15, No. 3, Jul., 1920, pp. 304–6.

27 In Boucicault's play, the term 'Octoroon' has come to stand in for mixed race: 'octoroon' specifically refers to one who has a black great-grandparent on one side – Zoe's mother, then, was also of a product of miscegenation. The implications of generational accretions of racial indeterminacy are not a specific focus, albeit fundamental to southern life and are certainly worthy of note in critical considerations of the play.

28 For a detailed account of Forrest's touring, see James Rees (Colley Cibbey) 1874. The biography is, overall, an exercise in hagiography, but provides a detailed account of where and when Forrest travelled.

29 Sections of this chapter on the nineteenth-century 'leg show' appeared in an article, 'A Pair of Handsome Legs: From Breeches to Burlesque on Nineteenth-century American Stages', for the *Hungarian Journal of English and American Studies*, Vol. 15, No. 1, 2009, pp. 27–44.

30 Sources: 'Richmond News and Gossip: Our Own Correspondent', *The Charleston Mercury*, 6 January 1862; 'The Great Fire', *The Charleston Mercury*, 12 December 1861.

31 William (Buffalo Bill) Cody had written the popular melodrama *Song of the Prairie* in 1873, which was one of the dramas from the last decades of the nineteenth century that contributed to the 'Wild West' of frontier mythology, alongside Augustin Daly's 1871 spectacular *Horizon*. Daly's melodrama features a character, Sundown Rowse (who was played by pantomimist George Lafayette Fox – a casting that could have contributed to the play's success, Fox still being a popular performer at that time), who sums up the constituent parts of the mythical 'West' towards the close of Act I: 'Native Americans, with a sprinkling of the injun and the least speck of Chinee' (1984: 112). The play sets out to destabilise tribal structures, and promote the assimilationist agenda, yet stages the ultimate defeat of Wannamucka at the hands of the cavalry, as the Native American remains unassimilated at the play's closure.

32 In the first edition of the *Cambridge Guide to American Theatre* (1997), there is no mention of this 'general' state of American theatre: this section was added to the extended second edition in 2007, suggesting that theatre scholarship has consolidated rather than challenged the theory of the 'feminisation' of the American stage in terms of domesticity and sentimentality in the early decades of the twentieth century.

33 Kim Marra builds on work undertaken by Wilde scholars to argue that Fitch and Wilde experienced 'a passionate physical love affair' during Fitch's travels to London in 1890 (2002: 250).

34 Deanna M. Toten Beard (2007) argues, though, that American expressionism had preceded O'Neill in dramas not normally associated with the form, such as David Belasco's *The Return of Peter Grimm* (1911).

35 The maenad were worshippers of Dionysus: the word translates as either 'mad' or 'raving'.

36 The New Federal Theatre Projects have included adaptations of Shakespeare's *Macbeth*, and a version of *In Dahomey*, adapted by Shauneille Perry in 1999, as well as new plays by African American writers.

37 The National Endowment for the Arts was established in 1965 to contribute federal funding to arts programmes. Various groups, both from marginal arts projects and from mainstream political agitants, have argued against the NEA, with very different objectives. The minority report from the House of Representatives 'could lead to attempts at political control of culture' (H.R. REP. NO. 618, 89th cong., 1st Sess. 21, 1965). In *Leaving Town Alive: Confessions of an Arts Warrior*, John Frohnmayer, chair of the NEA until expelled by Ronald Reagan, reported that key members of Congress were vocal in their belief that '"government shouldn't support art in the first place [...] we simply cannot afford art in an era of fiscal austerity [...] art isn't the government's business"' (1993: 45).

Bibliography

Ackerman, Alan (1999), *The Portable Theatre: American Literature and the Nineteenth-Century Stage*, Baltimore: The Johns Hopkins University Press.

Adams, Charles (ed.) (1876), *Familial Letters of John Adams and his Wife Abigail During the Revolution*, New York: Hurd and Houghton.

Addison, Joseph [1713] (1853), 'Cato: A Tragedy. As it is Acted at the Theatre Royal, Drury Lane, by His Majesty's Servants', in *The Works of Joseph Addison*, ed. George Washington Greene, New York: G. P. Putnam, pp. 365–467.

Adler, Thomas P. (2007), 'Fissures Beneath the Surface: Drama in the 1940s and 1950s', in David Krasner (ed.), *A Companion to Twentieth-Century American Drama*, 2nd edition, Oxford: Blackwell, pp. 159–74.

Agnew, Jean-Christophe (1986), *Worlds Apart: The Market and the Theater in Anglo-American Thought, 1550–1750*, Cambridge: Cambridge University Press.

Aiken, George L. (1858), *Uncle Tom's Cabin; or, Life Among the Lowly. A Domestic Drama in Six Acts*, New York: Samuel French.

Aleandri, Emelise and Maxine Schwartz Seller (1983), 'Italian-American Theatre', in Maxine Schwartz Seller (ed.), *Ethnic Theatre in the United States*, Westport, CT: Greenwood, pp. 237–77.

Alger, William R. [1877] (1977), *A Life of Edwin Forrest*, New York: Arno Press.

Allen, Paula Gunn (2000), 'The Sacred Hoop: A Contemporary Perspective', in Hanay Geiogamah and Jaye T. Darby (eds), *American Indian Theater in Performance: A Reader*, Los Angeles: UCLA American Indian Studies Center, pp. 50–75.

Allen, Robert Clyde (1991), *Horrible Prettiness: Burlesque and American Culture*, Chapel Hill: University of North Carolina Press.

Anderson, Marilyn J. (1977), '"Ponteach": The First American Problem Play', *American Indian Quarterly*, Vol. 3, No. 3, Autumn, pp. 225–41.

Andrews W. D. E. (1982), 'The Black Revolutionary Drama of LeRoi Jones', *Rocky Mountain Review of Language and Literature*, Vol. 36, No. 4, pp. 259–78.

Anon. [1764] (2003), *The Paxton Boys. A Farce Translated from the original*

French, by a Native of Donegall, Philadelphia: Anthony Armbruster; *American Drama Full-Text Online Database*, Cambridge: ProQuest Information and Learning.

Apess, William (1836), *Eulogy on King Philip, as Pronounced at the Odeon, in Federal Street, Boston*, Boston: published by the author.

Aptheker, Herbert (1943), *American Negro Slave Revolts*, Columbia: Columbia University Press.

Artaud, Antonin [1938] (1958), *The Theatre and Its Double*, trans. Mary Caroline Richards, New York: Grove Press.

—— (1968), *Collected Works*, trans. V. Corti, London: Balder and Boyars.

Avery, Laurence G. (1998), 'Introduction', in Laurence G. Avery (ed.), *A Paul Green Reader*, Chapel Hill: University of North Carolina Press, pp. 1–15.

Ballinger, Franchot (1991–2), 'Ambigere: The Euro-American Picaro and the Native American Trickster', *MELUS*, Vol. 17, No. 1, Native American Fiction: Myth and Criticism, Spring, pp. 21–38.

Bank, Rosemary K. (1993), 'Hustlers in the House: The Bowery Theatre as a Mode of Historical Information', in Ron Engle and Tice L. Miller (eds), *The American Stage*, Cambridge: Cambridge University Press, pp. 47–64.

—— (1997), *Theatre Culture in America, 1825–1860*, Cambridge: Cambridge University Press.

Barca, Dane (2004), 'Adah Isaacs Menken: Race and Transgendered Performance in the Nineteenth Century', *MELUS: Pedagogy, Canon, Context: Toward a Redefinition of Ethnic American Literary Studies*, Vol. 29, No. 3/4, Autumn/Winter, pp. 293–306.

Barlow, Judith E. (2001), 'Introduction', in Judith E. Barlow (ed.), *Plays by American Women: 1930–1960*, New York: Applause Books, pp. vii–xxxiv.

Barton, Andrew (Col. Thomas Forrester) [1764] (1976), 'The Disappointment: Or, the Force of Credulity', in Jerald C. Graue and Judith Layng (eds), *Recent Researches in American Music*, Madison: A-R Editions, pp. 1–133.

Bean, Annemarie (2007), 'Playwrights and Plays of the Harlem Renaissance', in David Krasner (ed.), *A Companion to Twentieth-Century American Drama*, 2nd edition, Oxford: Blackwell, pp. 91–105.

Beard, Deanna T. Toten (2007), 'American Experimentalism, American Expressionism, and Early O'Neill', in David Krasner (ed.), *A Companion to Twentieth-Century American Drama*, 2nd edition, Oxford: Blackwell, pp. 53–68.

Bell, Betty (2004), 'Gender in Native America', in Philip Joseph Deloria and Neal Salisbury (eds), *A Companion to American Indian History*, Oxford: Blackwell, pp. 307–20.

Bernbaum, Ernest (1958), *The Drama of Sensibility*, Gloucester: Peter Smith.

Bhabha, Homi (1994), *Location of Culture*, London and New York: Routledge.

Bigsby C. W. E. (1985), *A Critical Introduction to Twentieth-Century American Drama: Volume 3, Beyond Broadway*, Cambridge: Cambridge University Press.

Bigsby, Christopher and Don B. Wilmeth (1998), 'Introduction', in Don B. Wilmeth and Christopher Bigsby (eds), *The Cambridge History of American Theatre: Volume I, Beginnings to 1870*, Cambridge: Cambridge University Press, pp. 1–19.

Bilby, Kenneth M. (2202), 'Maroon Autonomy in Jamaica', *Cultural Survival Quarterly*, Issue 25.4, 31 January 2002, http://www.bnvillage.co.uk/black-roots-village/77735-maroon-autonomy-jamaica.html?langid=2, accessed 14 November 2010.

Black Elk [1953] (1989), *The Sacred Pipe: Black Elk's Account of the Seven Rites of the Oglala Sioux*, ed. Joseph Epes Brown, Oklahoma: University of Oklahoma Press.

Bordman, Gerald (1978), *Musical Theatre: A Chronicle*, New York: Oxford University Press.

—— (1992), *The Oxford Companion to American Theatre*, 2nd edition, New York and Oxford: Oxford University Press.

Bowdoin, James, Joseph Warren and Samuel Pemberton [1770] (1849), *A Short Narrative of the Horrid Massacre in Boston, Perpetrated in the Evening of the Fifth Day Of March, 1770, by Soldiers of the 29th Regiment, which with the 14th Regiment were then Quartered There; with some Observations on the State of Things Prior to that Catastrophe*, New York: J. Doggett, Jr.

Bowers, Rick (1989), '*The Theatre of Neptune*: Marc Lescarbot and the New World Masque', *Canadian Drama*, Vol. 15, No. 1, pp. 39–52.

Bradford, William (1908), *Of Plymouth Plantation, 1606–1646*, ed. William T. Davis, New York: Charles Scribner's Sons.

Brandão, F. A., Jr [1865] (1994), 'A escravatura no Brasil precedido d'um artigo sobre a agricultura e colonisação no Maranhão', in Robert Edgar Conrad (ed.), *Children of God's Fire: A Documentary History of Black Slavery in Brazil*, University Park, PA: Pennsylvania State University Press, pp. 397–9.

Brooks, Peter (1979), *The Melodramatic Imagination: Balzac, Henry James, Melodrama, and the Mode of Excess*, New Haven and London: Yale University Press.

Brown, Jared (1995), *The Theatre in American During the Revolution*, Cambridge: Cambridge University Press.

Brown, Joseph Epes (1976), 'The Roots of Renewal', in Walter Holden Cas (ed.), *Seeing with a Native Eye: Essays on Native American Religion*, New York: Harper and Row.

Brown, William Wells [1858] (1996), 'The Escape; Or, A Leap for Freedom', in James V. Hatch and Ted Shine (eds), *Black Theatre U.S.A.: The Early Period 1847–1938*, revised edition, New York: The Free Press, pp. 37–60.

Bryan, Mark Evans (2007), 'American Drama 1900–1915', in David Krasner (ed.), *A Companion to Twentieth-Century American Drama*, 2nd edition, Oxford: Blackwell, pp. 3–17.

Bryant, Lawrence M. (2007), 'A Savage Mirror: Power, Identity, and Knowledge in Early Modern France', *Renaissance Quarterly*, Vol. 60, No. 2, Summer, pp. 567–8.

Buckley, Peter (1993), 'The Culture of "Leg Work": The Transformation of Burlesque after the Civil War', in J. Gilbert, A. Gilman, D. Scott and J. Scott (eds), *The Mythmaking Frame of Mind: Social Imagination and American Culture*, Belmont: Wadsworth Publishing, pp. 113–34.

—— (1998), 'Paratheatricals and Popular Stage Entertainment', in Don B. Wilmeth and Christopher Bigsby (eds), *Cambridge History of American Theatre, Vol I: Beginnings to 1870*, Cambridge: Cambridge University Press.

Burdett, William (1801), *The Life and Exploits of Three-finger'd Jack, the Terror of Jamaica*, London: A. Neill.

Burgoyne, John (1776), *A Vaudvil: Sung by the Characters at the Conclusion of a New Farce called the Boston Blockade*, Boston: John Howe; Microform, *Early American Imprints*, Series I: Evans, 1639–1800, Readex, 15195.

Burkhart, Louise M. (1996), *Holy Wednesday: A Nahua Drama from Early Colonial Mexico*, Philadelphia: University of Pennsylvania Press.

Butler, Jon (2001), *Becoming America: The Revolution Before 1776*, Cambridge, MA: Harvard University Press.

Butsch, Richard (1994), 'Bowery B'hoys and Matinee Ladies: The Re-Gendering of Nineteenth-Century American Theater Audiences', *American Quarterly*, Vol. 46, No. 3, Sept., pp. 374–405.

Canby, Courtlandt (1949), 'Robert Munford's "The Patriots"', *The William and Mary Quarterly*, Third Series, Vol. 6, Jul., pp. 437–503.

Carlson, Marvin A. (1993), *Theories of the Theatre: A Historical and Critical Survey, from the Greeks to the Present*, Ithaca and London: Cornell University Press.

Carroll, Bret E. (2003), *American Masculinities*, London: Sage, Vol. I.

Carson, Herbert L. (1963), 'The Play That Would Not Die: George Lillo's *The London Merchant*', *Quarterly Journal of Speech*, Vol. XLIX, pp. 287–94.

Carvajal, Christa (1983), 'German-American Theatre', in Maxine Schwartz Seller (ed.), *Ethnic Theatre in the United States*, Westport, CT: Greenwood Press.

Carvajal, Michael de [1557] (2008), 'Complaint of the Indians in The Court of Death', in ed. Carlos A. Jáuregui, *The Conquest on Trial*, University Park, PA: Pennsylvania State University Press.

Castillo, Susan (2006), *Performing America: Colonial Encounters in New World Writing*, London and New York: Routledge.

Cave, Edward (Sylvanus Urban) (ed.) (1787), 'Select Poetry, Ancient and Modern', *Gentleman's Magazine and Historical Chronicle*, London, Vol. 58, pp. 913–16.

Chafe, William H. (1992), 'Women and American Society', in Luther S. Luedtke (ed.), *Making America: The Society & Culture of the United States*, Chapel

Hill: University of North Carolina Press, pp. 327–41.

Champagne, Duane (2000), 'Setting the Stage: An Historical Overview', in Hanay Geiogamah and Jaye T. Darby (eds), *American Indian Theater in Performance: A Reader*, Los Angeles: UCLA American Indian Studies Center, pp. 5–49.

Charles, John C. (2005), 'What Was Africa to Him? Alain Locke, Cultural Nationalism, and the Rhetoric of Empire during the New Negro Renaissance', in Australia Tarver and Paula C. Barnes (eds), *New Voices on the Harlem Renaissance: Essays on Race, Gender, and Literary Discourse*, Madison: Fairleigh Dickinson University Press, pp. 33–58.

Cibber, Colley (2001), *The Plays of Colley Cibber*, eds Timothy J. Viator and William J. Burling, Madison: Fairleigh Dickinson University Press, Vol. 1.

Clapp, William Warland [1853] (1968), *A Record of the Boston Stage*, New York: Benjamin Blom.

Clark, James Midgley (1950), *The Dance of Death in the Middle Ages and the Renaissance*, Glasgow: Jackson.

Cmiel, Kenneth (1990), *Democratic Eloquence: The Fight over Popular Speech in Nineteenth-Century America*, New York: William Morrow.

Coclanis, Peter A. (1985), 'The Sociology of Architecture in Colonial Charleston: Pattern and Process in an Eighteenth-Century Southern City', *Journal of Social History*, Vol. 18, No. 4, Summer, pp. 607–23.

Cohen, Hennig (1952), 'Slave Names in Colonial South Carolina', *American Speech*, Vol. 27, No. 2, May, pp. 102–7.

Cohen, Patricia (2008), 'Charging Bias by Theaters, Female Playwrights to Hold Meeting', *The New York Times*, 24 October 2008, http://www.nytimes.com/2008/10/25/theater/25women.html, accessed 28 March 2011.

Conrad, Robert Edgar (1994), *Children of God's Fire: A Documentary History of Black Slavery in Brazil*, University Park, PA: Pennsylvania State University Press.

Cook, Robert Allen (2008), *Sunwatch: Fort Ancient Development in the Mississippian World*, Tuscaloosa: The University of Alabama Press.

Covington, Richard (1997), 'The Salon Interview: David Mamet', reprinted from *Salon Magazine*, http://www.salonwanderlust.com/feature/1997/10/cov_si_24mamet.html, available at http://www.upstartfilmcollective.com/portfolios/jcharnick/mamet-museum/salon-interview.html, accessed 2 January 2010.

Creahan, John (1897), *The Life of Laura Keene: Actress, Artist, Manager, and Scholar, Together with Some Interesting Reminiscences of Her Daughter*, Philadelphia: Rodgers Publishing.

Cullen, Frank, Florence Hackman and Donald McNeilly (2006), *Vaudeville, Old & New: An Encyclopedia of Variety Performers in America*, London and New York: Routledge, Vol. 1.

Culp, Ralph Borden (1965), 'Drama-and-Theatre in the American Revolution', *Speech Monographs*, Vol. 32, No. 1, Mar., pp. 79–86.

Daly, Augustin [1871] (1984), 'Horizon', eds Don B. Wilmeth and Rosemary Cullen, *Plays by Augustin Daly*, Cambridge: Cambridge University Press.

Davis, Peter A. (1998), 'Plays and Playwrights to 1800', in Don B. Wilmeth and Christopher Bigsby (eds), *The Cambridge History of American Theatre, Vol I: Beginnings to 1870*, Cambridge: Cambridge University Press, pp. 216–49.

Davis, Thomas J. (1990), *A Rumor of Revolt: The 'Great Negro Plot' in Colonial New York*, Amherst: University of Massachusetts Press.

Deloria, Philip J. (1998), *Playing Indian*, New Haven and London: Yale University Press.

Deloria, Vine, Jr (1997), *Re, Earth, White Lies: Native Americans and the Myth of Scientific Fact*, Golden, CO: Fulcrum Publishing.

DeMallie Raymond J. (1982), 'The Lakota Ghost Dance: An Ethnohistorical Account', *Pacific Historical Review*, Vol. 51, No. 4, pp. 385–405.

—— (ed.) (1984), *The Sixth Grandfather: Black Elk's Teachings Given to John G. Neihardt*, Lincoln: University of Nebraska Press.

De Mille, William C. (1909), *Strongheart: An American Comedy Drama in Four Acts*, New York: S. French.

Dixon, Thomas, Jr (1905), 'Booker T. Washington and the Negro', *Saturday Evening Post*, 19 August 1905, p. 1.

Dolan, Jill, (2007), 'Lesbian and Gay Drama', in David Krasner (ed.), *A Companion to Twentieth-Century American Drama*, 2nd edition, Oxford: Blackwell, pp. 486–503.

Douglass, Frederick [1845] (2007), *Narrative of the Life of Frederick Douglass; An American Slave, Written by Himself*, Saint Louis Park: Filiquarian Publishing.

Du Bois, W. E. B. (1899), *The Philadelphia Negro*, New York: Lippincott.

—— [1913] (1996), 'Star of Ethiopia', in James V. Hatch and Ted Shine (eds), *Black Theatre U.S.A.: The Early Period 1847–1938*, revised edition, New York: The Free Press, pp. 89–92.

Dudden, Faye E. (1994), *Women in the American Theatre: Actresses and Audiences 1790–1870*, New Haven: Yale University Press.

Dunbar, Laurence and Jesse A. Shipp [1902] (1996), 'In Dahomey, A Negro Musical Comedy', in James V. Hatch and Ted Shine (eds), *Black Theatre U.S.A.: The Early Period 1847–1938*, revised edition, New York: The Free Press, pp. 65–85.

Dunlap, William [1832] (2005), *History of American Theatre from its Origins to 1832*, ed. Tice L. Miller, Urbana and Chicago: University of Illinois Press.

Durang, Charles (1854), 'History of the Philadelphia Stage', *Philadelphia Sunday Dispatch*, Vol. 3.

Dye, William S., Jr (1931), 'Pennsylvania Versus the Theatre', *The Pennsylvania Magazine of History and Biography*, Vol. 55, No. 4, pp. 333–72.

Edel, Leon (1989), 'Introduction', in Leon Edel (ed.), *The American Essays of Henry James*, New Jersey: Princeton University Press.

Edmunds, R. David (1980), *American Indian Leaders: Studies in Diversity*, Lincoln: University of Nebraska Press.

Edwards, Gus (2002), 'Caribbean Narrative: Carnival Characters – In Life and in the Mind', in Paul Carter Harrison, Victor Leo Walker II and Gus Edwards (eds), *Black Theatre: Ritual Performance in the African Diaspora*, Philadelphia: Temple University Press, pp. 108–14.

Edwards, Herbert (1951), 'Howells and Herne', *American Literature*, Vol. 22, No. 4, Jan., pp. 432–41.

Engle, Ron (1993), 'Introduction', in Ron Engle and Tice Miller (eds), *The American Stage*, Cambridge: Cambridge University Press, pp. 1–5.

Engle, Ron and Tice L. Miller (1993), 'Preface', in Ron Engle and Tice L. Miller (eds), *The American Stage*, Cambridge: Cambridge University Press, pp. xix–xx.

Faust, Albert Bernhardt (1909), *The German Element in the United States with special reference to its Political, Moral, Social, and Educational Influence*, Boston: Houghton Mifflin, Vol. II.

Fearnow, Mark (2007), '1980–1990: Disillusionment, Identity, and Discovery', in David Krasner (ed.), *A Companion to Twentieth-Century American Drama*, 2nd edition, Oxford: Blackwell, pp. 423–39.

Filewod, Alan (2002), *Performing Canada: The Nation Enacted in the Imagined Theatre*, Kamloops, BC: University College of the Cariboo.

Flora, Joseph M. and Lucinda H. Mackethan (eds) (2002), *The Companion to Southern Literature Themes, Genres, Places, People, Movements, and Motifs*, Baton Rouge: Louisiana State University Press.

Flores, Angel (ed.) (1991), *Great Spanish Plays in English Translation*, New York: Dover Publications.

Flynn, Joyce (1986), 'Melting Plots: Patterns of Racial and Ethnic Amalgamation in American Drama before Eugene O'Neill', *American Quarterly*, Vol. 38, No. 3, pp. 417–38.

Fordyce, Ehren (2007), 'Experimental Drama at the End of the Century', in David Krasner (ed.), *A Companion to Twentieth-Century American Drama*, 2nd edition, Oxford: Blackwell, pp. 536–51.

Fournier, Hannah (1981), 'Lescarbot's "Théâtre de Neptune": New World Pageant. Old World Polemic', *Canadian Drama*, Vol. 7, No. 1, Spring, pp. 3–11.

Fraden, Rena (1994), *Blueprints for a Black Federal Theatre 1935–1939*, New York and Cambridge: Cambridge University Press.

Frick, John (1999), 'A Changing Theatre: New York and Beyond', in Don B. Wilmeth and Christopher Bigsby (eds), *The Cambridge History of American Theatre: Volume II, 1870–1945*, Cambridge: Cambridge University Press, pp. 196–232.

Frick, John (2007), '"NOT from the Drowsy Pulpit!" The Moral Reform Melodrama on the Nineteenth-Century Stage', *Theatre Symposium: Theatre and Moral Order*, Vol. 15, pp.41–51.

Fritz, Jean (1972), *Cast for a Revolution: Some Friends and Enemies, 1728–1814*, Boston: Houghton Mifflin.

Frohnmayer, John (1993), *Leaving Town Alive: Confessions of an Arts Warrior*, Boston: Houghton Mifflin.

Furness, Horace Howard (ed.) (1892), *A New Variorum Edition of Shakespeare, Vol. 9: The Tempest*, Philadelphia: J. B. Lippincott.

Ganga Zumba, film, directed by Carlos Diegues. Brazil: Copacabana Filmes, 1963.

Gänzl Kurt (2002), *Lydia Thompson, Queen of Burlesque*, London and New York: Routledge.

Gates, Henry Louis (1994), 'Black Creativity: on the Cutting Edge', *Time*, 10 October 1994, http://www.time.com/time/magazine/article/0,9171, 981564,00.html, accessed 19 November 2009.

Geiogamah, Hanay, 'Introduction', in Hanay Geiogamah and Jaye T. Darby (eds), *Stories of Our Way: An Anthology of American Indian Plays*, Los Angeles: UCLA American Indian Studies Center.

Gibbon, Guy E. (2002), *The Sioux: The Dakota and Lakota Nations*, Oxford and New York: John Wiley.

Giles, Freda Scott (1996), 'Introduction to the *Star of Ethiopia*, 1913: W. E. B. Du Bois', in James V. Hatch and Ted Shine (eds), *Black Theatre U.S.A.: The Early Period 1847–1938*, revised edition, New York: The Free Press, pp. 87–8.

Gilmore, Glenda Elizabeth (1996), *Gender and Jim Crow: Women and the Politics of White Supremacy in North Carolina, 1986–1920*, Chapel Hill: University of North Carolina Press.

Godfrey, Thomas, Jr [1767] (1964), 'The Prince of Parthia', in Montrose J. Moses (ed.), *Representative Plays by American Dramatists: 1765–1819*, New York: Benjamin Blom, pp. 19–108.

Goffe, Marcus (2009), 'Protecting the Traditions of the Maroons and Rastafari: An Analysis of the Adequacy of the Intellectual Property Laws of Jamaica and Proposals for Reform', *SCRIPTed* 575, Vol. 6, No. 3, http://www.law.ed.ac.uk/ahrc/script-ed/vol6-3/goffe.asp, accessed 7 October 2010.

Goldman, Irving (1975), *The Mouth of Heaven: An Introduction to Kwakiua Religious Thought*, New York: John Wiley.

Gray, Christine (2001), 'Drama', in Gerald Horne and Mary Young (eds), *W. E. B. Du Bois: An Encyclopedia*, Westport, CT: Greenwood Press, pp. 53–5.

Graydon, Alexander (1811), *Memoirs of a Life, Chiefly Passed in Pennsylvania, within the last Sixty Years*, Harrisburgh: John Wyeth.

Graziano, John (1996), 'Introduction to *In Dahomey*', in James V. Hatch and

Ted Shine (eds), *Black Theatre U.S.A.: The Early Period 1847–1938*, revised edition, New York: The Free Press, pp. 63–5.

Green, Paul [1927] (1998), 'In Abraham's Bosom: The Tragedy of a Southern Negro', in Laurence G. Avery (ed.), *A Paul Green Reader*, Chapel Hill: University of North Carolina Press, pp. 17–79.

Green, Rayna (1975), 'The Pocahontas Perplex: The Image of Indian Women in American Culture', *The Massachusetts Review*, Vol. 16, No. 4, Autumn, pp. 698–714.

—— (1988), 'The Tribe Called Wannabee: Playing Indian in America and Europe', *Folklore*, Vol. 99, No. 1, pp. 30–55.

Grimsted, David (1968), *Melodrama Unveiled: American Theatre and Culture 1800–1850*, Berkeley, Los Angeles and London: University of California Press.

Grinde, Donald A., Jr and Bruce E. Johansen (1990), *Exemplar of Liberty: Native America and the Evolution of Democracy*, 7th draft 4/1/1990, http://www.ratical.org/many_worlds/6Nations/EoL/index.html, accessed 21 October 2010.

Haedicke, Janet V. (2007), 'David Mamet: American on the American Stage', in David Krasner (ed.), A *Companion to Twentieth-Century American Drama*, 2nd edition, Oxford: Blackwell, pp. 406–22.

Hamilton, Ross (2001), *The Mystery of the Serpent Mound: In Search of the Alphabet of the Gods*, Berkeley, California: Frog Books.

Hanson, Francis (1683), *The Laws of Jamaica: Passed by the Assembly, and Confirmed by His Majesty in Council, Feb. 23. 1683: To Which is Added a Short Account of the Island and Government Thereof: With an Exact Map of the Island*, printed by H. Hills for Charles Harper at the Flower de Luce over against St Dunstan's-Church in Fleet-street.

Hargrove, Richard J., Jr (1983), *General John Burgoyne*, Newark: University of Delaware Press.

Harrington, John P. (2009), *Irish Theatre in America: essays on Irish Theatrical Diaspora*, New York: Syracuse University Press.

Hatch, James V. (1989), 'Here Comes Everybody: Scholarship and Black Theatre History', in Thomas Postlewait and Bruce A. McConachie (eds), *Interpreting the Theatrical Past: Essays in the Historiography of Performance*, Iowa City: University of Iowa Press.

Hatch, James V. and Ted Shine (eds) (1996), *Black Theatre U.S.A.: The Early Period 1847–1938*, revised edition, New York: The Free Press.

Haugo, Ann (2000), 'Circles Upon Circles Upon Circles: Native Women in Theater and Performance', in Hanay Geiogamah and Jaye T. Darby (eds), *American Indian Theater in Performance: A Reader*, Los Angeles: UCLA American Indian Studies Center, pp. 228–55.

Hayes, Edmund M. (1976), 'Mercy Otis Warren: *The Defeat*', *The New England Quarterly*, Vol. 49, No. 3, Sept., pp. 440–58.

Hedrick, Donald Keith and Bryan Reynolds (2000), *Shakespeare Without Class: Misappropriations of Cultural Capital*, New York and London: Palgrave.

Heinemann, Margot (1980), *Puritanism and Theatre*, Cambridge: Cambridge University Press.

Henderson, Mary (2004), *The City and the Theatre: The History of New Playwrights, A 250-Year Journey From Bowling Green to Times Square*, New York: Back Stage Books.

Herbert, T. Walter (1980), *Marquesan Encounters: Melville and the Meaning of Civilization*, Cambridge, MA and London: Harvard University Press.

Hill, Errol G. (1992), *The Jamaican Stage, 1655–1900: Profile of a Colonial Theatre*, Amherst: University of Massachusetts Press.

Hill, Errol G. and James V. Hatch (2003), *A History of African American Theatre*, Cambridge: Cambridge University Press.

Hill, Frank Pierce (1934), *American Plays Printed 1714–1830: A Bibliographical Record*, New York: Burt Franklin.

Hill, Jonathan David (1996), *History, Power, and Identity: Ethnogenesis in the Americas, 1492–1992*, Iowa City: University of Iowa Press.

Hill, Randall T. G. (1997), 'Methodological Approaches to Native American Narrative and the Role of Performance', *American Indian Quarterly*, Special Issue: To Hear the Eagles Cry: Contemporary Themes in Native American Spirituality: Part III: Historical Reflections, Vol. 21, No. 1, Winter, pp. 111–47.

Hindle, Brooke (1946), 'The March of the Paxton Boys', *The William and Mary Quarterly*, Third Series, Vol. 3, No. 4, Oct., pp. 461–86.

Hipsher, Edward Ellsworth (1927), *American Opera and Its Composers*, Philadelphia: Theodore Presser.

Holler, Clyde (1995), *Black Elk's Religion: The Sun Dance and Lakota Catholicism*, New York: Syracuse University Press.

Hone, Philip (1910), *The Diary of Philip Hone, 1828–1851*, ed. Bayard Tuckerman, New York: Dodd, Mead.

Hoover, Herbert T. (1980), 'Sitting Bull', in David Edmund Russell (ed.), *American Indian leaders: Studies in Diversity*, Lincoln: University of Nebraska Press, pp. 152–75.

Hornblow, Arthur (1919), *A History of the Theatre in America from its Beginnings to the Present Time in Two Volumes*, Philadelphia and London: J. B. Lippincott.

Houchin, John H. (2003), *Censorship of the American Theatre in the Twentieth Century*, Cambridge: Cambridge University Press.

Howells, William Dean [1871] (2004), *Their Wedding Journey*, Whitefish, MT: Kessinger.

Hoxie, Frederick E. (1996), *Encyclopedia of North American Indians*, Boston: Houghton Mifflin Harcourt.

Huang, Guiyou (2006), *The Columbia Guide to Asian American Literature Since 1945*, New York: Columbia University Press.

Hughes, Langston (1956), *I Wonder As I Wander: An Autobiographical Journey*, New York: Thunder's Mouth Press.

Hunter Robert [1714] (2003), *Androboros. A Biographical Farce in Three Acts, Viz the Senate, the Consistory, and the Apotheosis*, New York: Publisher unknown; *American Drama Full-Text Database*, Cambridge: ProQuest Information and Learning.

Huntsman, Jeffrey (1983), 'Native American Theatre', in Maxine Schwartz Seller (ed.), *Ethnic Theatre in the United States*, Westport, CT: Greenwood Press.

Irving, Washington [1802–3] (1983), 'Letters of Jonathan Oldstyle, Gent', *History, Tales and Sketches*, ed. James W. Tuttleton, Washington, DC: The Library of America, Vol. I, pp. 1–44.

Isani, Mukhtar Ali (1972), 'Hawthorne and the Branding of William Prynne', *The New England Quarterly*, Vol. 45, No. 2, Jun., pp. 182–95.

Jacobs, Harriet (1861), *Incidents in the Life of a Slave Girl Written by Herself*, ed. L. Maria Childs, Boston: published for the author.

Jacobs, Sue-Ellen, Wesley Thomas and Sabine Lang (1997), 'Introduction', in Sue-Ellen Jacobs, Wesley Thomas and Sabine Lang (eds), *Two-Spirit People: Native American Gender Identity, Sexuality, and Spirituality*, Chicago: University of Illinois Press, pp. 1–18.

Jáuregui, Carlos A. [1557] (2008), *The Conquest on Trial: Carvajal's Complaint of the Indians in The Court of Death*, University Park, PA: Pennsylvania State University Press.

Johnson, Claudia D. (1975), 'That Guilty Third Tier: Prostitution in Nineteenth-Century American Theaters', *American Quarterly*, Vol. 27, No. 5, Special Issue: Victorian Culture in America, Dec., pp. 575–84.

Johnson, Katie N. (2006), *Sisters in Sin: Brothel Drama in America, 1900–1920*, Cambridge: Cambridge University Press.

Johnson, Odai (2006), *Fiorelli's Plaster: Absence and memory in Colonial American Theatre*, Basingstoke and New York: Palgrave Macmillan.

Johnson, Odai and William J. Burling (2003), *The Colonial Stage, 1665–1774: A Documentary Calendar*, Madison: Fairleigh Dickinson University Press.

Joseph, Frank (2010), *Advanced Civilizations of Prehistoric America: The Lost Kingdoms of the Adena, Hopewell, Mississippians, and Anasazi*, Rochester, VT: Bear.

Kan, Sergei (1990), 'The Sacred and the Secular: Tlingit Potlatch Songs outside the Potlatch', *American Indian Quarterly*, Vol. 14, No. 4, pp. 355–66.

Kent, R. K. (1965), 'Palmares: An African State in Brazil', *The Journal of African History*, Vol. 6, No. 2, pp. 161–75.

Kessler-Harris, Alice (2003), *Out to Work: A History of Wage-earning Women in the United States*, Oxford and New York: Oxford University Press.

Kevin, Kenny (2009), *Peaceable Kingdom Lost: The Paxton Boys and the Destruction of William Penn's Holy Experiment*, New York: Oxford University Press.

Koch, Frederick H. (1922), *Carolina Folk Plays*, New York: H. Holt.

Kochems, Lee M. and Sue-Ellen Jacobs (1997), 'Gender Statuses, Gender Features, and Gender/Sex Categories: New Perspectives on an Old Paradigm', Sue-Ellen Jacobs, Wesley Thomas and Sabine Lang (eds), *Two-Spirit People: Native American Gender Identity, Sexuality, and Spirituality*, Chicago: University of Illinois Press, pp. 255–64.

Kramnick, Isaac (ed.) [1788] (1987), *Alexander Hamilton, Isaac Kramnick, James Madison, John Jay – The Federalist Papers*, London and New York: Penguin Classics.

Kritzer, Amelia Howe (1999), 'Comedies by Early American Women', in Brenda Murphy (ed.), *The Cambridge Companion to American Women Playwrights*, Cambridge: Cambridge University Press.

Kruger, Loren (1996), 'Our Theater?: Stages in an American Cultural History', *American Literary History*, Vol. 8, pp. 699–714.

Kushner, Tony [2003] (2004), 'The Genius of O'Neill', *Times Literary Supplement*, 18 December 2003, reprinted in *Eugene O'Neill Review*, Vol. 26, pp. 248–56.

Land, Robert H. (1948), 'The First Williamsburg Theater', *The William and Mary Quarterly*, Third Series, Vol. 5, No. 3, Jul., pp. 359–74.

Landa, Diego [1579] (1941), *Relación de las cosas de Yucatán*, trans. and ed. Alfred M. Tozzer, Papers of the Peabody Museum of American Archaeology and Ethnology, Cambridge, MA: Harvard University Press, Vol. 18.

Lang, Sabine (1997), *Men as Women, Women as Men: Changing Gender in Native American Cultures*, Austin: University of Texas Press.

Leacock, John [1776] (1918), 'The Fall of British Tyranny; Or, American Liberty Triumphant', in Montrose J. Moses (ed.), *Representative Plays by American Dramatists: 1765–1819*, Boston: E. P. Dutton, pp. 277–350.

Léry, Jean, [1578] (1990), *History of a Voyage to the Land of Brazil, Otherwise Called America*, trans. and ed. Janet Whatley, Berkeley and Los Angeles: University of California Press.

Lescarbot, Marc [1606] [1927] (2006), 'Le Théâtre de Neptune en la Nouvelle France', *Spectacle of Empire*, trans. Harriet Taber Richardson (1927), ed. Jerry Wasserman, Vancouver: Talon Books.

—— [1609] (1907), *The History of New France in Three Volumes*, ed. W. L. Grant, Introduction H. P. Biggar, Toronto: The Champlain Society.

Levine, Laurence (1900), *Highbrow/Lowbrow: The Emergence of Cultural Hierarchy in America*, Cambridge, MA: Harvard University Press.

Levinger, Lee (1930), *A History of the Jews in the United States*, Rockville, MD: Wildside Press.

Lhamon, W. T., Jr (2003), *Jump Jim Crow: Lost Play Lyrics, and Street Prose of the First Atlantic Popular Culture*, Cambridge, MA: Harvard University Press.

Listengarten, Julia (2007), 'From Eccentricity to Endurance: Jewish Comedy and the Art of Affirmation', in David Krasner (ed.), *A Companion to Twentieth-Century American Drama*, 2nd edition, Oxford: Blackwell, pp. 456–72.

Litto, Fredric M. (1966), 'Addison's Cato in the Colonies', *The William and Mary Quarterly*, Third Series, Vol. 23, No. 3, Jul., pp. 431–49.

Loehlin, James N. (2002), *Romeo and Juliet: William Shakespeare*, Cambridge: Cambridge University Press.

Londré, Felicia and Daniel J. Watermeier (2000), *The History of North American Theatre, The United States, Canada, and Mexico: From Pre-Columbian Times to the Present*, New York: Continuum.

López-Rodríguez, Miriam (2004), *Women's Contribution to Nineteenth-Century American Theatre*, Valencia: Universitat de Valencia.

Lovgren, Stefan (2007), 'Clovis People Not First Americans, Study Shows', *National Geographic News*, 23 February 2007, http://news.nationalgeographic.com/news/pf/696856.html, accessed 19 November 2009.

Mails, Thomas E. (1998), *Sundancing: The Great Sioux Piercing Ritual*, Tulsa: Council Oak Books.

Marra, Kim (2002), 'Clyde Fitch's Too Wilde Love', in Robert A. Schanke and Kim Marra (eds), *Staging Desire: Queer Readings of American Theatre History*, Ann Arbor: University of Michigan Press.

Marshall, Herbert and Mildred Stock (1968), *Ira Aldridge, the Negro Tragedian*, Carbondale: Southern Illinois University Press.

Martin, Jay (1978), 'The Province of Speech: American Drama in the Eighteenth Century', *Early American Literature*, Vol. 13, No. 1, Mar., pp. 24–34.

Mather, Increase [1687], *A TESTIMONY Against several Prophane and Superstitious CUSTOMS, Now Practised by some in New-England, The Evil whereof is evinced from the Holy Scriptures, and from the Writings both of Ancient and Modern Divines*, http://www.covenanter.org/IMather/increasemathertestimony.htm, accessed 19 June 2009.

McAllister, Marvin (2003), *White People Do Not Know How to Behave at Entertainments Designed for Ladies & Gentleman of Colour*, Chapel Hill: University of North Carolina Press.

McConachie, Bruce A. (1982), 'H. J. Conway's Dramatization of "Uncle Tom's Cabin": A Previously Unpublished Letter', *Theatre Journal*, Vol. 34, No. 2, Insurgency in American Theatre, May, pp. 49–155.

—— (1998), 'American Theatre in Context, from the Beginnings to 1870', in Don B. Wilmeth and Christopher Bigsby (eds), *Cambridge History of American Theatre, Vol I: Beginnings to 1870*, Cambridge: Cambridge University Press, pp. 111–81.

McGowan, Margaret C. (1968), 'Form and Themes in Henri II's Entry into Rouen', *Renaissance Drama*, New Series, Vol. 1, pp. 199–252.

McInnis, Maurie Dee (2005), *The Politics of Taste in Antebellum Charleston*, Chapel Hill and London: University of North Carolina Press.

McLaughlin, Robert (1974), *Broadway and Hollywood*, Carlton: Arno Press.

Merrill, Lisa (2000), *When Romeo was a Woman: Charlotte Cushman and her Circle of Friends*, Ann Arbor: University of Michigan Press.

Merritt, Jane T. (1997), 'Dreaming of the Saviour's Blood: Moravians and the Indian Great Awakening in Pennsylvania', *The William and Mary Quarterly*, Third Series, Vol. 54, No. 4, Oct., pp. 723–46.

Meserve, Walter J. (1994), *An Outline History of American Theatre*, New York: Feedback Theatre Books.

Milleret, Margo (1987), 'Acting into Action: Teatro Arena's *Zumbi*', *Latin American Theatre Review*, Vol. 21, No. 1, pp. 19–27.

Mitchell, Loften (1996), 'Introduction to *The Escape; Or, A Leap for Freedom*, William Wells Brown', in James V. Hatch and Ted Shine (eds), *Black Theatre U.S.A.: The Early Period 1847–1938*, revised edition, New York: The Free Press, pp. 35–7.

Mooney, James [1896] (1973), *The Ghost-Dance Religion and Wounded Knee*, New York: Dover Publications.

Moore, S. J. (1997), 'Making a Spectacle of Suffrage: The National Woman Suffrage Pageant, 1913', *Journal of American Culture*, Vol. 20, No. 1, pp. 89–103.

Morgan, Kenneth (1998), 'Slave Sales in Colonial Charleston', *The English Historical Review*, Vol. 453, Sept., pp. 905–27.

Morton, Thomas [1637] (2000), *The New English Canaan*, ed. Jack Dempsey, Scituate, MA: Digital Scanning.

Moses, L. G. (1999), *Wild West Shows and the Images of American Indians, 1883–1933*, Albuquerque: University of New Mexico Press.

Moses, Montrose J. (ed.) (1924), *Clyde Fitch and His Letters*, New York: Little, Brown.

Moses, Montrose J. and John Mason Brown (eds) (1934), *The American Theatre As Seen by Its Critics, 1752–1934*, New York: W. W. Norton.

Mowatt, Anna Cora (1859), *Autobiography of an Actress; Or, Eight Years on the Stage*, Boston: Ticknor, Reed, and Fields.

Mullenix, Elizabeth Reitz (2000), *Wearing the Breeches: Gender on the Antebellum Stage*, New York: St. Martin's Press.

Mullin, Michael (1995), *Africa in America: Slave Acculturation and Resistance in the American South*, Chicago: University of Illinois Press.

Murdock, James (1880), *The Stage, or Recollections of Actors and Acting from an Experience of Fifty Years*, Philadelphia: J. M. Stoddard.

Murphy, Brenda (1999), 'Plays and Playwrights, 1915–1945', in Don B. Wilmeth and Christopher Bigsby (eds), *The Cambridge History of American Theatre: Volume II, 1870–1945*, Cambridge: Cambridge University Press, pp. 289–343.

Murphy, Maureen (1983), 'Irish-American Theatre', in Maxine Schwartz Seller (ed.), *Ethnic Theatre in the United States*, Westport, CT: Greenwood Press.

Nardocchio, Elaine Frances (1986), *Theatre and Politics in Modern Québec*, Edmonton, AB: University of Alberta Press.

Noah, Mordecai Manuel [1819] (1918), 'She Would Be a Soldier, or the Plains of Chippewa; an Historical Drama, in Three Acts', in Montrose J. Moses (ed.), *Representative Plays by American Dramatists: 1765–1819*, Boston: E. P. Dutton, pp. 629–78.

Odell, George C. D. (1927), *Annals of the New York Stage*, New York: Columbia University Press.

Oldfield, J. R. (1993), 'The "Ties of Soft Humanity": Slavery and Race in British Drama, 1760–1800', *Huntington Library Quarterly*, Vol. 56, No. 1, Winter, pp. 1–14.

Olson, James C. (1965), *Red Cloud and the Sioux Problem*. Lincoln: University of Nebraska Press.

Ostler, Jeffrey (2004), *The Plains Sioux and U.S. Colonialism from Lewis and Clark to Wounded Knee*, Cambridge: Cambridge University Press.

Page Eugene R. (ed.) (1940), *America's Lost Plays*, Princeton: Princeton University Press, Vol. XIV.

Paper, Jordan D. (2006), *Native North American Religious Traditions: Dancing for Life*, Westport, CT: Praeger.

Pauketat, Timothy R. and Thomas E. Emerson (1997), 'Introduction: Domination and Ideology in the Mississippian World', in Timothy R. Pauketat and Thomas E. Emerson (eds), *Cahokia: Domination and Ideology in the Mississippian World*. Lincoln: University of Nebraska Press, pp. 1–29.

Pauketat, Timothy R. and Thomas E. Emerson (eds) (1997), *Cahokia: Domination and Ideology in the Mississippian World*, Lincoln: University of Nebraska Press.

Pauketat Timothy R. and Neil Lopinot (1997), 'Cahokian Population Dynamics', in Timothy R. Pauketat and Thomas E. Emerson (eds), *Cahokia: Domination and Ideology in the Mississippian World*, Lincoln: University of Nebraska Press, pp. 103–123.

Pearce, Roy Harvey [1953] (1964), *Savagism and civilization: A Study of the Indian and the American Mind*, 2nd edition, Columbia and Princeton: University Presses of California.

Piersen, William W. (2002), 'African American Festive Style and the Creation of American Culture', in Matthew Dennis, Simon P. Newman and William Pencak (eds), *Riot and Revelry in Early America*, University Park, PA: Pennsylvania State University Press, pp. 255–72.

Poe, Edgar Allan (1845–6), 'The Theatre. The New Comedy by Mrs. Mowatt', *The Broadway Journal*, eds C. F. Briggs, Edgar A. Poe and Henry C. Watson, New York: John Brisco, Vol. 1, No. 13, pp. 203–5.

Pollard, Tanya (ed.) (2003), *Shakespeare's Theatre: A Sourcebook*, Oxford: Blackwell, pp. 279–97.

Pollock, Thomas Clark (1968), *The Philadelphia Theatre in the Eighteenth Century*, New York: Greenwood.

Porter, Susan L. (1991), *With an Air Debonair: Musical Theatre in America 1785–1815*, Washington, DC: Smithsonian Institution Press.

Postlewait, Thomas (1999a), 'From Melodrama to Realism: The Suspect History of American Drama', in Michael Hays and Anastasia Nikolopoulou (eds), *Melodrama: The Cultural Emergence of a Genre*, New York: St. Martin's Press.

—— (1999b), 'The Hieroglyphic Stage: American Theatre and Society, Post-Civil War to 1945', in Don B. Wilmeth and Christopher Bigsby (eds), *The Cambridge History of American Theatre: Volume II, 1870–1945*, Cambridge: Cambridge University Press, pp. 107–96.

Prucha, Francis Paul (1984), *The Great Father: The United States Government and the American Indians*, Lincoln: University of Nebraska Press.

Prynne, William [1633] (1974), *Histriomastix: The Player's Scourge*, ed. Arthur Freeman, New York: Garland.

Quilombo, film, directed by Carlos Diegues. Brazil: CDK, Embrafilme (co-production), Gaumont (co-production), 1984.

Quinn, Arthur Hobson (1927), *A History of the American Drama from the Civil War to the Present Day*, New York: Aleton-Century-Crofts, Vols I and II.

Quinn, Arthur Hobson (ed.) (1923), *Contemporary American Drama*, New York: Scribner's.

Rabson, Carolyn (1983), 'Disappointment Revisited: Unweaving the Tangled Web. Part I', *American Music*, Vol. 1, No. 1, Spring, pp. 12–35.

Radin, Paul (1956), *The Trickster: A Study in American Indian Mythology*, New York: Bell.

Ramos, Arthur (1939), *The Negro in Brazil*, Washington, DC: Associated Publishers.

Randall, E. O. [1907] (2003), *Serpent Mound Adams County*, Whitefish, MT: Kessinger.

Rankin, Hugh F. (1965), *The Theatre in Colonial America*, Chapel Hill: University of North Carolina Press.

Rede, Leman Thomas (1868), *The Guide to the Stage*, New York: Samuel French.

Reed, Peter (2007), '"There was no resisting John Canoe": Circum-Atlantic Transracial Performance', *Theatre History Studies*, Vol. 27, pp. 65–85.

Rees, James (Colley Cibber) (1874), *Life of Edwin Forrest, with Reminiscences and Personal Recollections*, Philadelphia: T. B. Peterson.

Richards, Jeffrey (1991), *Theatre Enough: American Culture and the Metaphor of the World Stage, 1607–1789*, Durham, NC: Duke University Press.

Richards, Sandra (2002), 'Horned Ancestral Masks, Shakespearean Actor Boys, and Scotch-Inspired Set Girls: Social Relations in Nineteenth-Century

Jamaican Jonkonnu', in Isidore Okpewho, Carole Boyce Davies and Ali A. Mazrui (eds), *The African Diaspora: African Origins and New World Identities*, Bloomington: Indiana University Press, pp. 254–72.

Riggs, Lynn [1931] (2003), 'Green Grow the Lilacs', *The Cherokee Night and Other Plays*, ed. Jace Weaver, Norman: University of Oklahoma Press.

—— [1932] (1999), 'The Cherokee Night', in Hanay Geiogamah and Jaye T. Darby (eds), *Stories of Our Way: An Anthology of American Indian Plays*, Los Angeles: UCLA American Indian Studies Center, pp. 7–102.

Riis, Thomas [1902] (1996), 'Introduction', in Thomas Riis (ed.), *The Music and Scripts of 'In Dahomey'*, Madison: A-R Editions.

Roach, Joseph (1996), *Cities of the Dead: Circum-Atlantic Performance*, New York: Columbia University Press.

—— (1998), 'The Emergence of the American Actor', in Don B. Wilmeth and Christopher Bigsby (eds), *The Cambridge History of American Theatre: Volume I, Beginnings to 1870*, Cambridge: Cambridge University Press, pp. 338–72.

Roaten, Darnell (1960), *Structural Forms in the French Theatre*, Philadelphia: University of Pennsylvania Press.

Robeson, Paul (1924), 'Reflections on O'Neill's Plays', *Opportunity*, December, pp. 368–70.

Robeson, Paul, Jr (2001), *The Undiscovered Paul Robeson: An Artist's Journey, 1898–1939*, New York: John Wiley.

Rogers, Robert [1766] (1964), 'Ponteach; or, The Savages of America', in Montrose J. Moses (ed.), *Representative Plays by American Dramatists: 1765–1819*, New York: Benjamin Blom, pp. 109–208.

Rogin, Michael Paul (1975), *Fathers and Children: Andrew Jackson and the Subjugation of the American Indian*, New York: Alfred A. Knopf.

Roper, John Herbert (2003), *Paul Green: Playwright of the Real South*, Athens, GA and London: University of Georgia Press.

Rosen, Robert N. (1992), *A Short History of Charleston*, Columbia: University of South Carolina Press.

Rothfuss, Hermann, E. (1951), 'The Beginnings of the German American Stage', *German Quarterly*, Vol. 24, pp. 93–102.

Rourke, Constance [1931] (1942), *The Roots of American Culture and Other Essays*, ed. Van Wyck Brooks, New York: Harcourt, Brace, Jovanovich.

Rowson, Susannah [1794] (2003), *Slaves in Algiers; or, A Struggle for Freedom: A Play Interspersed with Songs, in Three Acts. As Performed at the New Theatres, in Philadelphia and Baltimore*, Philadelphia: Wrigley and Berriman; *American Drama Full-Text Online Database*, Cambridge: ProQuest Information and Learning.

Rozik, Eli (2002), *The Roots of Theatre: Rethinking Ritual and Other Theories of Origin*, Iowa City: University of Iowa Press.

—— (2003), 'The Ritual Origin of Theatre – A Scientific Theory or Theatrical

Ideology?', *The Journal of Religion and Theatre*, Vol. 2, No. 1, Fall, http://www.rtjournal.org/vol_2/no_1/rozik.html, accessed 27 September 2010.

Sargent, Mark L. (1988), 'The Conservative Covenant: The Rise of the Mayflower Compact in American Myth', *The New England Quarterly*, Vol. 61, No. 2, Jun., pp. 233–51.

Savarese, Nicola (2001), '1931: Antonin Artaud Sees Balinese Theatre at the Paris Colonial Exposition', *The Drama Review*, Vol. 45, No. 3 (T171), Fall, pp. 51–77.

Savran, David (1997), 'Ambivalence, Utopia, and a Queer Sort of Materialism: How *Angels in America* Reconstructs the Nation', in Deborah R. Geis and Steven F. Kruger (eds), *Approaching the Millennium: Essays on Angels in America*, Ann Arbor: University of Michigan Press, pp. 13–49.

Schechner, Richard (1976), 'From Ritual to Theatre and Back', in Richard Schechner and Mady Schuman (eds), *Ritual, Play, and Performance: Readings in the Social Sciences/Theatre*, New York: Seabury Press, pp. 63–98.

—— (1985), *Between Theatre and Anthropology*, Philadelphia: University of Pennsylvania Press.

—— (1988), *Performance Theory*, New York: Routledge.

—— (2002), *Performance Studies: An Introduction*, New York: Routledge.

Schlueter, June (2007), *American Drama of the 1990s On- and Off-Broadway*, *A Companion to Twentieth-Century American Drama*, 2nd edition, Oxford: Blackwell, pp. 504–18.

Seed, Patricia (1995), *Ceremonies of Possession in Europe's Conquest of the New World, 1492–1640*, Cambridge: Cambridge University Press.

Sehat, David (2008), 'Gender and Theatrical Realism: The Problem of Clyde Fitch', *Journal of the Gilded Age and Progressive Era*, Vol. 7, No. 3, Jul., pp. 325–52.

Seilhamer, George O. [1891] (2005a), *A History of American Theatre: Before the Revolution*, Honolulu: University of Pacific Press.

—— (2005b), *A History of American Theatre: New Foundations*, Honolulu: University of Pacific Press.

Sell, Mike (2001), 'The Black Arts Movement: Performance, Neo-Orality, and the Destruction of the "White Thing"', in Harry J. Elam, Jr and David Krasner (eds), *African American Performance and Theatre History: A Critical Reader*, Oxford and New York: Oxford University Press, pp. 56–80.

Seller, Maxine Schwartz (1983), 'Introduction', in Maxine Schwartz Seller (ed.) *Ethnic Theatre in the United States*, Westport, CT: Greenwood Press, pp. 3–18.

Senelick, Laurence (2000), *The Changing Room: Sex, Drag and the Theatre*, London and New York: Routledge.

Shaffer, Jason (2007), *Performing Patriotism: National Identity in the Colonial and Revolutionary American Theatre*, Pennsylvania: University of Pennsylvania Press.

Sheldon, Edward (1910), *The Nigger: An American Play*, New York: Macmillan.

Shohat, Ella and Robert Stam (1994), *Unthinking Eurocentrism: Multiculturalism and the Media*, London: Routledge.

Silverman, Kenneth (1976), *A Cultural History of the American Revolution: Painting, Music, Literature, and the Theatre in the Colonies and the United States from the Treaty of Paris to the Inauguration of George Washington, 1763–1789*, New York: T. Y. Crowell.

Smith, Jeanne Rosier (1997), *Writing Tricksters: Mythic Gambols in American Ethnic Literature*, Berkeley: University of California Press.

Smith, John [1608], *True Relations*, in *American Journeys*, collection at Wisconsin Historical Society Digital Archives and Library: Document No.: AJ-074, http://content.wisconsinhistory.org, accessed 19 January 2008.

Smith, John [1624] (2006), *The Generall Historie of Virginia, New England & the Summer Isles*, Chapel Hill: University of North Carolina.

Smith, Michael P. (1994), *Mardi Gras Indians*, Gretna, LA: Pelican.

Smith, Page (1976), *A People's History of the American Revolution, Volume One: A New Age Now Begins*, New York: McGraw-Hill.

Smith, Susan Harris (1989), 'Generic Hegemony: American Drama and the Canon', *American Quarterly*, Vol. 41, pp. 111–22.

—— (1997), *American Drama: The Bastard Art*, Cambridge: Cambridge University Press.

Smith, Venture [1798] (1896), *A Narrative of the Life and Adventures of Venture, a Native of Africa, but Resident Above Sixty Years in the United States of America. Related by Himself. New London: Printed in 1798. Reprinted A. D. 1835, and Published by a Descendant of Venture. Revised and Republished with Traditions by H. M. Selden, Haddam, Conn., 1896*, electronic edition, Documenting the American South: Smith, Venture, 1729?–1805, Chapel Hill: University of North Carolina, http://docsouth.unc.edu/neh/venture2/menu.html, accessed 7 October 2010.

Squier, Ephraim G. and Edwin H. Davis (1848), *Ancient Monuments of the Mississippi Valley; Comprising the Results of Extensive Original Surveys and Explorations, Smithsonian Contributions to Knowledge, Vol. 1*, Washington, DC: Smithsonian Institution.

Stam, Robert (1997), *Tropical Multiculturalism: A Comparative History of Race in Brazilian Cinema and Culture*, Durham, NC and London: Duke University Press.

Stanton, William (1960), *The Leopard's Spots: Scientific Attitudes Toward Race in America 1815–1859*, Chicago: University of Chicago Press.

Stout, Harry S. (1991), *The Divine Dramatist: George Whitefield and the Rise of Modern Evangelicalism*, Grand Rapids, MI: Wm B. Eerdmans.

Stovall, Floyd (1953), 'Walt Whitman and the Dramatic Stage in New York', *Studies in Philology*, Vol. 50, No. 3, Jul., pp. 515–39.

Strang, Lewis (1899), *Famous Actresses of the Day in America*, Boston: L. C. Page.

Takaki Ronald (1992), 'The Tempest in the Wilderness: The Racialization of Savagery', *The Journal of American History*, Vol. 79, No. 3, Discovering America: A Special Issue, Dec., pp. 892–912.

Tate, Carolyn (2008), 'Landscape and a Visual Narrative of Creation and Origin at the Olmec Ceremonial Centre at La Venta', in John Edward Staller (ed.), *Pre-Columbian Landscapes of Creation and Origin*, New York: Springer, pp. 31–65.

Tedlock, Dennis (2003), *Rabinal Achi: A Mayan Drama of War and Sacrifice*, Oxford: Oxford University Press.

Thompson, Peter (1998), *Rum Punch & Revolution: Taverngoing & Public Life in Eighteenth-Century Philadelphia*, Philadelphia: University of Pennsylvania Press.

Tindall, George Brown and David E. Shi [1984] (1999), *America: A Narrative History*, 5th edition, New York and London: W. W. Norton.

Turner, Victor (1982), *From Ritual to Theatre: The Human Seriousness of Play*, New York: PAJ.

Tyler, Lyon G. [1907] (2009), *Williamsburg, the Old Colonial Capital*, Whitefish, MT: Kessinger.

Tyler, Royall [1787] (1970), *The Contrast*, New York: AMS Press.

Vestal, Stanley (1934), *New Sources of Indian History 1850–1891: The Ghost Dance, The Prairie Sioux*, Norman, OK: University of Oklahoma Press.

Vogel, Todd (2004), *Rewriting White: Race, Class, and Cultural Capital in Nineteenth-Century America*, New Brunswick, NJ: Rutgers University Press.

Waal, Carla (1962), 'The First Original Confederate Drama: *The Guerrillas*', *The Virginia Magazine of History and Biography*, Vol. 70, No. 4, Oct., pp. 459–67.

Walker, Ethel Pitts (1988), 'Krigwa, a Theatre by, for, and about Black People', *Perspectives in Theatre History*, Vol. 40, No. 3, Oct., pp. 347–56.

Walker, Juliet (2009), *The History of Black Business in America, Volume I: Capitalism, Race, Entrepreneurship to 1865*, Chapel Hill: University of North Carolina Press.

Wallendorf, Melanie and Eric J. Arnould (1991), '"We Gather Together": Consumption Rituals of Thanksgiving Day', *The Journal of Consumer Research*, Vol. 18, No. 1, Jun., pp. 13–31.

Walser, Richard (1955), 'Negro Dialect in Eighteenth-Century American Drama', *American Speech*, Vol. 30 No. 4, Dec., pp. 269–76.

Walsh, Martin W. (1997), 'May Games and Noble Savages: The Native American in Early Celebrations of the Tammany Society', *Folklore*, Vol. 108, pp. 83–91.

Ware, Susan (2005), *Notable American Women: A Biographical Dictionary –*

Completing the Twentieth Century, Cambridge, MA: Harvard University Press.

Warren, Mercy Otis [1773] (2003), 'The Adulateur. A Tragedy, as It Is Now Acted in Upper Servia', Boston: New Printing-Office; *American Drama Full-Text Online Database*, Cambridge: ProQuest Information and Learning.

Weiss, Judith A. (1993), *Latin American Popular Theatre: The First Five Centuries*, Albuquerque: University of New Mexico Press.

Weiss, M. Lynn (2001), 'Introduction', in Victor Séjour, *The Fortune Teller*, trans. Norman R. Shapiro, Urbana: University of Illinois Press.

White, Shane (2002), *Stories of Freedom in Black New York*, Cambridge, MA: Harvard University Press.

Wickham, Glynne (1963), *Early English Stages 1300 to 1660. Volume II. 1576–1660, Part I*, New York: Columbia University Press; London: Routledge.

Wilce, James M. (2008), *Crying Shame: Metaculture, Modernity, and the Exaggerated Death of Lament*, Oxford: John Wiley.

Williams, Gary Jay, Bruce A. McConachie, Carol Fisher Sorgenfrei and Phillip Zarrilli (2006), *Theatre Histories: An Introduction*, London and New York: Routledge.

Williams, Tennessee [1956] (1976), *Cat on a Hot Tin Roof*, London: Penguin.

Willis, Eola (1924), *The Charleston Stage in the XVIII Century*, Columbia, SC: The State Company.

Wilmer, S. E. (2002), *Theatre, Society and the Nation: Staging American Identities*, Cambridge: Cambridge University Press.

Wilmeth, Don B. [1983] (2000), 'Noble or Ruthless Savage? The American Indian on Stage and in the Drama', in Hanay Geiogamah and Jaye T. Darby (eds), *American Indian Theater in Performance: A Reader*, Los Angeles: UCLA American Indian Studies Center, pp. 127–56.

—— (1998), *Staging the Nation: Plays from the American Theatre 1787–1909*, Boston: Bedford Books.

—— (2007), *Cambridge Guide to American Theatre*, 2nd edition, Cambridge: Cambridge University Press.

Wilmeth, Don B. and Christopher Bigsby (eds) (1998), *The Cambridge History of American Theatre: Volume I, Beginnings to 1870*, Cambridge: Cambridge University Press.

Wilmeth, Don. B and Tice L. Miller (eds) (1993), *Cambridge Guide to American Theatre*, Cambridge: Cambridge University Press.

Wilson, Garff B. (1973), *Three Hundred Years of American Drama and Theatre, from Ye Bare and ye Cubb to Hair*, Englewood Cliffs, NJ: Prentice-Hall.

Windsor, Justin (1881), *The Memorial History of Boston: Including Suffolk County, Massachusetts. 1630–1880 Vol III: The Last Hundred Years*, Boston: Osgood.

Winter, William (1913), *The Wallet of Time; Containing Personal, Biographical, and Critical Reminiscence of the American Theatre*, New York: Moffat, Yard, Vol. II.

Wintroub, Michael (1998), 'Civilizing the Savage and Making a King: The Royal Entry Festival of Henri II (Rouen, 1550)', *The Sixteenth Century Journal*, Vol. 29, No. 2, Summer, pp. 465–94.

Wintroub, Michael (2006), *A Savage Mirror: Power, Identity, and Knowledge in Early Modern France*, Stanford: Stanford University Press.

Witham, Barry (2003), *The Federal Theatre Project: A Case Study*, Cambridge: Cambridge University Press.

Womack, Craig S. (1999), *Red on Red: Native American Literary Separatism*, Wisconsin: University of Minnesota Press.

Wood, Peter H. (1994), *Black Majority: Negroes in Colonial South Carolina from 1670 through the Stono Rebellion*, 2nd edition, New York: W. W. Norton.

Wormser, Richard (2003), *The Rise and Fall of Jim Crow*, New York: St. Martin's Press.

Wright, Louis B. [1957] (1962), The Cultural Life of the American Colonies, 1607–1763, New York: Harper and Row.

Wright, Thomas Goddard (1920), *Literary Culture in Early New England, 1620–1730*, New Haven, CT: Yale University Press.

Young, Alexander (ed.) (1841), *Chronicles of the Pilgrim Fathers of the Colony of Plymouth: from 1602–1625*, Boston: C. C. Little and J. Brown.

Zacharasiewicz, Waldemar (2007), *Images of Germany in American Literature*, Iowa City: University of Iowa Press.

Zamba (1847), *Life and Adventures of Zamba, an African Negro King; And His Experience of Slavery in South Carolina, Written by Himself*, ed. Peter Neilson, London: Smith Elder.

Zebrero, Izquierdo [1582] (1996), *Holy Wednesday: A Nahua Drama from Early Colonial Mexico*, ed. Louise M. Burkhart, Philadelphia: University of Pennsylvania Press.

Zinoman, Jason (2003), 'The Season of the Female Playwright', *The New York Times*, 21 December 2003, http://www.nytimes.com/2003/12/21/theater/theater-the-season-of-the-female-playwright.html, accessed 28 March 2011.

Zips, Werner (1999), *Black Rebels: African-Caribbean Freedom Fighters in Jamaica*, Kingston: Ian Randle.

Catalogues, Reports and Reviews

Catalog, 'American Indian Languages', *The National Museum of Natural History of the Smithsonian Institution*, Washington, DC, 1987, http://smithsonianlibraries.si.edu/smithsonianlibraries/anthropology-library, accessed 14 November 2008.

Charleston Gazette, 24 January 1736, *South Carolina Newspapers Collection 1732–1780 online*, Accessible Archives, http://www.accessible.com.

Pennsylvania Gazette, reports from *South Carolina Newspapers Collection 1732–1780 online*, Accessible Archives, http://www.accessible.com: 27 November 1762; 17 April 1767.

'Refuge of Oppression. Faneuil Hall', *The Liberator*, Boston, 6 June 1835.

'Richmond News and Gossip: Our Own Correspondent', *The Charleston Mercury*, 6 January 1862, *South Carolina Newspapers Collection 1732–1780 online*, Accessible Archives, http://www.accessible.com.

'Sons of Tammany', *Pennsylvania Gazette*, 18 May 1791, Accessible Archives, http://www.accessible.com.

South Carolina Gazette, unsigned reports from *South Carolina Newspapers Collection 1732–1780 online*, Accessible Archives, http://www.accessible.com: 18 January 1735; 6 March 1736; 23 June 1739; 27 November 1749; 10 October 1754; 1 January 1768; 29 April 1768.

'Terrible Riot in New York! – Twenty Persons Killed By the Military', *The Liberator*, Boston, 18 May 1849.

The New York Times reviews, http://query.nytimes.com

Unsigned review, 1 October 1868.

'Sapho in Chicago', 1 November 1899.

'Sapho stopped by Police', 6 March 1900.

Unsigned review, 5 April 1900.

Unsigned review, 27 July 1906.

Miscellaneous Reviews

'Death of Clyde Fitch', *The Independent*, 9 September 1909, p. 614.

'The Burlesque Mania', *Spirit of the Times*, 13 February 1869, p. 416.

'Uncle Tom at Barnum's', *New-York Daily Tribune*, 15 November 1853, American Social History Project/Centre for Media and Learning, The Graduate Centre, City University of New York in collaboration with Centre for History and New Media, George Mason University, http://chnm.gmu.edu/lostmuseum/lm/266, accessed 19 January 2009.

Unsigned Review, *New York Crier*, 31 November 1863, p. 243

Unsigned Review, *New York Herald*, 3 September 1852.

'Williamsburg November 17', *The Maryland Gazette*, 14 December 1752, *Maryland State Archives*, http://www.msa.md.gov/megafile/msa/speccol/sc2900/sc2908/html/mdgazette.html, accessed 14 January 2010.

Index

Series Editors: Simon Newman, Sir Denis Brogan Chair in American Studies at the University of Glasgow; and Carol R. Smith, Senior Lecturer in English and American Studies at the University of Winchester.

The British Association for American Studies (BAAS)

The British Association for American Studies was founded in 1955 to promote the study of the Unites States of America. It welcomes applications for membership from anyone interested in the history, society, government and politics, economics, geography, literature, creative arts, culture and thought of the USA.

The Association publishers a newsletter twice yearly, holds an annual national conference, supports regional branches and provides other membership services, including preferential subscription rates to the *Journal of American Studies*.

Membership enquiries may be addressed to the BAAS Secretary. For contact details visit our website: www.baas.ac.uk